Patriotic Information Systems

Todd Loendorf
North Carolina State University, USA

G. David Garson
North Carolina State University, USA

IGI PUBLISHING

Hershey • New York

Acquisition Editor:	Kristin Klinger
Senior Managing Editor:	Jennifer Neidig
Managing Editor:	Sara Reed
Development Editor:	Kristin Roth
Copy Editor:	Lanette Ehrhardt
Typesetter:	Lindsay Bergman
Cover Design:	Lisa Tosheff
Printed at:	Yurchak Printing Inc.

Published in the United States of America by
    IGI Publishing (an imprint of IGI Global)
    701 E. Chocolate Avenue
    Hershey PA 17033
    Tel: 717-533-8845
    Fax: 717-533-8661
    E-mail: cust@igi-global.com
    Web site: http://www.igi-global.com

and in the United Kingdom by
    IGI Publishing (an imprint of IGI Global)
    3 Henrietta Street
    Covent Garden
    London WC2E 8LU
    Tel: 44 20 7240 0856
    Fax: 44 20 7379 0609
    Web site: http://www.eurospanonline.com

Library of Congress Cataloging-in-Publication Data

Patriotic information systems / Todd Loendorf & G. David Garson, editors.
    p. cm.
  Summary: "This book discusses how, with its non-participatory enforcement ethos, its inherent bias against freedom of information, and its massive claims on IT budget resources, the information technology security system of the future may be even less hospitable to the democratic visions which some theorists once anticipated would be among the most important contributions of information technology to society"--Provided by publisher.
  Includes bibliographical references and index.
  ISBN-13: 978-1-59904-594-8 (hardcover)
  ISBN-13: 978-1-59904-596-2 (ebook)
  1. Computer security--Law and legislation--United States. 2. Data protection--Law and legislation--Untied States. 3. Information technology--Security measures--United States. 4. Electronic surveillance--United States. 5. Public records--Access control--United States. 6. Freedom of information--United States. 7. Privacy, Right of--United States. I. Loendorf, Todd. II. Garson, G. David.
  KF390.5.C6P38 2008
  342.7308'58--dc22
                      2007024490

British Cataloguing in Publication Data
A Cataloguing in Publication record for this book is available from the British Library.

Patriotic Information Systems

Table of Contents

Section I:
Introduction

Section II:
Freedom of Information and Access

Section IV:
Conclusion

Preface

It behooves every man who values liberty of conscience for himself, to resist invasions of it in the case of others: or their case may, by change of circumstances, become his own.

Thomas Jefferson (1803)

Written over 200 years ago in a letter to Dr. Benjamin Rush, the words of Thomas Jefferson still offer food for thought. Then, the issue was religious freedom. Today, the primary issue is the right to privacy. The right to privacy was not explicitly stated in the Constitution of the United States. However, many (including the Supreme Court) have argued that the right to privacy is an integral part of the constitution, as well as implicit in the thoughts and ideas of the Founding Fathers. In 1890, Samuel Warren and Louis Brandeis wrote an essay entitled "The Right to Privacy." At the time, the ease with which personal information, including photographs, could be disseminated to the public was beginning to make many citizens feel uneasy with respect to their own personal information. Warren and Brandeis argued that individuals should have control over their own personal information and that common law protects the right to privacy. Although the debate about whether, as citizens, we have a right to privacy has raged on for many decades since this famous essay, the decision in *Griswold v. Connecticut* (381 U.S. 479) in 1965 marked the beginning of constitutional protection for the right. This decision overturned the convictions of the director of Planned Parenthood and a doctor at Yale Medical School for dispersing contraceptive-related information, instruction, and medical advice to married persons. It has been used to protect the rights of many citizens including, most famously, the right to have an abortion in the case of *Roe v. Wade* (410 U.S. 113) in 1973. Although the applicability of this decision to specific activities has and will continue to be questioned, the "right to one's personality" discussed by Warren and Brandeis is an unmistakable part of the fabric of legal and political tradition in the United States of America.

The horrific events of September 11, 2001, have been an undeniable force affecting privacy. On this day, millions of people sat and watched in a state of disbelief as thousands of Americans lost their lives to the hate-inspired actions of others. How could this have happened? Why were we not protected? What should we do to make sure this does not happen again? Questions, anger, and more questions filled the public dialog. Unfortunately, this was not the first time the security of American citizens had been threatened on American soil. It was also not the first time that personal rights came under attack. The Alien and Sedition Acts, the suspension of habeas corpus during the Civil War, the internment of Japanese-Americans during World War II, the McCarthy era, and the surveillance and harassment of antiwar protesters, including Dr. Martin Luther King Jr., during the Vietnam War all mark serious transgressions against the right of privacy by those in power during different periods of our nations history. During times of crisis and war, two things can be expected. First, the power of the president will be at its highest, and personal liberties and freedoms will be at their lowest. This follows the political theory of Thomas Hobbes, who reasoned that citizens must expect to give up some of their freedoms in return for protection and a civil society.

The USA Patriot Act was signed into law October 26, 2001, after passing in the House of Representatives by a vote of 357-66, with nine not voting, and in the Senate by a vote of 98-1, with one not voting. Coming on the heels of 9-11, this law was rushed to a vote and provided the executive branch with the power it felt it needed to fight terrorism and those responsible for one of the darkest days in our nation's history. It was also, unfortunately, one of the greatest assaults on personal privacy ever launched upon the citizens of our nation. This sentiment is echoed by the words of the one Senator, Russ Feingold, who voted against the measure.

There is no doubt that if we lived in a police state, it would be easier to catch terrorists. If we lived in a country that allowed the police to search your home at any time for any reason; if we lived in a country that allowed the government to open your mail, eavesdrop on your phone conversations, or intercept your email communications; if we lived in a country that allowed the government to hold people in jail indefinitely based on what they write or think, or based on mere suspicion that they are up to no good, then the government would no doubt discover and arrest more terrorists. But that probably would not be a country in which we would want to live. That would not be a country for which we could, in good conscience, ask our young people to fight and die. In short, that would not be America.

Despite assurances to the contrary, the fears expressed by opponents of the Patriot Act have manifested themselves time and again. The abuse of prisoners at Abu Ghraib prison signaled that the Bush administration was willing to violate basic human rights in order to secure information. That studies indicate that torture as a means to collect information is unreliable, at best, appears to have been lost on the Bush administration. The warrantless wiretapping of American citizens reveals a sense of imperial power that many scholars and lawmakers viewed as unconstitutional long before it was rebuked by federal judges. The classification of investigations that collect and warehouse data on American citizens as being terrorism-related when there were no terrorism links present suggests a willingness to accumulate data on ordinary citizens. For citizens who believe that if they are doing nothing wrong then they have nothing to worry about, this should serve as a wake-up call. What is even more troubling is that when the investigations turn out to not be related to terrorism, the classification code used to mark the type of investigation is never changed to something that would indicate it is not terrorism-related. This indicates either a major problem with responsible management of personal information or a deliberate attempt to inflate antiterrorism statistics. Either is cause for concern. Finally, in March 2007, the abuse of power that is enabled by many of the provisions of the Patriot Act boiled to a head as an audit of the FBI use of National Security Letters (NSL) was made public.

The FBI issued about 8,500 NSLs in 2000, the last full year before the Patriot Act was passed. Four years later, the reported use of NSLs peaked at 56,000. Altogether, 143,000 NSL requests occurred from 2003-2005. NSL's are issued to organizations requesting that they turn over various record and data pertaining to individuals. NSL's require no judicial oversight. The original Patriot Act provision prohibited recipients from ever disclosing their receipt of an NSL to anyone. The Patriot Act expanded the use of NSL's by requiring that they only be relevant to an authorized investigation of international terrorism or foreign intelligence and that it not burden activities protected by the First Amendment. The lack of judicial oversight and the limits placed on free speech are troubling. The fact that the FBI misused this power several times, as found in a small audit of cases, is also troubling. These facts combined with the finding that "exigent letters," a letter that essentially circumvents the NSL process, were used over 700 times during the audit period, may have opened a policy window for change.

Many of the chapters in *Patriotic Information Systems* echo the sentiment of Senator Feingold in examining many of the current attacks on core democratic ideals, including the right to privacy. The first chapter in the book, entitled "Bush Administration Information Policy and Democratic Values," is written by G. David Garson and serves as an introduction to many of the issues presented in the course of the book. Discussions of the Total Information Awareness Act (TIA) and the USA Patriot Act are used to illustrate the concern over the survival of democratic values in what is increasingly a surveillance society. The chapter concludes with policy recommendations for fighting terrorism while protecting the freedoms of citizens.

The next five chapters comprise a section of the book that deals with the freedom of information and access. In his chapter "Less Safe: The Dismantling of Public Information Systems after September 11," Harry Hammitt analyzes how, in response to perceived security threats, government agencies have taken information down from Web sites, curtailed or restricted access to electronic sources of information, broadened the interpretation of FOIA exemptions, created or augmented new categories of restricted information, and prohibited public access for critical infrastructure information. These policy responses have been based both on the perceived security threat and an inhospitable attitude toward open government on the part of the Bush administration.

Next, Charles Davis, writing on "The Expanding of Privacy Rationales under the Federal Freedom of Information Act: Stigmatization as Talisman" focuses on the "War on Terror" and the handling of detainee and other information sought under the Freedom of Information Act suits by reporters.

Using two studies performed by the Library Research Center concerning the impact of the terrorist attacks and the USA PATRIOT Act on librarians and the patrons, Lauren Teffeau, Megan Mustafoff, and Leigh Estabrook combine to write a chapter entitled "Access to Information and the Freedom to Access: The Intersection of Public Libraries and the USA Patriot Act." The study finds a regional effect and points to the need for further research. The last chapter in the section on freedom of information and access is written by Abby A. Goodrum. The chapter serves as a national examination of librarians' perceptions of law enforcement activity in academic and public libraries and points to a possible chilling effect on the use and access of information.

The next section of chapters focuses on security, technology, and democracy. Brian S. Krueger, writing in "Resisting Government Internet Surveillance by Participating in Politics Online and Offline," argues that the growing use of the Internet for political participation and the government's expanded electronic surveillance capacities make increasingly dubious the assumption regarding political participation that citizens operate within an unproblematic surveillance context. Interestingly, Krueger finds that those who oppose the current administration, and who perceive the government monitors their Internet behavior, participate in politics online at the highest rates.

Jeffrey Roy's chapter on "Security, Sovereignty, and Continental Interoperability: Canada's Elusive Balance," discusses how U.S. antiterrorism and homeland security measures have raised international issues with respect to the appropriate scope of governmental action. As North American governance faces new and rising pressures to adapt to a post 9-11 nexus of security, technology, and democracy, the culture of secrecy already prevalent within U.S. national security authorities is being extended to the continental level under the guise of interoperability. Strikingly, this is happening without any corresponding political effort to ensure openness and public accountability, both within and between countries.

Akhlaque Haque, writing on "Information Technology and Surveillance: Implications for Public Administration in a New World Order," develops the thesis that the essential resolution of the Patriot Act has been to destabilize the status-quo, especially as it relates to diversity, by introducing control values. He argues that in trying to control apparent instability by surveillance methods, we could do more harm in the other branches of government, undermining the role of democracy in the information age. Finally, David C. Wyld, in "The Little Chip That Could: The Public Sector and RFID," provides a detailed examination of the current uses of RFID technology in the public sector. Like many things, the purpose for the technology will go a long way toward determining the effectiveness of the technology.

The final chapter entitled "Out of Control? The Real ID Act of 2005," is written by Todd Loendorf, and serves as the conclusion to the book. The chapter discusses the rationales for and arguments against the establishment of a Nation ID card, with particular attention paid to the issues revolving around the collection and mining of data. It concludes by illuminating the fact that this is a shining example of our federal system of government because, as of this writing, many states are actively seeking to repeal or amend this law.

In summary, the chapters in *Patriotic Information Systems* raise serious policy questions about current information policy of the U.S. government. It is now apparent that database technology can be used for various ends, ranging from promotion of democracy to strengthening of nationalism to shoring up authoritarian regimes through misinformation. When this is put in the context of the need for information technology (IT) security, with its nonparticipatory enforcement ethos, its inherent bias against freedom of information, and its massive claims on IT budget resources, the more secure IT systems of the future may well be even less hospitable to the democratic visions which some theorists once anticipated would be among the most important contributions of information technology to society.

References

Feingold, R. (2001, October 12). Address given to the Associated Press Managing Editors Conference, Milwaukee Art Museum, Milwaukee, WI.

Warren, S., & Brandeis, L. (1890). The right to privacy. *Harvard Law Review, 4,* 193-220.

Acknowledgment

The editors would like to acknowledge the help of all involved in the production of the book, without whose support the project could not have been satisfactorily completed.

Most of the authors of chapters included in this book also served as referees for articles written by other authors. Thanks go to all those who provided constructive and comprehensive reviews. Additionally, several other people helped the project by providing advice that was important in keeping the team moving forward. Especially important throughout the process were G. David Garson of North Carolina State University, Abby Goodrum of Ryerson University, David Wyld of Southeastern Louisiana University, and Walter Brasch of Bloomsburg University. Without your kind words, advice, and "gentle prodding" along the way, this book would not be the same. Support of the School of Public and International Affairs at North Carolina State University is acknowledged for computing resources used throughout this project.

Special thanks also go to all the staff at IGI Global, whose contributions throughout the whole process from inception of the initial idea to final publication have been invaluable. In particular, to Kristin Roth, who provided us with timely information, exceptional advice, and kept us on track via e-mail and phone calls.

Special thanks go to G. David Garson for providing me with this opportunity. I hope this book lives up to the vision you had for it. And last but not least, to my family, Siobhan, Jade, Brenna, and Joseph, for their unfailing support and encouragement during the months it took to give birth to this book. I love you very much.

In closing, I wish to thank all of the authors for their insights and excellent contributions to this book. I also want to thank all of the people who assisted me in the reviewing process. I learned much during the compilation of this book. I hope the readers of this book find it as interesting and informative as I do.

Todd Loendorf, Editor
Raleigh, North Carolina, USA
July 2007

Section I

Introduction

Chapter I

Bush Administration Information Policy and Democratic Values

G. David Garson, North Carolina State University, USA

Abstract

Bush administration information policy raises fundamental questions about the survival of democratic values in what is increasingly a surveillance society. After the terrorist attacks on the World Trade Center and the Pentagon in 2001, Bush administration information policy abandoned the transparency in government policies of the Clinton administration and the 1990s, moving the pendulum toward a policy of secrecy in government and massive classification of documents. From perpetuating core elements of the Congressionally-banned Total Information Awareness program to warrantless electronic searching on a mass basis to undermining provisions of the Freedom of Information Act, the Bush administration has sought as a matter of policy to curtail the democratic freedoms it purports to protect. A comprehensive civil remedies statute needs to be enacted in order to assure that citizens have a clear legal claim in litigation against the government when they suffer various forms of injury as a result of wrongful surveillance and intrusion into their privacy.

Introduction

In his last major work before his death in 2003, Senator Daniel Patrick Moynihan wrote *Secrecy: The American Experience* (1998), in which he advocated a culture of openness in decision making. Based on his chairmanship of the bipartisan Commission on Protecting and Reducing Government Secrecy, in this work Moynihan traced governmental secrecy since WWI through the failure to predict the collapse of the Soviet Union, arguing that many tragedies resulting from events he describes could have been prevented had the issues been clarified in an open exchange of ideas. Likewise, in the recent Abu Ghraib scandal, the *New York Times* quoted federal officials as saying that the 2004 scandals in the military justice system - abuses which severely damaged the credibility of American foreign policy—"are rooted in the secretive and contentious process from which it emerged" (Golden, 2004). Freedom of information, transparency, and openness in government are not niceties of a democratic society; they are fundamental to its survival and a major reason for the effectiveness of the democratic form of government.

Bush administration information policy raises fundamental questions about the survival of democratic values in what is increasingly a surveillance society. To take a recent instance, at the end of April 2006, the *Wall Street Journal* reported that Pentagon intelligence agencies had stepped up efforts to track the activities of American citizens, such as middle-aged Quakers participating in antiIraq war protests, on the justification they were "assessed to present a potential force protection threat" (Block & Solomon, 2006). Based on information collected, the Pentagon's activities included alerting local police forces for more active surveillance, such as following protesters in unmarked police cars—a form of attention understandably perceived by the protestors as political harassment and intimidation. At least 20 domestic antiwar groups have been tracked by the military, echoing the infamous FBI Cointelpro operations against Martin Luther King and assorted radical groups in the 1950s, 1960s, and 1970s (Wolf, 2004). Databases were amassed by the Pentagon based on intercepted e-mail, police databases, group Web sites, and FBI and other sources. While defending such hitherto-illegal domestic surveillance with an ingenuous claim that such efforts were directed toward keeping military personnel away from protest areas, the Pentagon also issued an apology, admitting some military databases contained inappropriate information.

The reinterpretation of the American legal environment with respect to privacy and databases has been influenced by the Bush administration's post 9/11 declaration of the continental United States as an official theater of military operations, something unprecedented since the Civil War. The reinterpretation, reflected in a 2001 directive from Army Deputy Chief of Staff for Intelligence General Robert Noonan, has been based on a new information policy rooted in a distinction between proscribed military "collection" of data on domestic civilians and the permitted "receiving" and electronic cross-referencing of information from such sources as e-mail, the Web, and law enforcement agencies. What under manual methods was collection, now under the methods of information technology is receiving. The military's CIFA (Counter Intelligence Field Activity) program has expanded dramatically since 2001 and works with the Department of Justice to implement "deep access data-mining techniques" (Block & Solomon, 2006). Since 2001, some military domestic receiving/spying has been organized under Talon (Threat and Local Observation Notice), a data-mining program established to detect threats based on disparate data bits. Talon data, in turn, was used to prompt Akron, Ohio, police to follow Quaker-organized antiwar protesters in the spring of 2006.

Limiting Freedom of Information after 9/11

Numerous authors have noted how, after the terrorist attacks on the World Trade Center and the Pentagon in 2001, Bush administration information policy abandoned the transparency in government policies of the Clinton administration and the 1990s, moving the pendulum toward a policy of secrecy in government and massive classification of documents (Fiorini, 2004). The Nuclear Regulatory Commission pulled its entire Web site. The U.S. Geological Survey removed maps of open water spaces. The EPA eliminated data on toxic waste sites needed by community groups to identify chemical hazards. The Department of Energy removed information on environmental impacts of nuclear plants and information on which communities are traversed by trucks carrying hazardous materials information previously used by public interest groups. According to the nonpartisan Working Group on Community Right-to-Know, over 6,000 public documents were removed from federal Web sites of over a dozen government agencies after 9/11. While some of this has been restored, there is little doubt that the United States now operates with less freedom of information than prior to 9/11. The EPA, for instance, denied twice as many FOIA requests in 2003 as it had in 2001. In terms of legislation, the Critical Infrastructure Information Security Act of 2001 (CIISA) exempted from FOIA disclosure any "critical infrastructure information that is voluntarily submitted" to one of 13 covered federal agencies (such as the EPA), and this has been cited as constituting a major new exemption to FOIA rights.

Immediately after the 9/11 tragedy, Bush's attorney general, John Ashcroft, issued a memorandum to all federal agency heads outlining how FOIA was to be implemented. Whereas Clinton and Janet Reno, Clinton's attorney general, had instructed agencies to promote freedom of information and to release documents even if they might arguably have been exempted under a FOIA exceptions clause, the Ashcroft memorandum reversed this policy. The new policy became one of encouraging agencies to look for reasons to deny access to information, and to expand secrecy in government by utilizing FOIA's exceptions as a way of denying access even beyond formal classification of documents. Moreover, public managers were assured that the resources of the Justice Department would be made available to them to defend refusals of FOIA requests should litigation occur (Public Citizen, 2004). A 2003 Government Accountability Office (GAO) report surveyed 183 FOIA officials at 23 federal agencies and found almost one third admitting that because of the Ashcroft memo, their agency subsequently was less likely to release information, a proportion OMB Watch found biased toward the low end (OMB Watch, 2003).

One function of the Freedom of Information Act (FOIA) requests is to keep a check on bureaucratic abuses of information rights. An example arose in 2004 when the Transportation Security Administration (TSA) sought to integrate commercial data on individuals with their Secure Flight data-mining system, in spite of an earlier promise by TSA that it would not do so. Every individual record purchased by TSA violated Privacy Act rights because of lack of proper disclosure to the individuals involved. Given the size of the commercial databases purchased, arguably there were tens of millions of violations of the act (Fink, 2005).

Aroused by the Electronic Frontier Foundation of other supporters of civil liberties, thousands of people submitted FOIA requests, seeking to determine what information the TSA had collected about them without their consent. In its defense, the TSA claimed it could not bring up individual records and could not comply with the FOIA demands. This, however, suggested either (1) TSA was not able to issue simple Structured Query Language commands to its databases, or (2) Secure Flight was incapable of identifying individuals, including terrorist suspects, using in part commercial data which had been purchased by TSA at great expense for the purpose. Either was an embarrassment to the TSA, which became an object of Congressional scrutiny as a result.

OMB Watch, based on a study by the American Bar Association (ABA), has reported that since 2001 there has been an "explosion in the use by federal agencies of Sensitive But Unclassified (SBU) designations to withhold information" (OMB Watch, 2006). The ABA has criticized the SBU designation, of which there are some 50 varying and inconsistent definitions in use by federal agencies, as being too vague and being wrongly used by agencies to deny FOIA requests for information.

While increasing the amount of information withheld from citizens, the Bush administration also experimented with increasing the amount of misinformation disseminated to citizens. In 2002, it resurrected the Eisenhower-era Office of Strategic Information (OSI) as part of the administration's anti-openness strategy to handle what some called "misinformation" to U.S. and foreign journalists and to citizens of Afghanistan (BBC, 2002). While deliberate misinformation has long been a weapon of information warfare, this marked a departure in expanding the strategy to an agency targeting American journalists and the American public, not just foreign enemies. In its short life, the OSI disseminated widely influential but false stories, such as a notable one about Iraqi soldiers yanking premature babies from their cribs and dashing them to the floor (Morano, 2002).

Pursuant to the Foreign Intelligence Surveillance Act of 1978, a 1980 document, "U.S. Signals Intelligence Directive 18," had prohibited the NSA from engaging in domestic spying, but after 9/11 President Bush ordered expanded electronic surveillance transcending former restrictions. Just before Christmas, 2005, the *New York Times* revealed that after the 9/11 terrorist attacks in 2001, President Bush had authorized the National Security Administration (NSA) to intercept telephone calls and e-mail traffic without benefit of court-issued warrants. The Bush administration defended its action on the grounds of homeland security and the need to pursue its antiterrorist efforts (Risen & Lichtblau, 2005).

As authority, Bush cited his presidential powers as commander-in-chief, his inherent powers to act to protect the American people, and Congress's post 9/11 resolution authorizing him to wage war on terrorists. The administration at first claimed that spying was limited to calls/e-mails in which at least one end of the communication was in another country, but later admitted that domestic-to-domestic traffic had also been surveilled, allegedly "by accident." The president's attorney-general, NSA advisor, and other administration officials rallied behind the president (Lichtblau, 2006a).

The issue of domestic spying and eavesdropping on U.S. citizens immediately became front-page news, with some Democrats calling for the creation of an independent counsel to investigate possible violations of the Fourth Amendment's prohibition against unreasonable searches and seizures, the constitutional provision which is the basis for the requirement for court authorization of warrants and wiretaps. The warrantless electronic surveillance program of the Bush administration had bypassed court approvals, even after-the-fact ones, even by the secretive Foreign Intelligence Surveillance Court (FISC, established in the 1970s under the Foreign Intelligence Surveillance Act). The USA PATRIOT Act had designated FISC as the only court authorized to issue surveillance orders in investigations of terrorism, and it was thought to approve almost all requests submitted to it.

In July 2005, an Islamic scholar and oncologist named Ali al-Timimi was given a life sentence plus 70 years, without possibility of parole, for having solicited followers to fight on the side of the Taliban's jihad against the United States (Pontoniere, 2005). The conviction was appealed to the federal district court in Alexandria, VA, which declined to hear evidence related to illegal eavesdropping. However, in April 2006, the 4th Circuit Court of Appeals remanded the case to the lower court, ordering to consider testimony related to charges that the conviction was based on illegally gathering evidence without a warrant (Lichtblau, 2006b). Still pending at this writing, the al-Timimi case may become the first to test the constitutionality of President Bush's warrantless search program.

Meanwhile, in January 2006, the Electronic Frontier Foundation filed a lawsuit based on testimony of Mark Klein. As an AT&T technician, Klein claimed that in 2003 he witnessed the construction of a secret room at AT&T's San Francisco headquarters, with wiring and equipment designed to tap Internet traffic in wholesale quantities (Hosenball & Thomas, 2006, p. 25). Allegedly, similar Internet-mining installations have been created in other cities.

Domestic spying seemed to be part of a general policy, not an aberration, since also in December 2005, the American Civil Liberties Union had released new FBI records (released as a result of a lawsuit over FBI activities in relation to the 2004 national political conventions) showing ongoing monitoring of antiwar, civil rights, environmental, and other activist groups. "Our government is spying on Americans —unapologetically, unnecessarily and with no regard for the Constitution," the ACLU stated (Fisher, 2005). Spying on reporters, inherently an activity which may be construed to intimidate a free press, is part of the pattern. In May 2006, ABC News revealed that two of its reporters were told by a senior federal law enforcement official that the government had obtained records of their calls. The reporters were working on stories about secret (and legally questionable) detention centers for terrorism suspects outside the United States, and related matters. At the same time, Vincent Cannistraro, a former CIA counterterrorism chief, told *The New York Sun* that FBI sources had confirmed to him the tracking of reporters' calls (Carlson & King, 2006).

While Congressional leaders, including Democrats, had been briefed about the domestic spying program, the briefings had bound them to secrecy, precluding even obtaining legal opinions regarding the constitutionality of the program. When the issue became public, various Senators made known that they had sent Vice President Cheney letters raising legal issues, but with no response. The no-discussions policy was further emphasized when, immediately after the domestic spying affair became public, the Bush Justice Department moved to investigate and prosecute the whistle-blowers who had leaked the story.

Supporting the Cheney position, in May 2006, in the case of *Garcetti v. Ceballos*, the U.S. Supreme Court ruled that "job-related" speech is unprotected by the First Amendment. This reversal of prior law, made possible by new conservative Court appointments made by President Bush, was based on elevating the rights of employers, including the federal government, over the rights of employees not to be penalized for exposing fraud, waste, or simply bad policy in reports and communications performed as part of their jobs. Whistleblower.org, a public interest group promoting the protection of whistle-blowers, stated, "This ruling will have a serious chilling effect on the willingness of public employees to risk their livelihood to expose government fraud and waste. Our democratic traditions and the American taxpayer are sacrificed to the alter of 'employer control'" (Blaylock, 2006). Implications for the sphere of information technology are clear, since virtually everything appearing on a .gov Web site can be seen as work performed for hire. From an information systems viewpoint, *Garcetti v. Ceballos* institutionalizes information control: there is no legal protection for government employees who might be tempted to post on the Web anything critical of the administration, their employer. Moreover, since all e-mail on the job is supposed to be "job-related," the logical implication is that there is also no legal protection for government employees using e-mail from a government computer to criticize the administration.

In May 2006, *USA Today* reported that the NSA had created a massive database of billions of domestic phone call records (number calling, time, date, to what number, duration) which it was using to identify suspect patterns for further possible investigation and eavesdropping (Hosenball & Thomas, 2006, p. 24). Verizon, BellSouth, and AT&T surrendered their huge databases voluntarily, without warrant and without informing their customers, and in apparent violation of Section 222 of the Communications Act, which prohibits telephone companies from disclosing customer's calling information without a warrant (Cauley, 2006). Congress was not briefed, setting the scene for criticism from both political parties when the press revealed the project (CBS News, 2006).

The defense of this and related domestic spying has taken two contradictory forms. First, it is argued that it is essential to combat terrorism and prevent "another 9/11, but has to remain ultra-secret to prevent Al Quaida from getting an advantage. U.S. Attorney General Alberto Gonzales cited the Patriot Act as authority for the executive order giving the NSA authorization for domestic spying (Cauley, 2006). The weakness of this argument is that Al Quaida already has access to state-of-the-art throw-away encrypted phones; specific instances of preventing other "9/11s" have not been cited, and even if there has been some antiterrorist value, there is no empirical comparison with equivalent investment in other forms of spying which may be less inimical to the privacy rights of Americans (e.g., many call for a shift of funds from electronics to old-fashioned human agents).

The second, contradictory defense is virtually the opposite: that the NSA's information systems for dealing with massive amounts of tapped data is of dubious effectiveness. The NSA Trailblazer software system, designed to datamine voluminous amounts of communications traffic, has been described by one CIA veteran as "a complete and abject failure" which reporters describe as producing "nearly a billion dollars' worth of junk hardware and software" (Hosenball & Thomas, 2006, p. 29). The implication is that Americans need not worry about what does not work anyway (except, possibly, worry about their tax dollars!). Likewise, the *Washington Post* found that the NSA examined millions of records, flagging thousands of suspect cases (about 5,000 according to one source), finding about 10 per year worth-recording phone conversations, and winding up dismissing "nearly all" of these (Gellman, Linzer, & Leonnig, 2006).

In September, 2006, the split within the Republican Party over warrantless searches seemed to be healed when Senator John McCain and other Republicans reached a much-criticized compromise with President Bush. In a vote in the Senate Judiciary Committee with all Republicans supporting Bush and all Democrats opposed, the Committee approved a bill which allowed (but did not require) the president to submit the NSA's warrantless wiretapping program to secret court review. The Center for Technology and Democracy condemned the so-called compromise as a sham, noting it gutted FISA requirements, making them merely voluntary and giving the president sweeping new powers (CTD, 2006). While the bill did provide that individuals identified by warrantless searches as terrorism suspects would have to be submitted to the Foreign Intelligence Security Court, such review would be voluntary, would not apply to individuals identified in nonterrorist contexts, and would be applied post-hoc in seeming violation of the spirit of the Fourth Amendment, which was to require a priori court approval of such searches.

The Republican compromise bill was widely perceived to ratify the warrantless wiretapping program. As such, it undercut the argument that the president was unconstitutionally disregarding Congress's express wishes under FISA to have all such programs reviewed by FISA courts. The new bill, in contrast, was designed to be cited as Congressional support for the president's constitutional authority to conduct foreign intelligence surveillance, including the warrantless wiretap program (Weisman, 2006).

How Information Systems Transcend Congressional Oversight

Much as drug culture assures that the trafficking in prohibited substances suppressed in one location pops up in another, so in a surveillance culture in those rare instances when congressional oversight of the bureaucracy does terminate the invasion of privacy in one area, similarly invasive information systems crop up in another. A good illustration arises in efforts of Congress to deal with the 2002 report that the Pentagon's Defense Advanced Research Projects Office (DARPA) was developing a "Total Information Awareness System"(TIA) which would use information technology to create a virtual database with instant access to information on an individual's phone call records, e-mail transcripts, Web search histories, financial records, store purchases, health prescriptions and medical records, educational records, travel history, and all transactions involving passports and drivers' licenses.

Part of the TIA project incorporated technology for extracting information about people from e-mail and other message traffic, raising the specter of "Big Brother" reading one's personal mail. The effort, later renamed the "Terrorism Information Awareness" project to make it more politically palatable, was initially budgeted for $10 million in FY 2003 and headed by Bush administration official John Poindexter. That Poindexter had been involved in the 1980s Iran-Contra scandal and had been found guilty of obstruction of justice and destruction of evidence did nothing to increase confidence in the Bush administration's commitment to protection of privacy under the TIA program.

Criticism of the TIA came not only from the expected civil liberties direction (ACLU, 2002a), but also from the conservative think tank, the CATO Institute (Onley, 2002). CATO director of technology studies, Wayne Crews, argued that the TIA was "bad on three fronts: civil liberties, compromising the future of electronic commerce, and it's bad for security." That is, the TIA was seen as bad for business because consumers would be wary of making electronic purchases, knowing this information was given to the government for secret domestic surveillance purposes. The CATO Institute also put forward the secondary argument that by consolidating information in a single system, the TIA database would become a prime target for hackers, and thus the TIA would actually weaken security.

By January, 2003, the combination of civil liberties and business criticism of the TIA project led Congress to begin de-funding the effort. A rider to the Senate bill providing funding for the TIA made funding dependent on a report on the project's civil liberties aspects, to come later in 2003. In the meantime, the TIA continued anyway with funds under the discretion of President Bush. The July 2003 TIA report from the Pentagon emphasized that the Palo Alto Research Center, Inc., had been awarded a $3.5 million contract to develop "privacy appliance" software as a filtering gateway to TIA databases, blocking unauthorized access and preventing the release of individually identifiable data. Civil libertarians were not satisfied. Even if DOD or other analysts were required to have a court order for each access to individually identifiable data (mentioned as a possibility but not promised and not deemed practical), David Sobel, general counsel for Washington's Electronic Privacy Information Center, noted even with the "privacy appliance," the system would be "completely alien to our judicial system" because it would involve court-ordered surveillance for a crime that had not actually been committed (Jackson, 2003, p. 32).

Unmoved by the DOD report, Congress voted to de-fund the TIA project in September 2003. As one TIA critic, Erick Schonfeld, noted, de-funding the TIA did not stop similar efforts in the private sector, nor governmental access to and utilization of them. He wrote:

Commercial data aggregators such as Accurint, Acxiom, and Choicepoint bring together hundreds of publicly and privately available databases filled with information on people's addresses, phone numbers, driver's licenses, bankruptcy histories, accident histories, and property. These databases are used by police departments and debt collectors to find deadbeats and crime suspects, as well as their assets. And while the technologies they use are primitive versions of what Poindexter wants to create, they are pretty far-reaching nevertheless. For instance, a search in

one of those databases for 'John M. Poindexter' comes up with the address of his
house in Rockville, Md.; how much he paid for it on March 30, 1971 ($42,000); its
assessed value today ($269,050); his known associates (mostly family members),
along with their current addresses and phone numbers; and the hull number of
his 42-foot boat, the Bluebird. I could go on. But even Poindexter deserves some
privacy. (Schonfeld, 2003)

Commenting on the TIA de-funding vote, DARPA chief Anthony Tether noted that
Congress's Joint Inquiry into 9/11 had called for data mining of the TIA type and
that this mandate to the DOD and other federal agencies was still there (Levy, 2003).
Although the TIA was dropped from the Defense Department's appropriations bill,
the *Government Computer News* reported that the de-funding bill "still states that
a similar system could be used to collect data on non-U.S. citizens or residents for
counter-terrorism and intelligence purposes. That seems to leave wiggle room for
grabbing data from any source if it seems important enough" (McCarthy, 2004).

In 2006, investigative journalists brought to light several ongoing data mining pro-
grams which were direct descendants of the Total Information Awareness project.
Block and Solomon (2006), writing in the *Wall Street Journal*, discovered that
"Many computer programs and techniques developed during the Total Information
Awareness project quietly survived" (p. 14). At least three systems of TIA were
taken up by the nation's largest military counterintelligence unit, the Army's 902nd
Military Intelligence Group, which was the source of reports fed to Akron, Ohio,
police to track Quaker-organized antiwar protest groups, as discussed above. Like-
wise, in an article headed, "The Total Information Awareness Project Lives On,"
Technology Review reported how at least two "principal components of the overall
TIA project have migrated to the Advanced Research and Development Activity
(ARDA), which is housed somewhere among the 60-odd buildings of 'Crypto City,'
as NSA headquarters in Fort Meade, MD, is nicknamed" (Williams, 2006). One of
these components was the core TIA system designed to integrate massive personal
databases. Congressional oversight seemed to uphold privacy values over surveillance values in 2003, but now in retrospect seems to have served as a symbolic act
defusing civil libertarian and popular protest while allowing the substance of the
information technology-based surveillance state to advance almost unimpeded.

In October 2006, the United Press International Homeland and National Security
Editor reported that a TIA-like mass data mining project had been resurrected by
John Negroponte, the new Director of National Intelligence. The 4-year experimental
program, named Tangram, was immediately criticized by the American Civil Liberties Union, both on privacy grounds and as a waster of taxpayer dollars. Anonymous
official sources told UPI that the types of information to be searched remained
secret but that Tangram built on previous data-mining projects undertaken by the
intelligence community to fight terrorism. Tangram was placed under the Advanced

Research and Development Activity office, the same office which had overseen the TIA project. Referring to Congress's "termination" of the TIA in 2003, an ACLU lawyer stated, "The administration has flat out ignored Congress. They renamed it, re-tied the bow around it and off they went" (Waterman, 2006).

A conceptual issue with Tangram, TIA, and other data mining systems is that they revolve around link analysis, which critics call a form of "guilt by association." Particularly given its use on datasets with errors, link analysis targets possible suspects on a mass basis without the need for any evidence of any crime. Once targeted, individuals may find themselves investigated, their privacy compromised, and their lives disrupted, sometimes for a prolonged period of time. In the course of investigation, the fact they are "suspected" may be given to various law enforcement authorities. Interviews with friends, associates, and mere acquaintances can lead to suspects suffering irreparable damage to reputations and standing in the community and in jobs. Civil libertarians thus find inherent in TIA a threat to the fundamental fairness which was previously upheld by the requirement of court-approved warrants prior to intrusive searches. However, under data mining link analysis, there is no warrant process or, indeed, any court process for protecting citizen rights, only self-regulation by those doing the investigating, which involves clear conflict of interest.

Bush domestic information policy was also reflected in the Republican-sponsored Real ID Act of 2005, passed largely along party lines and largely without debate in Congress and without much attention from the media. It was embedded in an emergency military appropriations bill for Iraq, to make it hard for opponents to vote against it. Its purpose is "to establish and rapidly implement regulations for State driver's license and identification document security standards." The Real ID act would compel states to design their driver's licenses by 2008 to comply with federal antiterrorist standards. Federal employees would then reject licenses or identity cards that don't comply, which could curb Americans' access to airplanes, national parks, federal courthouses, Social Security, and even opening bank accounts. In short, the Real ID Act comes close to being a national ID card. It is slated to take effect in 2008, so its impacts are speculative at this point.

Under the Real ID Act, the Department of Homeland Security is given authority to specify standards for state drivers' licenses, which could include biometrics (fingerprint, iris scans), RFID tags, and DNA information; it will also include basic identity information and a digital photo. State DMVs will have to require much more identification than in the past (another unfunded mandate to the states). DMV's will require most license applicants to show a photo ID, a birth certificate, proof of their Social Security number and a document showing their full name and address. All of the documents then would have to be checked against federal databases.

From the point of view of national information policy, the significance of the Real ID Act centers on the likelihood that it will involve creation of a massive national database on individuals. While there is still a chance the Real ID cards will only be checked locally on an individual basis (e.g., does the cardholder have the fingerprints the card says they have?), at this writing it seems more likely that cards will be checked against a national database. Vast public policy issues pertain to the unresolved questions of what will be in the database, who will have access to it, and what privacy protections and remedies may or may not exist.

Resistance to Bush Information Policy

Writing of the unprecedented level of secrecy in the administration of George W. Bush, John Dean, former counsel to President Nixon, wrote to Karl Rove, Bush's chief political strategist:

The continuing insistence on secrecy by your White House is startlingly Nixonian. I'm talking about everything from stiffing Congressional requests for information and witnesses, to employing an executive order to demolish the 1978 law providing public access to presidential papers, to forcing the Government Accountability Office to go to court to obtain information on how the White House is spending tax money when creating a pro-energy industry Vice Presidential task force. The Bush Administration apparently seeks to reverse the post-Watergate trend of open government. (Dean, 2004, pp. 12-13)

Of the Bush administration, Dean wrote, "Government under a virtual gag order became their standard operating procedure" (Dean, 2004, p. xv).

Bush administration undermining of freedom of information principles led to opposition, even within the Republican Party (Nakashima, 2002; Schmitt & Pound, 2003). In 2004, a bipartisan group led by Senators Trent Lott (R-MS) and Ron Wyden (D-OR) proposed the establishment of an Independent National Security Classification Board which might function as a check on overclassification of federal documents. However, Bush's national security advisor Condoleeza Rice and Budget Director Joshua Bolten wrote to House-Senate conferees on the bill, "The Administration ... opposes section 226 of S. 2845, which would...create a Congressional right to appeal classification decisions made by an executive agency with respect to national security information" (Federation of American Scientists, 2004).

A 2004 survey of open government laws by Rep. Henry A. Waxman concluded that under the Bush administration there had been a consistent pattern of undermining laws designed to promote public access, while laws that authorize the government to withhold information or to operate in secret were expanded. Waxman called the result "an unprecedented assault on the principle of open government" (Government Reform Minority Office, 2004). Specifically, the Waxman committee found that Bush had limited the scope of the Freedom of Information Act and had used procedural tactics and delays to resist information requests; had issued an executive order undermining the law making presidential records available to historians and the public; had evaded and undermined the Federal Advisory Committee Act, which requires openness and a balance of viewpoints on government advisory bodies; had reversed Clinton efforts to declassify information; had instead expanded the classification powers of executive agencies, resulting in a dramatic increase in the volume of classified government information; had expanded the definition of "sensitive security information" to allow the withholding of information about the safety of any mode of transportation; had proposed a pending directive to allow the Department of Homeland Security to conceal information about environmental impacts of its activities; had expanded authority to conduct law enforcement operations in secret with limited or no judicial oversight through the USA PATRIOT Act and through new interpretations of existing law; had repeatedly refused to provide members of Congress, the GAO, and congressional commissions with information needed for meaningful congressional oversight; had repeatedly challenged the authority of the GAO to review federal records or investigate federal programs; and had resisted providing information to senior committee members of Congress and to the National Commission on Terrorist Attacks. The Waxman report concluded, "The Bush Administration has systematically sought to limit disclosure of government records while expanding its authority to operate in secret. Taken together, the Administration's actions represent an unparalleled assault on the principle of open government" (Government Reform Minority Office, 2004).

In 2005, Rep. Waxman also spoke out against the unusual decision of the Bush administration to suppress the State Department's *Patterns of Global Terrorism* report, even though the report was mandated under a law that requires it to be submitted to the House and to the Senate Foreign Relations Committee. The report, published and released publicly since 1986, detailed on a country-by-country basis all known incidents of terrorism. When the 2005 report covering 2004 revealed that there were more incidents of terrorism in 2004 than at any time since 1985, facts which implied criticism of Bush policy, the Bush administration suddenly declared the methodology of the report to be "flawed" and ordered the State Department's National Counterterrorism Center to stop publishing the report. "This is the definitive report on the incidence of terrorism around the world," Waxman stated. "It should be unthinkable that there would be an effort to withhold it—or any of the key data—from the public." However, Bush administration information policy centered on control, not access.

Under Bush policy, the Patriot Act has been used to access statistical records for which privacy and nondissemination were promised to individual respondents at the time of data collection based on a statutory guarantee of confidentiality, as in the case of records of the National Center for Educational Statistics (Gellman, 2002). Although a court order is required to open these records for investigative uses, the courts are obliged to issue the order if the government certifies there are facts leading investigators to believe that the statistical records are relevant to their investigation. That is, the Patriot Act has been used to override statutory guarantees of privacy and to do so retroactively, breaking federal confidentiality promises made to citizens. Data from Real ID Act licenses may well become a component of the post TIA dataveillance discussed above.

By the middle of George W. Bush's presidential term, his administration had become severely criticized for its erosion of FOIA. This was illustrated in 2006, when the CIA was given the satirical Rosemary Award for "the most dramatic one-year drop-off in professionalism and responsiveness to the public" in 20 years of monitoring compliance with FOIA by the National Security Archive, the openness advocacy group making the awards (*Washington Post*, 2006).

In December 2005, President Bush issued an executive order calling on agencies to "streamline" their handling of FOIA requests (Executive Office of the President, 2005). Following up on this, an OMB memo (OMB, 2005) gave agencies until January 13, 2006, to designate a chief Freedom of Information Act officer. Also required was a new review and revision of agency FOIA processing policies and requirements by mid-June 2006, and submission of an "improvement plan" with concrete milestones for FY 2006 and FY 2007 (Thormeyer, 2006). In addition, the OMB memo called on each agency to establish one or more FOIA Requester Service Centers, where requesters could track the status of their FOIA requests. And the OMB memo required agency FOIA officers to designate one or more agency FOIA Public Liaisons to handle requests, comments, and complaints pertaining to the agency's FOIA procession. The stated purposes of the "streamlining" reforms were to better serve citizens, and to minimize FOIA lawsuits against agencies.

At this writing, it was too early to ascertain the outcome of the "streamlining" reforms of agency FOIA process. Some concern was raised about the governance structure, however. The agency FOIA officers, apart from reporting to the agency head and agency legal counsel, reported to and were required to submit their "streamlining" plans to the attorney general. Given that it was the Attorney General's office which led the Bush administration in establishing an antitransparency policy from its beginning, skepticism seemed warranted to some. As OMB Watch observed at the time, "Attorney General John Ashcroft issued a policy memo to agencies in October 2001 regarding implementation of the Freedom of Information Act. That memo turns on its head the previous policy, which, in essence, was, where possible, disclose. The Ashcroft memo tells agencies where possible do not disclose information to the public" (OMB Watch, 2002a). "Streamlining" was designed to promote efficiency in government, but efficiency always raises the question, "Efficiency toward what end?" The 2005-2006 streamlining policy could be seen as a reversal of Bush information policy regarding FOIA and transparency, or it may be seen as an exercise in damage control if the servicing of FOIA requests does not actually improve access.

Patriot Act Renewal

In October 2004, a federal court ruled unconstitutional the part of the Patriot Act which required Internet Service Providers and phone companies to comply with secret FBI orders to turn over subscriber information, including phone calls made, e-mail subject lines, and logs of Web sites visited. The basis for the decision was the holding that a mandatory gag provision prevented companies from ever informing customers or others that their privacy had been breached. The court held that the gag orders were an unconstitutional violation of free speech rights under the First Amendment (McCullagh, 2004). Also in 2004, international criticism of the Patriot Act increased, with Latin American countries objecting to providing voter and census data to U.S. law enforcement officials, and Canada warning that Patriot Act compliance would violate that nation's constitution. Nonetheless, the Bush administration pressed ahead with further expansion of Patriot Act surveillance powers, having "Patriot Act II" prepared by the Department of Justice.

In mid-December 2005, the Senate rejected the reauthorization of the Patriot Act by a vote of 52:47, with opposition coming largely on privacy rights grounds. A week later, a 5-week extension was granted and then on February 2, 2006, another 5-week extension was also approved by Congress. Finally, on March 2, 2006, the Senate passed a modified version of the renewal act by a vote of 89:10. Fourteen of sixteen Patriot Act provisions were made permanent, with two others (including roving wiretaps) given a renewal for 4 years.

Particularly controversial was Section 605 of the House version of the Patriot Act renewal, which created a permanent national police force under the Secret Service with the power to make arrests without warrant for any offense against the United States committed in their presence or for any felony under the laws of the United States. While the Secret Service has already exercised such powers in the District of Columbia, Section 605 nationalized the scope of a secret police force with powers of warrantless arrest, all with surprisingly little public debate! The renewal of the Patriot Act made Section 605 permanent. Other controversial aspects of Patriot Act renewal included:

- **"Sneak and peek" searches:** Physical searches of homes and offices without notice, before or after, that privacy was being invaded. At issue was whether such searches would have to be followed by notice 7 or 30 days after the search. The renewal bill continued "sneak and peak" searches and provided for 30 day notification, but law enforcement appeals could delay notification indefinitely.

- **Roving wiretaps:** General wiretaps of selected premises. At issue was whether enforcement authorities would have to determine that a specific target was probably present before surveillance was initiated. The renewal bill extended roving wiretaps for four more years.

- **Section 215 records searches:** Patriot Act Section 215 authorized the FBI to take out secret court orders forcing businesses and organizations to disclose personal records (e.g., library records, Internet service provider records, bank records). At issue was whether the FBI should be required to show a connection between the records and suspected terrorism. The renewal bill imposed no such requirement, but renews Section 215 for only 4 years.

- **Section 215 gag orders:** Section 215 also criminalized the disclosure by librarians, ISP's, or others of searches of their records. At issue was whether organizations should have a right to inform their members, clients, or customers that their privacy had been violated. The renewal as passed extended the gag order for 1 year, after which it gave subpoena recipients in terrorist investigations the right to challenge in court the requirement that they refrain from telling anyone. As few libraries or other subpoena recipients would be willing to undertake an expensive court fight with the government, which would claim secrecy was required by national security, critics called this concession to civil liberties merely "cosmetic."

- **NSL records searches:** Between passage of the Patriot Act in 2001 and 2005, over 30,000 National Security Letters (NSLs) were issued by the FBI, forcing businesses and organizations to turn over records. At issue was whether the current requirement of "relevance" needed to be tightened to restrict wholesale use of NSLs. One proposal was to require NSLs to be approved by the FISA Court or a federal judge. The renewal continued NSLs, but did stipulate that libraries could not be recipients of NSLs unless they ran Internet servers; and that the FBI could not demand the name of a lawyer consulted about a National Security Letter, as had been the practice. The renewal law makes explicit that judicial review of NSLs is allowable.

- **NSL disclosure penalties:** Also at issue was a proposal to make disclosure of an NSL a crime with a 5-year jail term, if there was intent to obstruct an investigation (in the view of enforcement authorities, not in the view of the organization). The renewal bill retains NSL disclosure penalties. The renewal law also provides that nondisclosure orders are no longer attached to NSL requests on an automatic basis.

- **Appeal rights:** At issue was whether organizations would have the right to appeal Section 215 and NSL records search requests, and if so, whether the appeal process would be pro forma or meaningful. The renewal bill did provide for individuals receiving Section 215 orders to seek judicial review. The renewal bill supported the right of NSL recipients to seek legal counsel, but did not spell out any appeal rights apart from appealing gag orders.

- **Definition of terrorism:** The Patriot Act employs a vague and expansive definition of terrorism, to include a broad range of political activities. Domestic terrorism is defined to include acts "dangerous to human life" in violation of criminal law, if the act involves intimidation or coercion of a civilian population, influence of government policy by intimidation or coercion, or affecting the conduct of government through mass destruction, assassination, or kidnapping. The ACLU has noted that Greenpeace, Operation Rescue, Vieques Island, and WTO protesters and the Environmental Liberation Front had all engaged in activities that could subject them to being investigated as engaging in domestic terrorism (ACLU, 2002b). The renewal act did not alter the definition of terrorism.

- **Criminal trials:** The Patriot Act allowed information gathered in warrantless searches to be used in criminal trials, where such information would otherwise be inadmissable as having been illegally obtained. The renewal act left this intact.

The Bush administration pushed for permanent expansion of relatively unrestricted police powers, in the name of antiterrorism, but faced opposition from Democrats, joined by libertarian Republicans opposed to conferring further police state powers on the president (Associated Press, 2006). In the end, however, the Patriot Act was renewed with expansive executive powers for domestic spying, with most areas of controversy resolved in favor of executive power at the expense of civil liberties.

Conclusion and Policy Recommendations

Public managers are legally responsible to assure privacy in their electronic transactions. Privacy assurance is essential to the effective implementation of electronic public services and to the growth of e-government. Failure to have well-designed privacy systems in place beforehand was a significant obstacle to information sharing in the response to the 9/11 terrorist attack on the World Trade Center (Dawes, Cresswell, & Cahan, 2004). The potential threat to privacy has been one of the significant barriers to progress in providing consumers with electronic health services, for instance (Anderson, 2004). Nearly half of Americans presently believe that if they submit personal information to government Web sites, it may risk the security and privacy of their personal information. As a corollary, a majority (54%) think that government should proceed slowly in relying on the Internet for communication between citizens and government (Council for Excellence in Government, 2003). Until policy leaders and public managers do a better job on privacy protection, as well as transparency in public management, the full potential of electronic government will never be reached.

Current trends raise serious questions about information policies of the Bush administration. It is now apparent that database technology can be used for various ends, ranging from the promotion of open democracy to the strengthening of nationalism to the shoring up of authoritarian regimes through misinformation. When this is put in the context of the need for IT security, with its nonparticipatory enforcement ethos, its inherent bias against freedom of information, and its massive claims on IT budget resources, the more secure IT systems of the future may well be even less hospitable to the democratic visions which some theorists once anticipated would be the most important societal contributions of information technology.

What needs to be done? Unfortunately, the scales have tipped so heavily in favor of surveillance and security and so much against privacy and freedom, that proposals for reform seem almost utopian. Nonetheless, if there were to be a minimum program to uphold the values of a free and democratic society against those who would erode it through "patriotic" information systems, there would have to be three elements: reintroducing independent checks and balances, creating a bureaucratic culture favorable to civil liberty, and rendering the rights of citizens enforceable.

Reintroducing Independent Checks and Balances

In February 2005, the Office of Management and Budget issued a memorandum requiring all federal departments and agencies to designate "the senior official who has the overall agency-wide responsibility for information privacy issues" (OMB, 2005). The OMB noted that consistent with the Paperwork Reduction Act of 1995, the agency's chief information officer could perform this role. The controversy, of course, was that the CIO also is responsible for information access, security, and other matters which may well conflict with privacy goals and thus incur a conflict of interest. The OMB memo fell short of requiring separate, let alone independent, privacy officers in each department. Moreover, a 1998 memorandum (OMB, 1998) had earlier required designation of departmental privacy officers and the conducting of privacy reviews. The issuance of the 2005 memo was an admission that there were grave shortcomings in earlier implementation of the Privacy Act of 1974, the Computer Matching and Privacy Protection Act of 1988, the Paperwork Reduction Act of 1995, and the Commerce Department's "Principles for Providing and Using Personal Information" ("Privacy Principles"), published by the Information Infra-structure Task Force in June 1995.

What is needed is a genuinely independent federal privacy commission with powers of investigation and subpoena, authorized to undertake not only inquiry into reported abuses but to initiate investigations under their own authority. While Canada, New Zealand, and other countries offer existing models of national privacy commissions, an American version would have to be qualitatively different and much better funded in order to cope with the grand scope of the surveillance bureaucracy in the United States. In addition, courts established under the Foreign Intelligence Surveillance Act (FISA) of 1978 need resources and restructuring to assure they are not the rubber stamp for the intelligence bureaucracy which they seem to be at present. (The FISA Court approved 1,754 surveillance orders in 2004 and rejected none and had only rejected four in its history [OpenTheGovernment.org, 2005]). If it were judged that creation of democratic checks and balances was worth funding through just 1% of the estimated $40 billion intelligence budget (Kellerhals, 2004), adequate levels of technical, legal, and other forms of expertise could be made available to make the work of a federal privacy commission meaningful.

Creating a Bureaucratic Culture Favorable to Civil Liberty

A system of checks and balances is only as good as the people who comprise the system. Creating a bureaucratic culture favorable to civil liberty requires explicit and forceful advocacy by agency leadership, independent formal training of agency employees, and a system which rewards rather than punishes whistle-blowers.

Leadership advocacy of the protection of privacy and civil liberty: The single most-commonly cited success factor in implementation of any information technology change process is the active and open support of the leaders of the organization (Garson, 2006, p. 393). By the same token, when leadership is perceived to give low priority to or be hypocritical about some objective, implementation failure is almost sure to follow. For the Bush administration, it is instructive to note that protection of privacy is not one of the president's formal management objectives. In the 64-page *President's Management Agenda,* privacy is mentioned only twice, in obscure locations (OMB, 2002). When checked by the author in May 2006, the Office of Management and Budget home page does list a link to "Privacy Guidance," but this leads only to a series of documents predating the Bush administration. Privacy also does not even appear in the rankings when federal information technology officials are surveyed about their top three priorities (CDW-Inc., 2006). In contrast to these indicators, meaningful reform requires that privacy become a significant priority advocated at the leadership level within the federal government.

Independent formal training in civil liberties: In Chicago, even convenience store surveillance camera operators are supposed to receive formal training in civil liberties and the law (*Newsweek*, 2006). So why shouldn't federal officials responsible for domestic spying receive at least as much? The answer is that they do, or at least statements by President Bush claim civil liberties training is "extensive" (Associated Press, 2005). The difference, which may contribute to accounting for the existence of extensive abuses in spite of such training, is that the convenience store does not hire the trainers, whereas the NSA does. There is a clear conflict of interest when those charged with training employees in civil liberties are not independent of the control of an agency in which abuses may occur. Trainers should be independent in any meaningful reform. They could, for instance, report to the above-proposed privacy commission.

Rewarding rather than punishing whistle-blowers: Violation of privacy rights should be taken as seriously as fraud in the expenditure of government funds, and those who report such violations deserve commendation, not retribution. Whistle-blower protection is, of course, a government-wide issue. Reform starts with the admission that the Whistleblower Protection Act of 1989 and amended in 1994 has been a failure. Citing data from the Government Accountability Project, Merrill Goozman (2006) has noted that not only are the resources of the Justice Department used to defend agencies against whistle-blowers, but also the Justice Department has won all but one of the 95 whistle-blowing cases which have reached the U.S. Court of Appeals.

At this writing, in summer 2006, there were five bills before Congress to reform whistle-blower protection, including proposals to eliminate current loopholes and afford whistle-blower protection to the quarter million employees of the FBI and other intelligence agencies (for a comparison of pending bills, see http://www. whistleblower.org/doc/GAP%20Legislative%20Whistleblower%20Chart.pdf).

Other reforms embedded in proposed legislation include overturning antiwhistle-blower case law, prohibiting removal of security clearance as a form of antiwhistle-blower retaliation, banning retaliatory investigations against whistle-blowers, institutionalizing statutory whistle-blowing rights in spite of agency gag orders and nondisclosure agreements, affording whistle-blowers access to all federal courts and to jury trials to challenge retaliation, reforming due process and other procedures of the Merit Systems Protection Board to make disciplinary action against retaliating officials more likely, and giving whistle-blowers the right to seek punitive damages. While passage of these reforms is unlikely under the present Congress, in actuality they represent only part of what needs to be accomplished. Beneath the tip of the iceberg represented by these legal protections is the iceberg itself, which is reforming bureaucratic culture to look upon whistle-blowing as a good thing, one which makes organizations more effective, and thus one which deserves promotion within the agency.

Rendering the Rights of Citizens Enforceable

A comprehensive civil remedies statute needs to be enacted in order to assure that citizens have a clear legal claim in litigation against the government when they suffer various forms of injury as a result of wrongful surveillance and intrusion into their privacy, much as the Computer Fraud and Abuse Act of 1984 was amended in 1994 to provide civil remedies for employers against present and former employees who may violate the privacy of corporate information.

This recommendation is similar to that made 3 decades ago a U.S. Senate committee, which recommended that civil remedies should be expanded (U.S. Senate, 1976). Section VII of its report, *Intelligence Activities and the Rights of Americans*, called for "establishing a legislative scheme which will afford effective redress to people who are injured by improper federal intelligence activity." Remedy was to apply not only to deprivation of constitutional rights to privacy and free speech, but also to "the loss of a job or professional standing, break-up of a marriage, and impairment of physical or mental health."

The committee also believed that institution of such remedies would "deter improper intelligence activity without restricting the sound exercise of discretion by intelligence officers at headquarters or in the field" (U.S. Senate, 1976). Part of the committee proposal was that procedures under which federal officers and agents operate should be "structured to encourage intelligence officers to obtain written authorization for questionable activities and to seek legal advice about them." Further, the committee recommended that a fund be established to indemnify attorney fees and reasonable litigation costs for federal officers and agents for the exercise of discretion when they are held not to be liable. Finally, the committee also recommended in Section VIII of their report that criminal penalties be instituted for willful and knowing violations of statutes regulating intelligence activities.

The rights abuses of the infamous FBI Cointelpro operations (Wolf, 2004), against which the Senate committee was reacting 3 decades ago, are now mirrored on a much larger scale by threats to civil liberties emanating from various aspects of Bush administration information policy. The failure of Congress to enact the committee's recommendations, then, is one factor now among many which has allowed the recurrence of abuse. Rendering meaningful the rights of citizens against the intelligence bureaucracy is an essential dimension of the three-fold reforms advocated in this chapter.

In public administration, there is an emphasis on the difference between efficiency and effectiveness. Efficient agencies may process much but do not necessarily achieve their goal, while effective agencies define their efforts in terms of progress toward the goal. Bush administration information and intelligence policies have indeed led agencies to process massive, indeed unprecedented, amounts of information, but at the end of the day it only offers Americans a choice between fighting terrorism or defending domestic liberty. The purpose of this chapter and of the reforms it advocates has been to suggest that an effective nation is one which fights terrorism *while* defending freedom at home.

References

ACLU. (2002a, November 15). *Stop the plan to mine our privacy.* Retrieved July 1, 2007, from www.aclu.org/Privacy/Privacy.cfm?ID=11323&c=130

ACLU. (2002b, December 6). *How the USA PATRIOT Act redefines "Domestic Terrorism."* Retrieved July 1, 2007, from http://www.aclu.org/natsec/emergpowers/14444leg20021206.html

Anderson, James G. (2004). Consumers of e-health: Patterns of use and barriers. Social Science Computer Review, 22(2), 242-248.

Associated Press. (2005, December 17). *Bush defends secret spying in the U.S. KUTV Web site.* Retrieved July 13, 2007, from http://kutv.com/national/topstories_story_350200457.html

Associated Press. (2006, February 7). *Congress extends Patriot Act 5 weeks.* Retrieved July 13, 2007, from http://www.cnn.com/2006/POLITICS/02/02/patriot.act.ap/

BBC News (2002). US closes 'disinformation' unit. Feb. 26, 2002. Retrieved 5/14/07 from http://news.bbc.co.uk/2/hi/americas/1843201.stm.

Blaylock, D. (2006, May 30). *Supreme Court rules against government whistleblowers.* Retrieved July 13, 2007, from www.whistleblower.org

Block, R., & Solomon, J. (2006). Pentagon steps up intelligence efforts inside U.S. borders. *Wall Street Journal, 247*(98), 1-12.

Carlson, D., & King, B. (2006). Government tracking of reporters' calls "outrageous, frightening." *SPJ News.* Retrieved July 13, 2007, from http://www.spj.org/news.asp?ref=583

Cauley, L. (2006, May 10). NSA has massive database of Americans' phone calls. *USA Today.* Retrieved July 13, 2007, from http://www.usatoday.com/news/washington/2006-05-10-nsa_x.htm

CBS News. (2006, May 14). Battlelines drawn over NSA program. *CBS News.* Retrieved July 13, 2007, from http://www.cbsnews.com/stories/2006/05/13/politics/,ain1616387.shtml

CDT. (2006). CDT calls changes to Senate wiretapping bill "meaningless." *PolicyBeta—Digital Policy in Process* (Sept.). Washington, DC: Center for Technology and Democracy. Retrieved July 13, 2007, from http://blog.cdt.org/2006/09/

CDW-Inc. (2006, March). *Federal IT landscape, survey.* Retrieved July 13, 2007, from http://newsroom.cdwg.com/features/2006-03ITLandscapeReport.pdf

Council for Excellence in Government. (2003, April). *The new e-government equation: Ease, engagement, privacy & protection.* Retrieved July 13, 2007, from http://www.excelgov.org/usermedia/images/uploads/PDFs/egovpoll2003.pdf

Dawes, S.S., Cresswell, A.M., & Cahan, B.B. (2004). Learning from crisis: Lessons in human and information infrastructure from the World Trade Center response. *Social Science Computer Review, 22*(1), 52-66.

Dean, J.W. (2004). *Worse than Watergate: The secret presidency of George W. Bush.* New York: Little, Brown.

Executive Office of the President. (2005). *Improving agency disclosure of information. Executive Order 13392.* Retrieved July 13, 2007, from http://www. whitehouse.gov/omb/memoranda/fy2006/m06-04.pdf

Federation of American Scientists. (2004, October 21). *Secrecy News. FAS Project on Government Secrecy 2004,* (92). Retrieved July 13, 2007, from http://www. fas.org/sgp/news/secrecy/2004/10/102104.html

Fink, R. (2005, October 24). If they take your personal info but can't find it, do you really exist? *Government Computer News, 24*(31). Retrieved July 13, 2007, from http://www.gcn.com/24_31/log-off/37389-1.html

Fiorini, A. (2004, Spring). Behind closed doors: Governmental transparency gives way to secrecy. *Harvard International Review, 26*(1), 18-21.

Fisher, W. (2005, December 21). Congress to probe domestic spying. *Inter Press Service News Agency.* Retrieved July 13, 2007, from http://www.ipsnews. net/news.asp?idnews=31530

Garson, G.D. (2006). *Public information technology and e-governance: Managing the virtual state.* Sudbury, MA: Jones and Bartlett.

Gellman, R. (2002). Perspectives on privacy and terrorism: All is not lost—yet. *Government Information Quarterly, 19,* 255-264.

Gellman, R. (2003). Flap is brewing over federal Web privacy policies. *Government Computer News, 32.*

Gellman, B., Linzer, D., & Leonnig, C.D. (2006, February 5). NSA's hunt for terrorists scrutinizes thousands of Americans, but most are later cleared. *The Washington Post,* p. A01.

Golden, T. (2004, October 10). After terror, a secret rewriting of military law. *New York Times.* Retrieved July 13, 2007, from http://www.nytimes.com/2004/10/24/ international/worldspecial2/24gitmo.html

Goozman, M. (2005). Blowing the whistle. *Gooznews.com.* Retrieved July 13, 2007, from http://www.gooznews.com/archives/000103.html

Government Reform Minority Office. (2004). *Secrecy in the Bush Administration.* U.S. House of Representatives, Committee on Government Reform, Minority Office. Retrieved July 13, 2007, from http://democrats.reform.house.gov/features/secrecy_report/index.asp

Hosenball, M., & Thomas, E. (2006). Hold the phone. *Newsweek* 147(21), 22 32. May 22.

Jackson, W. (2003). Privacy enforcement tool could become a TIA boon. *Government Computer News, 32.*

Kellerhals, M.D., Jr. (2004). 9/11 Attacks prompting intelligence overhaul: Legislation pending in several Senate committees. *Washington File.* U.S. Information Programs, U.S. Department of State. Retrieved July 13, 2007, from http://usinfo. state.gov/xarchives/display.html?p=washfile-english&y=2004&m=August& x=20040824125446dmslahrellek0.2199823&t=livefeeds/wf-latest.html

Levy, S. (2003). Can snooping stop terrorism? *Newsweek, 65.*

Lichtblau, E. (2006a). Bush defends spy program and denies misleading public. *New York Times.* Retrieved July 13, 2007, from http://www.nytimes.com/2006/01/02/ politics/02spy.html

Lichtblau, E. (2006b). Cleric wins appeal ruling over wiretaps. *New York Times.* Retrieved July 13, 2007, from http://pewforum.org/news/display. php?NewsID=10409

McCarthy, S.P. (2004, January 26). Government shouldn't break its privacy promises. *Government Computer News, 23*(2), 38.

McCullagh, D. (2004, September 29). Judge disarms Patriot Act proviso. Bush stumps for Patriot Act extension. *CNET News.com.* Retrieved, July 13, 2007, from http://news.zdnet.com/2100-1009_22-5388764.html?tag=default

Morano, L. (2002, February 26). Propaganda: Remember the Kuwaiti babies? *United Press International.* Retrieved, July 13, 2007, from http://www.propaganda-critic.com/articles/examples.osi.html

Nakashima, E. (2002, March 3). Bush view of secrecy is stirring frustration. Disclosure battle unites right and left. *The Washington Post,* p. A04.

Newsweek. (2006). Big brother's business. *Newsweek Web site.* Retrieved July 13, 2007, from http://www.msnbc.msn.com/id/11832024/site/newsweek/page/3/

OMB. (1998, May 14). *Privacy and personal information in federal records.* Office of Management and Budget, Memorandum. Washington, DC. Retrieved July 13, 2007, from http://www.whitehouse.gov/omb/memoranda/m99-05-a.html

OMB. (2002a). *The president's management agenda, FY 2002.* Washington, DC: Office of Management and Budget. U.S. Superintendent of Documents, S/N 041-001-00568. Retrieved, July 13, 2007, from http://www.whitehouse.gov/ omb/budget/fy2002/mgmt.pdf

OMB Watch. (2002b). *OMB Watch 2002 annual report.* Washington, DC: OMB Watch. Retrieved July 13, 2007, from http://www.ombwatch.org/pdfs/OMB %20Watch%20Biennial%20Report.pdf

OMB Watch. (2003, September 22). *GAO report indicates less FOIA information under Ashcroft.* Retrieved July 13, 2007, from http://www.ombwatch.org/ar-ticle/articleview/1821

OMB. (2005, February 11). *Designation of senior agency officials for privacy.* Washington, DC: Office of Management and Budget Memorandum—M-05-08. Retrieved July 13, 2007, from http://www.whitehouse.gov/omb/memoranda/fy2005/m05-08.pdf

OMB Watch. (2006, February 22). *Sensitive but unclassified info: You can't have it. Why? Because they say so.* Retrieved July 13, 2007, from http://www.ombwatch.org/article/articleview/3295

Onley, D.S. (2002, December 16). DARPA's plans for data mining draw criticism. *Government Computer News, 36.*

OpenTheGovernment.org. (2005). *Secrecy report card 2005: Quantitative indicators of government secrecy.* Washington, DC: OpenTheGovernment.org. Retrieved July 13, 2007, from http://www.openthegovernment.org/otg/SRC2005.pdf

Pontoniere, P. (2005, December 1). *Islam put on trial in terrorism cases, U.S. Muslims say.* Pacific News Service. Retrieved July 13, 2007, from http://news.pacificnews.org/news/view_article.html?article_id=626af5d0e2191bdbb03fe12aaa65ae8a

Public Citizen. (2004). *Freedom of Information Act.* Washington, DC: Public Citizen. Retrieved July 13, 2007, from http://www.bushsecrecy.org/PageIndex.cfm?ParentID=2&CategoryID=2&PagesID=15

Risen, J., & Lichtblau, E. (2005, December 16). *Bush lets U.S. spy on callers without courts.* The New York Times. Retrieved July 13, 2007, from http://www.nytimes.com/2005/12/16/politics/16program.html

Schmitt, C.H., & Pound, E.T. (2003, December 22). Keeping secrets: The Bush administration is doing the public's business out of the public eye. *U.S. News and World Report, 18-22*(24), 27-29.

Schonfield, E. (2003, February 3). *Total information delusion. Business 2.0.* Retrieved July 13, 2007, from http://www.business2.com/articles/web/0,1653,46876,00.html

Thormeyer, R. (2006, January 3). *OMB issues further guidance on FOIA executive order.* Government Computer News. Retrieved July 13, 2007, from http://www.gcn.com/vol1_no1/daily-updates/37851-1.html

U.S. Senate. (1976, April 26). *Intelligence activities and the rights of Americans, book II: Final report of the Select Committee to Study Governmental Operations with Respect to Intelligence Activities.* Retrieved July 13, 2007, from http://www.icdc.com/~paulwolf/cointelpro/churchfinalreportIId.htm

Washington Post. (2006, March 14). Openness advocates single out CIA. *News & Observer*, p. 5a.

Waterman, S. (2006, October 26). Total information lives again. *UPI*. Retrieved July 13, 2007, from http://www.spacewar.com/reports/Total_Information_Lives_Again_999.html

Weisman, J. (2006, September 14). GOP leaders back Bush on wiretapping, tribunals. *The Washington Post,* p. A13. Retrieved July 13, 2007, from http://www.washingtonpost.com/wp-dyn/content/article/2006/09/12/AR2006091201252_pf.html

Williams, M. (2006, April 26). The total information awareness project lives on. *Technology Review*. Retrieved July 13, 2007, from http://www.technologyreview.com/read_article.aspx?ch=infotech&sc=&id=16741&pg=1

Wolf, P. (2004). *Cointelpro*. Retrieved July 13, 2007, from http://www.icdc.com/~paulwolf/cointelpro/cointel.htm

Section II

Freedom of Information
and Access

Chapter II

Less Safe:
The Dismantling of Public Information Systems after September 11

Harry Hammitt, Access Reports, Inc., USA

Abstract

Since the terrorist attacks of September 11, 2001, there has been a tightening of public access. In response to perceived security threats, government agencies have taken information down from Web sites, curtailed or restricted access to electronic sources of information, broadened the interpretation of FOIA exemptions, created or augmented new categories of restricted information, and prohibited public access for critical infrastructure information. These policy responses have been based both on the perceived security threat and an inhospitable attitude toward open government on the part of the Bush administration.

Introduction

By the end of the Clinton administration, government at all levels was becoming a major source of information on the Internet. After the technological barriers were conquered, agencies began to realize that Internet dissemination, or at least availability, was a wonderful model for disseminating information, for making routine information readily available, and for allowing consumers to conduct a variety of interactions with government without actually having to deal with an individual employee. The prospects for increased convenience, efficiency, and cost-savings seemed endless and, as a result, agencies provided a broad array of information, often without much forethought as to whether the information was essential. The mantra seemed to be to post as much information as possible and let users sort it out; whatever feedback the agency might get as to the usefulness of their Web sites could then be used to modify them accordingly, with the goal being to make the information as useful and convenient as possible.

This model abruptly changed in the aftermath of the terrorist attacks of September 11, 2001, as agencies began to rethink the availability of information. Because the Internet allowed universal access and made tracking individual users nearly impossible, agencies worried about how publicly available information might be used. It was clear that the terrorists had used public information sources in developing their plan. Suddenly, the idea that the more knowledge and information that was available the better was abandoned, and replaced with an essentially contrary conclusion, that information in the wrong hands could be used to hurt us. The immediate conclusion was that information should be restricted and, as a result, one of the consequences of 9/11 was to dismantle many public information resources.

The headlong rush to post information on the Internet during the 1990s was something of an anomaly as far as government information policy is concerned. Rather than being driven primarily by a political conclusion tied to the tradition of the right to know—that government is a repository of a vast wealth of information that it stockpiles and creates on behalf of the people and thus the people should have a presumptive right of access unless there are specific reasons for exempting certain types of information—the policy seems to have been driven more by a model derived from good business practices tied to the ideas of reinventing government and customer-friendly government services. The reinventing government policy, most closely identified with Vice President Al Gore, aimed to remake a bureaucracy that was typically seen as lethargic and inhospitable and to streamline it through the use of technology to make it more efficient and responsive to its customers. Information was an asset that allowed government to distinguish itself from the private sector. By making its huge repository of information more readily available, government provided resources and solutions that promised to make government more efficient and responsive. As a result, agencies pursued a policy of posting information because it could be posted, without much thought about the consequences of disclosure.

The response to the attacks of September 11, 2001, was not a reasoned debate as to what information should be made public, but, instead, a reflexive conclusion that information was harmful in the wrong hands. In a repeat of the worst-case scenario model that has frequently driven reactive government information policy, electronic information sources were dismantled wholesale. The Nuclear Regulatory Commission closed down its Web site completely, although it eventually put much of it back online.

As a practical matter, information policy has never been based on a broad view of the public interest. The value of a well-informed public does not figure into the equation. Instead, disclosure has traditionally gravitated to the lowest common denominator and disclosure decisions are generally made based on what would happen if the most unsavory element—previously the KGB or the Mafia, now terrorists—got hold of the information. Because "any person" is be treated equally under the provisions of the Freedom of Information Act, the government has consistently viewed any disclosure decision as having the potential of falling into the hands of the worst requester. Under such a model, information that might truly be of value to the vast majority of people—the likelihood of a chemical accident, a bridge or dam failure, or whether entry points into the country are secure and well-patrolled—is withheld because in the hands of a terrorist the information could be misused. Although in the aftermath of September 11, Rep. Tom Davis (R-VA) claimed that American troops in Afghanistan found GAO reports in abandoned terrorist strongholds, there is no credible evidence that al-Qaeda has ever used the FOIA; it is likely, however, that terrorists could have used public information available on the Internet.

Dismantling the Internet

Aside from the temporary shut-down of the NRC Web site, many agencies quickly removed information they felt should not be public in light of the terrorist threat. The FAA removed databases, including its Enforcement Information System, which provided information on enforcement actions. The Office of Pipeline Safety discontinued open access to its National Pipeline Mapping System. One incident that received considerable press and public interest attention was the request by the U.S. Geological Survey that depository libraries destroy a previously disseminated CD-ROM entitled "Source Area Characteristics of Large Public Surface-Water Supplies in the Coterminous United States: An Information Resource for Source-Water Assessment." The Defense Department removed more than 6,600 technical documents for review dealing with germ and chemical weapons.

In an article for the online magazine *Slate*, Steve Aftergood, director of the Secrecy Project for the Federation of American Scientists, noted that the Defense Department no longer made its phone directory available, that a number of documents had been removed from password-protected sites run by the Army and the Air Force, and that the budget for the Office of Intelligence at the Energy Department had been recently classified.

One problem with withdrawing information that had been available to the public previously is that much of it was already in the hands of nongovernmental sources. The journalism group Investigative Reporters and Editors was criticized shortly after 9/11 when it announced that its database that described problems with bridges and highways would remain public. In another instance, although the White House discontinued publication of its telephone directory, the newsletter publisher Bureau of National Affairs continued to publish it privately.

The *Washington Post* and several public interest publications focused on the curious story of a PhD student in computer science at George Mason University who, using public sources, had put together a program that allowed a detailed mapping of various elements of the local and national infrastructure. When the student and his advisor demonstrated the program to national security officials, the common advice was to destroy the project, or at least classify it.

Certainly part of the dismantling of electronic information sources after 9/11 was because agencies had made too much information available without much thought about potential consequences. However, in taking down large chunks of information there was never any sense that agencies were going through a thoughtful process in analyzing whether information should be taken down and balancing the legitimate societal value of the information against the heightened sensitivity of some information after 9/11.

Sensitive but Unclassified Information

Shortly after the September 11 attacks, letters containing trace amounts of anthrax showed up in the office of Sen. Tom Daschle (D-SD), at a nearby post office in Washington, and at the offices of the *National Enquirer* in Florida, causing several deaths and requiring the evacuation of Senate office buildings for a period of weeks. Although the parties responsible for sending the anthrax have yet to be discovered, at the time it seemed like a second front in the war on terrorism and most people assumed that terrorists were behind the incident. Examining the public availability of information about biological toxins, largely in the scientific literature, the *New York Times* ran a prominent article suggesting that such information might be too easily available.

Following on the heels of the *Times* article, White House Chief of Staff Andrew Card issued a memorandum March 19, 2002, to the heads of executive department and agencies on "Action to Safeguard Information Regarding Weapons of Mass Destruction and Other Sensitive Documents Related to Homeland Security." Card discussed the need to safeguard sensitive but unclassified information pertaining to homeland security. Because such undefined information did not qualify for classification on national security grounds, Card attached two short memos from Laura Kimberly, Acting Director of the Information Security Oversight Office, explaining the standards for classification and how information was safeguarded as a result, and from Richard Huff and Daniel Metcalfe, codirectors of the Justice Department's Office of Information and Privacy. The Huff-Metcalfe memo explained possible FOIA exemptions that could be used to withhold such information. Primary among them was Exemption 2, which allows an agency to withhold records "related solely to the internal personnel rules and practices of an agency." Over the years, courts have interpreted this exemption to allow agencies to withhold information, the disclosure of which could allow circumvention of a law or regulation.

The FOIA does not contain any exemptions that readily cover security issues unless they are law enforcement matters. The courts have acquiesced in broadening Exemption 2 largely to provide a justification for withholding legitimately sensitive material that could be used in circumventing a law or regulation. Such cases have focused on protecting agency guidelines or manuals which provide criteria for deciding when a case should be investigated or prosecuted. The theory is that if requesters had access to such information, they could accommodate their behavior to remain just below the threshold of breaking a law or regulation and thus avoid prosecution. But application in a terrorist context presupposes that a much broader range of information is dangerous, that information that might suggest vulnerability could lead to a terrorist attack.

Critical Infrastructure Information

Even before the terrorists appeared in the New York and Washington skies on September 11, business interests were already pursuing a straw-man terrorist policy and had successfully persuaded Congress to take action on their speculation. Under amendments to the Clean Air Act, the EPA was required to make public worst-case scenarios for production and storage facilities that housed toxic substances. The scenarios were to describe the potential catastrophic events if such toxics were to explode or corrode or somehow pose a real threat to the community. These scenarios were to project the potential casualties from such an incident, indicate how the facility would deal with such a problem if it occurred, and provide a basis for discussion to develop community security and evacuation plans. As the Internet took off in the 1990s, the EPA decided to post such plans online so that they could be readily available. At least at this point, the agency believed it had an affirmative obligation under the Clean Air Act to make these plans widely available to the public.

Business, led by the Chemical Manufacturers Association, strongly opposed such dissemination and, instead of initially making its case to Congress, went to the FBI and convinced the agency that such widespread disclosure would aid terrorists in targeting vulnerable locations that could produce maximum casualties. By the time the issue was aired before Congress, industry had enlisted the FBI on its side and the story took on a heightened level of plausibility. The Clinton administration, not wanting to scrap the public dissemination component altogether, but not wanting to appear soft on terrorism, agreed to a compromise study commission to report back to Congress. No report has ever been produced, and today the availability of worst-case scenarios is very limited at local agency reading rooms and other community locations. The longer term consequences of the incident were to establish a policy mind-set that public information whose disclosure could in any way aid terrorists was a danger that should be checked.

Another short-term policy with long-term implications was the Y2K legislation designed to foster information sharing on the part of technology companies while absolving them of liability for computer failures that might be caused when the date changed to 2000. As the new century approached, there was concern that computers, which had never been programmed to recognize dates other than those in the 20th century, might fail to recognize the year 2000 and might stop working as a result. Although the dimensions of the potential problem were unknown, the government was worried enough about the consequences to recommend legislation to encourage companies to share information about potential vulnerabilities so that they could be addressed before the date change. The legislation that emerged made information sharing voluntary and encouraged such sharing by assuring companies that information related to vulnerabilities that was voluntarily provided to the government would not be subject to public disclosure. For good measure, Congress also insulated companies from any potential antitrust violations that might arise as a result of the Y2K problem.

The Y2K legislation, designed to address a specific finite problem, became the model for broader legislation to encourage industry to provide critical infrastructure information. Protecting critical infrastructure information evolved as a legislative initiative from the EPA worst-case scenario experience. Policymakers realized that the country's infrastructure was vulnerable to failures of all kinds and that dams, bridges, power-grids, and many other critical junctures could be targeted by terrorists. Most of the infrastructure was held privately and the government believed those companies needed an incentive to share information about the state of the infrastructure with government agencies. The incentive, again, would be confidentiality, a blanket prohibition on public disclosure on critical infrastructure information voluntarily submitted to the government. Antitrust liability was thrown in for good measure, although it was dropped later on.

The critical infrastructure information legislation was moving slowly but inevitably through Congress when the events of September 11 occurred. In the legislative flurry of activity shortly after September 11, Congress first substantially broadened law enforcement powers by passing the USA PATRIOT Act. But the next large piece of security legislation, the Homeland Security Act, which created the Department of Homeland Security, included a slightly toned-down provision protecting critical infrastructure information. Rather than provide protection for any critical infrastructure information provided to a government agency, the protection would only apply to such information provided to the Department of Homeland Security. The House version of the amendment granted protection for critical infrastructure information provided to the agency by companies without establishing any procedure by which the information would be measured. By contrast, with considerable help from the public interest sector, the Senate agreed to a bill sponsored by Sen. Patrick Leahy (D-VT) and Sen. Robert Bennett (R-UT), which provided the same measure of protection, but allowed requesters to challenge the decision to designate information as critical infrastructure information based on a test developed by the U.S. Court of Appeals for the District of Columbia in *Critical Mass v. NRC*, 975 F.2d 871 (D.C. Cir. 1992), allowing agencies to withhold information voluntarily submitted by companies as long as it was the kind of information not customarily made public by the company. Although the *Critical Mass* test is not difficult to meet, public interest advocates hoped such a test would at least help keep submitters honest. However, when the two bills were reconciled in conference the House version prevailed. Both Leahy and Rep. Henry Waxman (D-CA) currently have bills that would restore the original Senate language, but neither is given much chance of passing.

Since passage of the critical infrastructure amendment, the Department of Homeland Security has issued a proposed rule for submission of critical infrastructure information. While the proposed rule generally tracks the legislation, it also suggests that companies could submit information to other agencies, which would then submit the information to Homeland Security. Such a procedure seems to be specifically prohibited by the legislation itself, and Homeland Security has since backed down from its original position. However, as a matter of convenience, it does not seem unlikely that Homeland Security will ultimately rationalize the submission of information through another agency. Ironically, the anecdotal evidence so far indicates that industry is reluctant to provide such information, not because it is worried the information will be made public, but rather because it is worried that the information will be shared too freely within the government.

The Federal Energy Regulatory Commission established its own rules to protect what it calls critical energy infrastructure information. Although most if not all of this information was made public when used as part of regulatory proceedings, FERC performed its own legal legerdemain by assuming, without any conclusive legal support, that all information that could be categorized as critical energy infra-structure information was exempt under FOIA. The only basis for this conclusion was the theory constructed by the Justice Department's Office of Information and Privacy that, as a general matter, infrastructure information could be protected by invoking Exemption 2 and Exemption 7, which covers law enforcement records. FERC initially claimed the information also fell under Exemption 4, which protects confidential business information, because if a terrorist was to blow up a commercial facility, it would cause the company commercial harm; the agency later dropped that argument, but used Exemption 2 and Exemption 7 as the basis for withhold-ing critical energy infrastructure information. The tricky part for FERC is that the agency needs to use the information during regulatory proceedings. To accomplish that goal, the agency uses a nondisclosure agreement between the agency and par-ties who have a "need to know" as part of regulatory proceedings.

The Freedom of Information Act

The Bush administration has not been friendly to FOIA, but it has not used the events of September 11 to bring about any direct changes in the law. The infamous Ashcroft Memorandum, issued October 12, 2001, showed the administration's disdain for open government, but its philosophy placing protection of information ahead of disclosure is historically in line with the previous Attorney General's memorandum issued by the Reagan administration. Generally speaking, Democratic administrations tend to emphasize a concept of maximum responsible disclosure and stress that certain exemptions designed more to protect institutional interests than the interests of third parties should be used only where the agency can identify a foreseeable harm from disclosure. In other words, exemptions like Exemption 5, which protects information that qualifies for various privileges, particularly the deliberative process privilege, and Exemption 2, which allows an agency to withhold what it considered trivial information, should only be used if disclosure could cause a foreseeable harm. Other exemptions, like Exemption 4, which covers confidential business information, and Exemption 6, which covers personal privacy, are designed to protect the interests of other parties, and in the case of both Exemption 4 and Exemption 6, discretion to disclose information is severely restricted by other statutes: the Trade Secrets Act for Exemption 4, and the Privacy Act for Exemption 6.

While there is little empirical evidence that attorney general memoranda have a significant impact on agency implementation of FOIA, they clearly set the tone. The Ashcroft memo, after giving a brief description of the values of open gov-ernment, quickly changes gears and stresses "other fundamental values," among which are "safeguarding our national security, enhancing the effectiveness of our law enforcement agencies, protecting sensitive business information and, not least, preserving personal privacy." The memo really betrays its difference with that of former Attorney General Janet Reno when it addresses Exemption 5. The memo indicates that "our citizens have a strong interest as well in a government that is fully functional and efficient. Congress and the courts have long recognized that certain legal privileges ensure candid and complete agency deliberations without fear that they will be made public. Other privileges ensure that lawyers' deliberations and communications are kept private. No leader can operate effectively without confidential advice and counsel. Exemption 5 of the FOIA incorporates these privileges and the sound policies underlying them." He adds that "I encourage your agency to carefully consider the protection of all such values and interests when making disclosure determinations under the FOIA. Any discretionary decision by your agency to disclose information protected under the FOIA should be made only after the full and deliberate consideration of the institutional, commercial, and personal privacy interests that could be implicated by disclosure of the information." This language not only reminds agencies of the analytical process required in making FOIA determinations, but implicitly suggests the outcome.

The memo then indicates the basis for defending an agency's action in court. "When you carefully consider FOIA requests and decide to withhold records, in whole or in part, you can be assured that the Department of Justice will defend your decisions unless they lack a sound legal basis or present an unwarranted risk of adverse impact on the ability of other agencies to protect important records." Agencies occasionally dig in their heels and adopt a stance that is unsupported by either the statutory language or the case law, but those cases are the exception, not the rule. For the Justice Department to say it will support any agency's claim if there is a "sound legal basis," is a rather low threshold.

With the Ashcroft Memo as the basis for government FOIA policy, the emphasis has been on withholding rather than on disclosure. However, FOIA has not ground to a halt by any means, and after September 11, it looked like the federal courts were going to come to the rescue of the cause of open government by rebuffing the attempts of the administration to withhold many aspects of the domestic war against terrorism.

As in any moment of national security crisis, after September 11 the government instinctively elevated national security above civil liberties. With a preoccupation with security, it became clear that certain civil liberties were likely to be sacrificed in the short run and the first major legislative product from Congress was the controversial USA PATRIOT Act, a mish-mash of law enforcement ideas, many of which had been contentious for years but seemed acceptable now as part of a strategy to fight a war against terrorism. In a hasty round-up that had eerie echoes of the Japanese internment camps during World War II and even the Red Scare raids after World War I, the government detained a number of Arabic men, keeping many of them incarcerated without charge for months. Although the government frequently had nothing more than a generalized suspicion for detaining these individuals, and the vast majority of those shown to have broken the law were guilty of immigration violations, the government was unwilling to identify any of the individuals detained, telling a coalition of public interest groups that to identify the detainees or their attorneys would be an invasion of their privacy. At the same time, the Immigration and Naturalization Service announced that it would close hearings for all individuals "of interest."

The first case to be heard in court involved a suit brought by the ACLU of New Jersey for the names of detainees being held in local jails. Although the government argued that the detainees were federal prisoners and not subject to state access laws, the court agreed with the ACLU that state law required publication of the names of individuals being held in state and local jails. However, the INS then promulgated a rule, which was applied retroactively, prohibiting state and local officials from disclosing information about federal prisoners being held under contract with the agency without permission, effectively preventing New Jersey officials from disclosing the information.

The next round of litigation involved two separate challenges to the validity of instructions, issued by chief INS judge Michael Creppy, closing any immigration proceeding which the government indicated would involve an individual of interest. Although defendants and the press traditionally can challenge decisions to close public proceedings, the Creppy memo made no allowances for any such challenges. Cases were taken to federal court in Detroit and in New Jersey. In both cases, the district court ruled that a decision to close a previously open proceeding could be challenged in court and that the government would need to show the court on a case-by-case basis why the proceeding needed to be closed. Ruling in the government's appeal of the Detroit case, the U.S. Court of Appeals for the Sixth Circuit issued a ringing endorsement of the need for open court proceedings and emphasized that, while the proceedings could be closed, the government was required to provide evidence to substantiate such a request. Not long after the Sixth Circuit ruling, the U.S. Court of Appeals for the Third Circuit issued its ruling in the New Jersey appeal. That court strongly disagreed with the ruling of the Sixth Circuit, finding no historical tradition of openness in immigration proceedings, and approving of the policy enunciated in the Creppy memo.

A separate FOIA suit requesting the names of detainees and their attorneys, filed by a group of public interest organizations, was decided in federal court in Washington, D.C. At issue in district court was the extent to which the round-up of Arabic men qualified as a law enforcement investigation, and whether disclosure of identities of detainees and attorneys would constitute an invasion of privacy. The court ruled that the public interest in identifying and learning more about the detainees far outweighed any privacy interest in withholding the identities. However, the court suggested that if detainees affirmatively indicated that they did not want to be identified publicly, those names could be withheld. The case then went up on appeal to the U.S. Court of Appeals for the District of Columbia. In its decision, the D.C.

Circuit ruled that all the records were protected by Exemption 7(A), which allows an agency to withhold law enforcement records where disclosure could interfere with an ongoing investigation or proceeding. Without reaching the privacy implications, the court readily accepted that the investigation was for law enforcement purposes and, further, that the traditional deference shown to agency expertise in national security matters should be extended to encompass law enforcement records that pertained to a national security investigation.

In another case brought by the ACLU to get information about the implementation of certain controversial sections of the Patriot Act, the district court in Washington ruled that the information was not available under FOIA, and that by requiring the Justice Department to report to Congress on the use of these sections, Congress had established a separate accountability process that lessened the public interest in disclosure under FOIA.

There is still ongoing litigation concerning detainees rounded up in Afghanistan and Iraq. A federal court in New York has ordered the Defense Department, the CIA, and other agencies to process records responsive to the request, although no decision has yet been made on disclosure of any records.

The greatest worry for access advocates was the extent to which the government would withhold previously public information on the basis that its disclosure could be useful to terrorists. Two district court cases have upheld this practice so far. The problem with both cases is the extent to which the government is willing to go to speculate about the uses of information for evil ends, without considering the public interest in maintaining the availability of such information for other useful purposes.

In *Coastal Delivery Corp. v. Customs Service*, a district court judge in Los Angeles allowed the Customs Service to withhold information about the number of off-site inspections of cargo conducted at the Port of Long Beach. The case originated as a business dispute. Coastal Delivery had been subcontracted by the company that had the contract for hauling cargo at Long Beach to move freight to off-site locations. Coastal Delivery believed the contractor was short-changing it and asked the Customs Service for information about the number of off-site inspections conducted for the year at Long Beach. Although such information had been available under FOIA previously, the agency withheld the information under Exemption 2 and Exemption 7(e), which allows a law enforcement agency to withhold information about investigative methods and techniques, and Exemption 7(f), which allows a law enforcement agency to withhold information, the disclosure of which could harm the safety of an individual. The government's argument was not that the information itself was harmful, but that a terrorist could request such information for all ports of entry in the United States, analyze and quantify the information, and then be able to pinpoint the most vulnerable entry points. With little analysis, the court accepted all the exemption claims.

In *Living Rivers, Inc. v. Bureau of Reclamation*, a federal court in Utah allowed the Bureau of Reclamation to withhold a flood-plain inundation map for Grand Coulee and Echo Canyon dams. Again, such maps had been public before 9/11. The agency told Living Rivers, a local grassroots environmental organization, that the map would allow a terrorist to understand the projected consequences of a dam break. The court rejected Exemption 2 because in the Tenth Circuit, which includes Utah, the exemption only applies to information related to personnel. The court also was unable to accept that the map constituted an investigative method or technique. However, the court concluded that if either dam was destroyed as a result of disclosure of the map, people would be put in harm's way and, therefore, it could be protected by Exemption 7(f). The court was ultimately persuaded by an affidavit filed by the Bureau's security chief, a position created after 9/11, but it is not completely clear what law enforcement function the Bureau performs in terms of protecting dams.

What is particularly disconcerting about cases like these is that the courts accepted such speculative claims in the first place. Commenting on attempts to dismantle information sources on the Internet, William Martel, a professor of national security affairs at the Naval War College, told the Associated Press: "Think of how many mundane pieces of information can be used for ill purposes." Martel's comments are well-taken, and a case could be made that virtually any piece of information could ultimately be used for bad purposes. However, that is a poor basis for information policy, and ignores the public value of the information for perfectly legitimate purposes.

State Secrets Privilege

Another tactic used more frequently since 9/11 has been the state secrets privilege, a claim invoked by the attorney general asserting that the national security implications of allowing a civil suit against the government to continue are so great because of their potential to reveal sensitive national security information that the court must dismiss the suit altogether. As long as the procedural requirements for making the claim are followed, a court faced with a claim of state secrets privilege will dismiss the suit. The privilege was used at least once during the Clinton administration to stop litigation against the EPA for information concerning environmental hazards at the military installation at Groom Lake; the suit was brought by the widows of two former Groom Lake employees who died of cancer. In the first 4 years of the Bush administration, the state secrets privilege has been invoked at least three times, including the suit brought by FBI contract translator Sibel Edmonds, who in the aftermath of 9/11 accused the translation department at the FBI of allowing an Arabic translator with possible ties to a terrorist organization to continue to review classified information. She also alleged that the department was purposely going slow to increase its backlog so that it would have a better case for requesting an increased budget. Edmonds went public with her claims, including an interview on "60 Minutes," and was subsequently fired as a result. She filed suit against the Justice Department, and although an investigation by the Department's own Inspector General largely supported her claims, the agency continued to resist the suit, finally claiming the state secrets privilege. The agency also took the highly unusual step of trying to reclassify a memo provided earlier to members of Congress and subsequently made public on the Web sites of two Senators. Just before claiming the state secrets privilege in court, the agency informed the Senate that the memo was now classified and should be removed from the public record. After the Senate resisted the claim, the agency backed down. As to the state secrets privilege, the district court judge concluded that as long as the procedural requirements had been followed he was foreclosed from questioning its validity. Edmonds then appealed to the D.C. Circuit, which initially closed the oral argument in Edmonds' case and subsequently issued a one-page order affirming the district court ruling.

The use of the state secrets privilege often appears to be just another tactical device used by the government to stop litigation that it does not want to proceed. Particularly in Edmonds' case, where her allegations were well-known and focused largely on misconduct or incompetence on the part of the agency rather than on national security issues, a claim of state secrets seems suspect at best. There are other procedural alternatives, such as controlled disclosure and closed proceedings where necessary, that could be used to manage such litigation to safeguard sensitive information.

Conclusion

There is no doubt that 9/11 has had a dramatic impact on the availability of public information. Information has been removed from the Internet, and, although much of it has been put back, the policy now certainly emphasizes erring on the part of caution and withholding information whenever there is a plausible basis for connecting its disclosure to terrorist threats. Information that does not qualify for classification under the executive order, but that appears to be sensitive in some way, has also been withheld, often without any clearly legal basis. The Freedom of Information Act has continued to be an important avenue of disclosure, but agencies have tightened their attitudes toward disclosure and tend to use exemptions somewhat more aggressively than was the case before the terrorist attacks. There has been a retrenchment of information policy that is based more on a response to a security threat than on an objective appraisal of information policy. The result has been a diminution in the availability of public information that has serious long-term consequences for information policy if it remains the status quo.

References

Coastal Delivery Corp. v. Customer Service, No. 02-3838 WMB (C.D. Cal., March 14, 2003).

Critical Mass v. NRC, 975 F2d 871 (D.C. Cir. 1992).

Living Rivers, Inc. v. Bureau of Reclamation, No. 2:02-CV-644TC (D. Utah, March 25, 2003).

An earlier version of this chapter appeared in Social Science Computer Review, 23(4), pp. 429-438, copyright 2005 by Sage Publications. Reprinted by permission of Sage Publications Inc.

Chapter III

Expanding Privacy Rationales under the Federal Freedom of Information Act:
Stigmatization as Talisman

Charles N. Davis, University of Missouri School of Journalism, USA

Abstract

Access to government information in a post-September 11 often involves the resolution of conflicts between privacy rights and the public interest inherent in information flow. On the one hand, information about any individual investigated by the government, or merely landing in an investigative file, might very well invade the privacy of the detainees by unduly stigmatizing them. In fact, such reasoning reflects a line of argumentation central to the federal government's justification for denial of access: privacy interests, particularly the risk of stigmatization. This chapter reviews the origins and expansion of stigmatization as grounds for protection of information under the FOIA. Examination of several key post-Reporters Committee cases decided by the federal courts illustrates the scope of the problem, as stigmatization has gained a great deal of legal traction in recent years.

Introduction

In the days and months following the terrorist attacks of September 11, 2001, United States Justice Department agents detained more than 1,000 people for immigration violations and criminal violations. A small number were arrested as material witnesses who authorities believe may have information vital to prosecutors. In most cases, officials declined to release any information about the detainees, including where they were being held, the names of their lawyers, or the progress of their cases.

On November 27, 2001, at the height of the controversy over detainee secrecy, then-U.S. Attorney General John Ashcroft defended his refusal to release the names of hundreds of people detained in connection with the September 11 terrorist attacks, saying that doing so would create "a public blacklist" that would violate the detainees' privacy rights (Eggen, 2001).[1]

"The law properly prevents the department from creating a public blacklist of detainees that would violate their rights," Ashcroft said at a news conference, adding that none of those detained had been denied access to a lawyer. "They are not being held in secret," he said.[2]

Such a contention depends entirely upon one's conceptualization of secrecy. Certainly, those entrusted with detaining and prosecuting those swept up in the post-September 11 investigation knew the identities of those in custody; equally certainly, the public and press did not.

It is important to note that the basis of Attorney General Ashcroft's contention—that providing public access to the names of those detained after the terrorist attacks would invade the privacy of the detainees by unduly stigmatizing them—was a well-calculated legal position and not the posturing of a public official defending secrecy for secrecy's sake. Rather, this language reflects a line of argumentation central to the Justice Department's most common justification for denial of access: privacy interests as defined by the United States Supreme Court in *Reporters Committee for Freedom of the Press v. Department of Justice*, a 1989 decision that dominates the FOIA landscape before and certainly after September 11.

Until *Reporters Committee*, courts weighing privacy claims made by federal agencies seeking to block a FOIA disclosure request had balanced the public and social interest in disclosure against the individual's interest in protecting personal privacy.[3] However, in *Reporters Committee*, the Department of Justice successfully argued for a change in this analysis.[4] This new judicial analysis expands the scope of privacy under the FOIA while it restricts the scope of acceptable public interest arguments in favor of disclosure.[5]

The expansion of a central tenet of *Reporters Committee*—that disclosure of information about private individuals contained in certain investigative records can "stigmatize" those individuals and thus violate their right to privacy—constitutes a threshold issue in information policy in the age of the Internet. If access under the federal Freedom of Information Act gives rise automatically to stigmatization, the balancing of interests mandated by the act must yield in nearly every instance to privacy interests. Examination of several key post-*Reporters Committee* cases decided by the federal courts illustrates the scope of the problem, as stigmatization has gained a great deal of legal traction in recent years.

The Origins of the "Stigmatization Doctrine"

The facts of *Reporters Committee* are noteworthy only because they illustrate the nature of the privacy interests at stake and the shrinking notion of the public interest in access inherent in the information sought by a CBS journalist following a rather newsworthy story. The reporter had filed a FOIA request[6] asking for the FBI's "rap sheet" on Charles Medico, a Pennsylvania businessman whose company had received defense contracts allegedly in exchange for political contributions to former U.S. Representative Daniel J. Flood.[7] Flood, who eventually left office in disgrace, pleaded guilty on February 26, 1980, to conspiracy to violate federal campaign laws. This clearly was no journalistic fishing expedition, but a clear clash of privacy vs. access.

The FBI released information on three of Charles Medico's brothers, all deceased, but the agency refused to release Charles Medico's records on privacy grounds because he was still alive.[8] The reporter sued to gain access to the records, but the U.S. District Court for the District of Columbia granted the FBI's motion for summary judgment to dismiss the suit. On appeal, however, the U.S. Court of Appeals for the D.C. Circuit ruled in favor of the CBS journalist and the Reporters Committee. The appeals court reasoned that the government could not claim a privacy interest in an FBI compilation of law enforcement agency records when those same records would be available as public records from the individual agencies themselves.[9]

The Department of Justice appealed to the Supreme Court, which, after weighing Medico's right of privacy against the public interest in disclosure, reversed the appellate court ruling and allowed the FBI to withhold the information.[10] Refuting its earlier balancing test for privacy cases which took into consideration the broader public interest in the information contained in governmental information, the *Reporters Committee* Court said that the only aspect of public interest to be balanced against the privacy interest is that of disclosing only official information that "directly reveals the operations or activities of the government."[11]

Writing for the Court, Justice John Paul Stevens said the FOIA's "central purpose is to ensure that the government's activities be opened to the sharp eye of public scrutiny, not that information about private citizens that happens to be in the warehouse of the government be so disclosed."[12] Because a computerized compilation of an individual's criminal records does not directly reveal governmental operations or performance, it falls "outside the ambit of the public interest that the FOIA was enacted to serve."[13]

The Court's definition of the FOIA's "central purpose" created in *Reporters Committee*—is the genesis of much of the government's FOIA posture in a post-September 11 world. The "central purpose" test leads inevitably to the position that government-held information that does not necessarily reveal government operations but that still holds great public interest is not subject to disclosure under the FOIA.

Contrast *Reporters Committee* with *U.S. Dept. of the Air Force v. Rose*,[14] a 1976 case that marked the government's first try at arguing privacy as a potential bar to disclosure under the FOIA.[15] The *Rose* Court flatly denied such a narrow conceptualization of the public interest under the FOIA, declaring that the act's legislative history makes clear that the statute was "broadly conceived" and that Congress intended for the statute to permit access to official information and open as much agency action as possible to public scrutiny.[16] The *Rose* Court did not say that disclosure was predicated on any conditions that a requested record must reveal agency performance or illuminate agency conduct. Instead, the *Rose* Court weighed the broader public interest in any and all information held by government, whether or not the information revealed government operations. While the *Reporters Committee* Court never explicitly mentioned the term "stigmatization," it created the supposition that the mere mention of an individual in a government record might give rise to privacy interests that outweigh the public interest in access to information.

In holding that a computerized compilation of records is different in nature from the individual records themselves, the *Reporters Committee* Court introduced the concept that there actually are inherent benefits to the kind of "practical obscurity" that existed before the emergence of the computer.[17] According to this theory, it is a good thing that all criminal records on a single individual—stored in police stations and courthouses scattered throughout the nation—are difficult to compile. This situation creates a "practical obscurity" inherent in these records, thus giving privacy protection to the records.[18] In other words, if information is difficult or time-consuming to acquire, that is, not "freely available,"[19] it takes on a mantle of privacy, cloaking it from public examination. The Court also noted that the "practical obscurity" of information is an especially useful quality in cases when official government information is sought not for the purposes of examining government performance but rather for private use.[20] Clearly concerned with the rise of computerized information and the ease with which such information may be accessed through the FOIA, the Court's opinion in *Reporters Committee* set the stage for further expansion of privacy rationales, including the argument that access might "stigmatize" third parties mentioned in government records.

Stigmatization as Privacy Rationale

Exemption 6 of FOIA permits an agency to withhold "personnel and medical files and similar files the disclosure of which would constitute a clearly unwarranted invasion of personal privacy."[21] The terms "similar files" has been interpreted broadly to include all information that applies to a particular individual.[22] In determining whether the exemption applies, the court must find that there is a privacy interest that outweighs the public interest in disclosure. The mere assertion that a privacy interest is threatened is insufficient to withhold information under Exemption 6. The requirement that disclosure be "clearly unwarranted" instructs this Court to "tilt the balance [of disclosure interests against privacy interests] in favor of disclosure."[23]

Exemption 7(c) permits the withholding of the records or information that have been compiled for law enforcement purposes, but only to the extent that production could "reasonably be expected to constitute an unwarranted invasion of personal privacy."[24] The threshold determination of what constitutes an invasion of privacy under Exemption 7(c) is not as high as that which is required under Exemption 6.[25] This is in large measure due to two reasons. First, there is a public interest in nondisclosure of this type of information to the extent that disclosure impairs the ability of law enforcement agencies to gather information and conduct investigations. Second, courts have long been concerned that the mere mention of an individual's name in the context of a law enforcement investigation may carry a stigmatizing connotation.[26] Finally, in assessing whether Exemption 7(c) has been properly invoked, courts must balance the privacy interest at stake against the public interest in disclosure. The government need not prove with certainty that disclosure will lead to an unwarranted invasion of privacy, but only that there is a reasonable expectation that such an invasion will occur.

Agencies subject to FOIA have used the holding in *Reporters Committee*, and its expansive dicta, to withhold a wide variety of documents on privacy grounds, and the lower federal courts have, for the most part, enlarged upon its already expansive doctrine. In a 1998 report prepared for a House committee, the Reporters Committee for Freedom of the Press said that ever since the Reporters Committee decision was handed down, the scales of balance in the test between the individual right to privacy and the public interest in disclosure has tipped heavily in favor of privacy over public access.[27] The *Reporters Committee* report concluded that the Supreme Court came up with a "narrow and crabbed interpretation" of the FOIA's congressional intent, critically impairing the ability of requesters to receive government information.[28]

It thus should come as no surprise that the federal government has, in recent years, successfully denied access to a list of federal inmates in an Illinois county jail because it feared the "stigmatization" of the inmates should their names be made public;[29] and shut down access to the records of a long-completed investigation of a West Texas sheriff convicted for helping a drug-runner smuggle 2,421 pounds of cocaine -- with a street value of $1.1 billion -- into the United States.[30] In that case, the court further expanded the *Reporters Committee* holding: the court said that in order to trigger the sort of public interest that would outweigh privacy concerns, the request must "put forward compelling evidence" that the agency involved is engaged in illegal activity.[31] In other words, unless the requester can prove wrongdoing, no public interest exists that would outweigh the privacy interests at stake.

Judicial treatment of stigmatization predates *Reporters Committee* by nearly a decade. For example, in *Fund For Constitutional Government v. National Archives*, the United States Court of Appeals for the District of Columbia Circuit upheld the government's decision to withhold records of grand jury matters and names of unindicted individuals, finding that revelation of the fact that an individual has been investigated for suspected criminal activity represents a significant intrusion on that individual's privacy under the FOIA.[32]

At issue in the case were approximately 500,000 pages of documents generated in the course of six investigations conducted by the Watergate Special Prosecution Force (WSPF). After reviewing the entire file, WSPF released a few documents but withheld the vast majority in reliance on one or more FOIA exemptions. The district court, treating the motion as one for partial summary judgment, ordered the release of certain documents to FCG but upheld the claimed exemptions as to the majority of the information.[33]

In balancing the privacy interests against the right of access, the court first noted that Exemptions 6 and 7 of the FOIA are distinguishable in two significant respects. First, while Exemption 6 refers to "a clearly unwarranted invasion of personal privacy," Exemption 7(c)'s reference is to an "unwarranted invasion of personal privacy." The omission of the word "clearly" from the Exemption 7(c) standard was a legislative choice made during the passage of the 1974 amendments to that section[34] and was intended to provide somewhat broader protection for privacy interests under Exemption 7(c) than normally afforded under Exemption 6.

Second, the threshold criterion governing applicability of FOIA Exemption 6 is that the information be contained in personnel, medical, or similar files. By contrast, Exemption 7 is applicable to information contained in investigatory records compiled for law enforcement purposes. In Exemption 6 cases, applicability of the exemption has been limited to information of an intimate or personal nature similar to that usually contained in an individual's personnel or medical files. No such limitation applies to Exemption 7 claims, which concern criminal investigative matters.[35]

Thus, having found the documents in question ripe for analysis under Exemption 7(c), the court reasoned that the decision to prosecute an individual for a crime that has attracted general notoriety typically provokes widespread speculation attended by at least some damage to the reputation of the individual involved. Typically, the decision not to prosecute insulates individuals who have been investigated but not charged from this rather significant intrusion into their lives. In finding that the public interest in disclosure was insufficient to overcome the legitimate privacy interests of the individuals in question, the court observed:

We might be persuaded under appropriate circumstances that an individual's status as a "public figure" would tip the 7(c) balance in favor of disclosure. This is not, however, such a case. While such a status might somewhat diminish an individual's interest in privacy, the degree of intrusion occasioned by disclosure is necessarily dependent upon the character of the information in question. As we have already indicated, revelation of the fact that an individual has been investigated for suspected criminal activity represents a significant intrusion on that individual's privacy cognizable under Exemption 7(c). The degree of intrusion is indeed potentially augmented by the fact that the individual is a well known figure and the investigation one which attracts as much national attention as those conducted by the WSPF. The disclosure of that information would produce the unwarranted result of placing the named individuals in the position of having to defend their conduct in the public forum outside of the procedural protections normally afforded the accused in criminal proceedings.[36]

While the D.C. Circuit never mentioned the word "stigmatization" in its opinion in *Fund For Constitutional Government*, the concept clearly was at play. The court's concern that the release of documents mentioning those investigated, but not charged with crimes, clearly troubled the court and it rejected the FCG's arguments that the public interest in the Watergate investigation outweighed the privacy interests of those public officials implicated, but never charged, in the investigation.

Typically, exemption 7(c) has been used to protect from disclosure the identities of and information concerning individuals in whom the FBI has an investigative interest.[37] It has also been used to protect the identities of FBI agents, other government personnel, and those who have provided information as part of an investigation. Few disagree with the protection of that information in the context of a criminal investigation; the "stigma" created by disclosure of such information seems fairly obvious. The problem with the rationale lies not with its application in cases such as *Fund For Constitutional Government*; instead, issues arise where the public interest in governmental information is more intense and the privacy interests less obvious.

The Supreme Court's decision in *Reporters Committee* substantially altered the judicial approach to balancing privacy interests under the FOIA. While recognizing that "official information that sheds light on an agency's performance of its statutory duties falls squarely within [FOIA's] statutory purpose," the court also noted that requests solely about the activities of private persons mentioned in government records rarely would "shed any light on the conduct of any governmental agency or official."[38]

Although the *Reporters Committee* Court stopped short of rejecting the balance of interests required by the reference to "unwarranted" invasions privacy in the FOIA, it said "categorical decisions may be appropriate and individual circumstances disregarded when a case fits into a genus in which the balance characteristically tips in one direction."[39] Applying the categorical approach to rap sheets, the Court concluded that the "privacy interest in maintaining the practical obscurity of rap-sheet information will always be high."[40] Thus, when the subject of a requested record is a private citizen and the information is in the government's control as an electronic compilation, "…the FOIA-based public interest in disclosure is at its nadir."[41]

Since *Reporters Committee*, the D.C. Circuit has steadfastly followed the opinion, applying categorical balancing to withhold names, addresses, and other identifying information contained in government databases. In fact, the D.C. Circuit has gone so far as to declare that "unless the names and addresses of private individuals appearing in files within the ambit of Exemption 7(c) is necessary to refute compelling evidence that the agency is engaged in illegal activity, such information is exempt from disclosure."[42] The vast majority of federal courts have generally followed this line of reasoning, greatly reducing disclosure under 7(c).[43] In many of the opinions, the threat of stigmatization is cited as a reason for closure.

Under Exemption 6, as noted earlier, the standard—whether disclosure would constitute a clearly unwarranted invasion of privacy"—is higher than in 7(c) by design. For Exemption 6 to support closure, then, the privacy invasion must be substantial; as the United States Supreme Court has noted, the privacy interests at stake must be "more palpable than mere possibilities."[44] The *Reporters Committee* Court, in extending the holding of the case beyond 7(c) to Exemption 6, altered the public interest analysis under Exemption 6 as well. By stating that the only public interest to be weighed in the balance with privacy concerns is the FOIA's "core purpose" of contributing to public understanding of government operations or activities, *Reporters Committee* also altered the calculus of Exemption 6.

In cases decided after the Supreme Court's decision in *Reporters Committee*, there clearly is judicial recognition in the public interest in favor of release of some documents, so long as they trigger only broad privacy claims under Exemption 6. Files that involve law enforcement-based privacy claims under 7(c) rarely have been disclosed.

For example, federal courts have routinely held that there is a strong public interest in the release of information identifying individuals owed money by the federal government.[45] The courts have also released photographs of a murder victim from a requester who was court-martialed 25 years earlier, rejecting claims under Exemptions 7(c) and 6.[46] Similarly, in 1996, a federal appellate court allowed disclosure of individual mug shots, finding that the release could lead to greater oversight of governmental activities.[47] Stigmatization thus does not always carry the day, although it is a far more effective argument post-*Reporters Committee*.

As for names, addresses, and other identifying information of federal employees contained in government databases, the post-*Reporters Committee* courts split on the issue, until a subsequent United States Supreme Court opinion in 1994 clearly held that only when such requests are made in the context of the "core purpose" of FOIA—understanding governmental activities and operations—can they overcome privacy interests.[48] Again, the implication is that disclosure of such information would somehow implicate privacy interests, even in the context of federal employment.

Still other courts have taken privacy interests even further, siding with "stigmatization" arguments reminiscent of Attorney General Ashcroft's defense of detainee secrecy in the wake of September 11. For example, in a 2002 Illinois district court case, the federal government denied a newspaper reporter's request for the names of federal inmates serving under a bed-for-hire agreement with a county jail.[49] The reporter sought the names of all inmates held in the DeWitt County jail under the Illinois Freedom of Information Act. The reporter obtained the names of the Illinois state prisoners, but the jail refused to release the names of the federal prisoners, and the federal government intervened to prevent the release of the names of federal prisoners. The government removed the case to federal district court in Illinois, and the district judge held that the names of federal prisoners could be withheld on privacy grounds.

The court cited *Reporters Committee*'s declaration: "as a categorical matter that a third party's request for law enforcement records or information about a private citizen can reasonably be expected to invade that citizen's privacy, and that when the request seeks no "official information" about a Government agency, but merely records that the Government happens to be storing, the invasion of privacy is 'unwarranted.'"

Using that categorical approach, the district court said that "[l]ike disclosing a 'rap sheet,' providing a list of inmates' names here would be an unreasonable invasion of privacy," because some of the inmates under federal control are merely witnesses and detainees who have not been charged with or convicted of crimes. Releasing their names to the press, the court said:

> ...*would stigmatize these individuals and cause what could be irreparable damage to their reputations. Thus, any watchdog function that disclosure would serve here is clearly outweighed by inmates' privacy interests.*[50]

The district court's opinion illustrates the problems inherent in applying categorical reasoning to FOIA requests. Such an approach devalues the public interest in access—in this case, the rather obvious interest of the citizens of Bloomington, Illinois, in who was residing in their county jail. County jails, after all, seldom house federal prisoners, and clearly there is a legitimate public discussion that should take place when federal inmates appear in county facilities. What are the inmates charged with? Why are they being detained? On what grounds are they being held? How can the public assess the risk of federal prisoners in a county jail?

Historically, such a conflict between privacy and access would have required the judge in the case to carefully weigh those interests when deciding whether the privacy interests of witnesses and detainees in custody trump the rather substantial public interest in knowing the names, and thus the offenses, of federal inmates in the county jail.

Here, however, we see the power of *Reporters Committee* and its categorical approach. No discussion of the public interest in access appears in the opinion; rather, the court concludes, with no analysis, that "any watchdog function that disclosure would serve here is clearly outweighed by inmates' privacy interests."[51] Thus, to the court, the privacy rights of prisoners categorically outweighs the public interest in access to information about them, and the court assumes that information about the prisoners no "watchdog function."

Quite the contrary, the request was made entirely for watchdog purposes: a reporter wanted to know the kinds of federal inmates who had appeared, with little warning, in a county jail.[52] Readers of the Bloomington, Illinois, *Pantagraph* were interested in the details of the agreement made to house the federal prisoners, and the newspaper was interested in the safety issues raised by the prisoners. Yet the court dismissed those interests without analysis. Categorical approaches, by their very structure, devalue counterarguments in conflicts between oppositional rights, and that is their downfall where the public interest in access may well outweigh privacy interests.

Conclusion

The emergence of the categorical approach, with its frequent reliance on potential stigmatization as a rational for closure, raises novel issues of privacy and access. Taken together, the rise of database technology and the resultant reinvigoration of the privacy debate threaten the most effective check citizens have on their elected representatives and their legislatively created agencies—the statutory right of individuals to inspect the records of government (Mauro, 2000; O'Reilly, 1998; Westin, 1974).[53] This principle of accountability is embodied in the federal Freedom of Information Act[54] and in analogous state open-records laws (Cross, 1953).[55]

When weighing privacy claims made by federal agencies seeking to block a FOIA disclosure request, courts historically had balanced the public and social interest in disclosure against the individual's interest in protecting personal privacy until the *Reporters Committee* ruling.[56] However, in *Reporters Committee*, the Department of Justice successfully argued for a change in this analysis, resulting in a narrower definition of disclosable records.[57] This new judicial analysis expands the scope of privacy under the FOIA, while it restricts the scope of acceptable public interest arguments in favor of disclosure.[58]

The stigmatization argument fits the *Reporters Committee* rubric nicely, as it benefits mightily from categorical approaches that present privacy interests as a bar to access to records, while severely limiting judicial scrutiny of the underlying arguments for the potential stigmatization. In conflicts between privacy and access, the threshold question historically, and under the FOIA's statutory language, is whether there has been "an unwarranted invasion of privacy," for purposes of Exemption 7(c), and a "*clearly* unwarranted invasion" for purposes of satisfying Exemption 6. Stigmatization short-circuits that critical analysis by rendering entire classes of information withheld under the FOIA, greatly reducing the public interest in access.

References

Albuquerque Publishing Co. v. Department of Justice, 726 F. Supp. 851 (D.D.C. 1989).

Aronson v. IRS, 767 F. Supp. 378 (D. Mass., 1991), affirmed in part, reversed in part, 973 F. 2d 962 (1st Cir. 1992).

Brady-Lunny v. Department of Justice, 185 F. Supp. 2d 928 (C. Dist. Ill. 2002).

Cross, H. (1953). *The people's right to know.* New York: Columbia University Press.

Department of Defense v. Federal Labor Relations Authority, 510 U.S. 487 (1994), reversing 975 F.2d 1105 (5th Cir. 1992).

Department of State v. Washington Post Co., 456 U.S. 595, 599-603, 102 S. Ct. 1957, 72 L. Ed. 2d 358 (1982).

Detroit Free Press v. Department of Justice, 73 F.3d 93 (6th Cir. 1996).

Ditlow v. Shultz, 170 U.S. App. D.C. 352, 517 F.2d 166, 169 (D.C. Cir. 1975).

Eggen, D. (2001, November 27). Ashcroft defends not listing detainees: Privacy rights at issue, he says. *The Washington Post*, p. A4.

Federal Freedom of Information Act, 489 U.S. 749 (1989).

Federal Freedom of Information Act, 5 U.S.C. § 552(b)(6) (1996).

Fund for Constitutional Government v. National Archives and Records Service, 485 F. Supp. 1 (D.D.C., 1978).

Fund for Constitutional Government v. National Archives and Records Service, 211 U.S. App.

D.C. 267, 656 F.2d 856, 862 (D.C. Cir., 1981).

KTVY-TV v. United States, 919 F.2d 1465 (10th Cir. 1990).

Landano v. Department of Justice, 956 F.2d 422 (3d Cir. 1992).

Lesar v. U.S. Department of Justice, 204 U.S. App. D.C. 200, 636 F.2d 472, 488 (D.C. Cir., 1980).

Mauro, T. (2000, March). Press overlooked in DPPA ruling. *QUILL*, 24-24.

McNamera v. Department of Justice, 974 F.Supp. 946 (W.Dis. Tex. 1997).

O'Reilly, J.T. (1998). Expanding the purpose of federal records access: New private entitlement or new threat to privacy. *Administrative Law Review*, *50*(2), 371-373.

Outlaw v. Department of Justice, 815 F. Supp. 505 (D.D.C. 1993).

Reporters Committee for Freedom of the Press v. U.S. Department of Justice, 816 F.2d 730, 740 (D.C. Cir. 1987).

Reporters Committee for Freedom of the Press. (1998, July 2). Report on responses and non-response of the executive and judicial branches to congress' finding that the FOI Act serves "any purpose." Prepared by request of Rep. Steven Horn, chairman, Subcommittee on Government Management, Information and Technology, of the House Committee on Government Reform and Oversight. Retrieved July 13, 2007, from www.rcfp.org

Robert A. Holland v. U.S. Department of Justice, 1986 U.S. Dist. LEXIS 28345 (E.Dist. Pa. 1986).

SafeCard Services v. SEC, 926 F.2d 1197, 1206 (D.C. Cir. 1991).

U.S. Department of the Air Force v. Rose, 425 U.S. 352 (1976).

Washington Post Co. v. Department of Health and Human Services, 223 U.S. App. D.C. 139, 690 F.2d 252, 261 (D.C. Cir. 1982).

Westin, A.F. (1974). The technology of secrecy. In S. Gillers & N. Dorsen (Eds.), *None of your business* (pp. 305-312). New York: Viking.

Endnotes

[1] Dan Eggen, "Ashcroft Defends Not Listing Detainees; Privacy Rights At Issue, He Says," The Washington Post, November 27, 2001; Page A4.

[2] Ibid.

[3] *See* U.S. Dep't of the Air Force v. Rose, 425 U.S. 352 (1976). The *Rose* decision marks the first time that the Supreme Court considered invasion of privacy as a potential bar to disclosure under the FOIA. The *Rose* court established that a balancing test between the individual value of personal privacy against

the social value of public disclosure must be the device to determine whether information should be disclosed. The Court held that the act's exemptions are limited, and they must be narrowly construed. *See id.* at 361. The opinion emphasized that the exemptions' existence should not "obscure the basic policy that disclosure, not secrecy, is the dominant object of the Act." *See id.*

4   *See* 489 U.S. 749, 780.

5   *See id.* at 772-74.

6   *See id.*

7   *See id.*

8   *See* 489 U.S. at 757.

9   *See* Reporters Comm. for Freedom of the Press v. U.S. Dep't of Justice, 816 F.2d 730, 740 (D.C. Cir. 1987).

10   *See* 489 U.S. at 772-73 (citing 425 U.S. at 372.)

11   *See id.*

12   *See id.* at 774.

13   *See id.* at 775.

14   *See id.*

15   *See* 425 U.S. 352 (1976).

16   *See id.* at 361 (citing EPA v. Mink, 410 U.S. 73, 80 [1973]).

17   *See* 510 U.S. at 496, n. 6. (J. Ginsburg, concurring).

18   *See* 489 U.S. 749, 764, 780 (1989).

19   *See id.* at 764.

20   *See id* at 771.

21   5 U.S.C. § 552(b)(6).

22   See Department of State v. Washington Post Co., 456 U.S. 595, 599-603, 102 S. Ct. 1957, 72 L. Ed. 2d 358 (1982); Washington Post Co. v. Department of Health and Human Services, 223 U.S. App. D.C. 139, 690 F.2d 252, 261 (D.C. Cir. 1982).

23   See Ditlow v. Shultz, 170 U.S. App. D.C. 352, 517 F.2d 166, 169 (D.C. Cir. 1975).

24   5 U.S.C. § 552(b)(7)(C).

25   See Fund for Constitutional Government v. National Archives and Records Service, 211 U.S. App. D.C. 267, 656 F.2d 856, 862 (D.C. Cir. 1981).

26   See, e.g., Fund for Constitutional Government, supra; Lesar v. U.S. Department of Justice, 204 U.S. App. D.C. 200, 636 F.2d 472, 488 (D.C. Cir. 1980).

27   *See* Reporters Committee for Freedom of the Press, *Report on Responses and Non-Response of the Executive and Judicial Branches to Congress' Finding*

that the FOI Act Serves 'Any Purpose' 2 (July 2, 1998)(Prepared by request of Rep. Steven Horn, chairman, Subcommittee on Government Management, Information and Technology, of the House Committee on Government Reform and Oversight.)

[28]   *See id.* at 10.

[29]   Brady-Lunny v. Dept. of Justice, 185 F. Supp. 2d 928 (C. Dist. Ill. 2002).

[30]   McNamera v. Dept. of Justice, 974 F.Supp. 946 (W.Dis. Tex. 1997).

[31]   *See id.* at 960.

[32]   211 U.S. App. D.C. 267 (D.C. 1981).

[33]   Fund for Constitutional Government v. National Archives and Records Service, 485 F. Supp. 1 (D.D.C.1978).

[34]   Id., at 14, citing Pub.L. No. 93-502, § 2(b), 88 Stat. 1563.

[35]   Id. At 15.

[36]   Id. At 20-21.

[37]   See, e.g., Robert A. Holland v. U.S. Dept. of Justice, 1986 U.S. Dist. LEXIS 28345 (E.Dist. Pa. 1986).

[38]   Reporters Committee, at 773 & n. 21.

[39]   Id. at 776.

[40]   Id. at 780.

[41]   Id.

[42]   SafeCard Services v. SEC, 926 F.2d 1197, 1206 (D.C. Cir. 1991).

[43]   See Landano v. Dept. of Justice, 956 F.2d 422 (3d Cir. 1992); KTVY-TV v. United States, 919 F.2d 1465 (10th Cir. 1990); Albuquerque Publishing Co. v. Dept. of Justice, 726 F. Supp. 851 (D.D.C. 1989).

[44]   Air Force v. Rose, 425 U.S. 352, at 380 n. 19 (1976).

[45]   See Aronson v. IRS, 767 F. Supp. 378 (D. Mass. 1991), affirmed in part, reversed in part, 973 F. 2d 962 (1st cir. 1992).

[46]   Outlaw v. Dept. of Justice, 815 F. Supp. 505 (D.D.C. 1993).

[47]   Detroit Free Press v. Dept. of Justice, 73 F.3d 93 (6th Cir. 1996).

[48]   Dept. of Defense v. Fed. Labor Relations Auth., 510 U.S. 487 (1994), reversing 975 F.2d 1105 (5th Cir. 1992).

[49]   Brady-Lunny v. Massey, 185 F. Supp. 2d 928, 930 (C.D. Ill. 2002).

[50]   Id. at 932.

[51]   Id.

[52]   Interview with Edith Brady-Lunny, reporter, Bloomington, Illinois, Pantagraph, Nov. 13, 2003.

⁵³ *See* James T. O'Reilly, *Expanding the Purpose of Federal Records Access: New Private Entitlement or New Threat to Privacy,* 50 ADMIN. L.REV. 371 (1998); Tony Mauro, *Press overlooked in DPPA ruling,* QUILL, Mar. 2000, at 24. The tremendous advances in information technology over the last decade without doubt have stimulated growing alarm about protecting personal privacy. However, concern over how computerization may contribute to government secrecy dates back at least to the mid-1970s. Congress acknowledged in 1974 that maintenance of federal agency records in computerized formats could potentially alter the calculus of information disclosure requirements under the FOIA. *See* S. REP. No. 854, 93d Cong., 2d Sess. 12 (1974). Also in 1974, Professor Alan F. Westin called for federal computerization and information policy, and raised the issue that computerization of records could create a new form of government secrecy and posed a potentially great danger to the right to know. *See* Alan F. Westin, *The Technology of Secrecy, in* STEVEN GILLERS AND NORMAN DORSEN, EDS., NONE OF YOUR BUSINESS 305, 317 (1974).

⁵⁴ *See* 5 U.S.C. § 552 (1994).

⁵⁵ State open-records statutes were in effect for decades before Congress passed the FOIA, which opened to public inspection the records of the executive branch administrative agencies. President Lyndon B. Johnson signed the Freedom of Information Act into law on July 4, 1966. *See* Wkly COMP. PRES. DOC. 895 (July 4, 1966). By 1950, at least 11 states had already enacted limited open-records statutes. Among the earliest were Tennessee, 1934; Delaware, 1935; Maryland, 1939; Louisiana, 1940; Idaho, 1941; North Carolina, 1943; Utah, 1945; Montana, 1947; New Jersey, 1947; California, 1949; and Kansas, 1949. *See* HAROLD CROSS, THE PEOPLE'S RIGHT TO KNOW 328-36 (1953). Today, every state has an open-records statute.

⁵⁶ *See* U.S. Dep't of the Air Force v. Rose, 425 U.S. 352 (1976). The *Rose* decision marks the first time that the Supreme Court considered invasion of privacy as a potential bar to disclosure under the FOIA. The *Rose* court established that a balancing test between the individual value of personal privacy against the social value of public disclosure must be the device to determine whether information should be disclosed. The Court held that the act's exemptions are limited, and they must be narrowly construed. *See id.* at 361. The opinion emphasized that the exemptions' existence should not "obscure the basic policy that disclosure, not secrecy, is the dominant object of the Act." *See id.*

⁵⁷ *See* 489 U.S. 749, 780.

⁵⁸ *See id.* at 772-74.

This chapter was previously published in in Social Science Computer Review, 23(4), pp. 453-462, copyright 2005 by Sage Publications. Reprinted by permission of Sage Publications Inc.

Chapter IV

Access to Information and the Freedom to Access:
The Intersection of Public Libraries and the USA PATRIOT Act

Lauren Teffeau, University of Illinois at Urbana-Champaign, USA

Megan Mustafoff, University of Illinois at Urbana-Champaign, USA

Leigh Estabrook, University of Illinois at Urbana-Champaign, USA

Abstract

This chapter discusses two studies performed by the Library Research Center at the University of Illinois concerning the impact the terrorist attacks and the USA PATRIOT Act has had on the librarians and the patrons they serve. Results are compared with findings from a Pew Internet and American Life survey to analyze differences between library directors and the public at large. Together, these studies illustrate the chilling effect's impact on libraries and their patrons, as well as question the fundamental freedom to read all ideas. Libraries in the North Atlantic region of the United States were far more likely to report changes in staff attitudes, collection development, and security and policy changes that were influenced by September

11 and the passage of the USA Patriot Act as compared to the rest of the country. This tendency could be reflective of many issues, but the libraries' proximity to the terrorist attacks does seem to stand out. In addition to region, library size was also prognostic. The two surveys presented in this chapter clearly highlight the regional effects of the attacks over time and point to additional avenues of investigation. Continued research on library changes in response to the USA PATRIOT Act and terrorism needs to continue in order to understand better how American information habits are being both protected and compromised in today's public libraries. today's public libraries.

Introduction

The foundation of public libraries is a belief that an informed citizenry is critical to a democracy, and that being informed means having the opportunity to consider all points of view. Librarians have long believed that freedom of inquiry is only guaranteed if people can be assured that the subject of their inquiry is kept private. In the United States, 48 states have laws guaranteeing the confidentiality of library records. When the USA PATRIOT Act was passed in October 2001, librarians immediately began to consider the implications of its provisions on public library service and on their users. Under the act, law enforcement agencies in the course of an investigation can scrutinize business records, and library records are just one type of business records that fall under its jurisdiction.

This chapter discusses two studies performed by the Library Research Center concerning the impact of the terrorist attacks and the USA PATRIOT Act on librarians and the patrons they serve. Together, these studies illustrate the chilling effect's impact on libraries and their patrons, as well as question the fundamental freedom to read all ideas. Originally conducted in late 2001 and 1 year later, results of these studies have not until this time been fully analyzed, although the findings have received public attention, including the investigator being called "scurrilous" by an FBI spokesperson (Kronholz, 2003). Until now, they have only been summarized in brief on the Library Research Center Web site.

As background to the analysis, we review provisions of the USA PATRIOT Act of particular concern and relevance to libraries, as well as focus on the research that has been conducted on libraries subsequent to the events of September 11, 2001.

Literature Review

As the first reports of the terrorist attacks on September 11, 2001 started to reach the American public, people sought information. They wanted to learn more about the attacks, who perpetrated them and why, and whether or not their loved ones were safe. In addition to news media coverage and the Internet, "[l]ibraries played an important role in meeting this sudden demand for information on so many diverse subjects," (Matthews & Wiggins, 2001). This development was remarkable because "libraries in many cities have become the place of last resort for information and access, and they remain a political afterthought except in times of crisis," (Wheeler, 2005, p. 90). Libraries' part in this time of "crisis" was reframed in the public eye when Delray Beach, Florida, librarian Kathleen Hensmen told authorities that she recognized one of the suspected terrorists based on computer sign-up sheets in her library (Pressley & Blum, 2001). The discovery that the hijackers were potentially using public library Internet terminals to facilitate their terrorist plans placed libraries in the center of the USA PATRIOT Act controversy, between the right to freedom of speech and the need for domestic security.

The USA PATRIOT Act was set in place on October 26, 2001, just 6 weeks following the terrorist attacks. With the only opposition from Senator Russ Feingold (D—Wisconsin), the passage of the act modified many previous laws and statutes, and these changes have transformed the ways in which library and patron information can be used. By examining the political atmosphere leading up to the passage of the USA PATRIOT Act and its provisions, the act's relevance to libraries, the attempts by the American Library Association (ALA) and the Department of Justice to spread awareness of the act, and how the act has impacted the library environment, we can better understand the placement of the public library in the information landscape after September 11.

The USA PATRIOT Act is a combination of two bills, the Uniting and Strengthening America Act initiated by then-Senator Tom Daschle (D—South Dakota) and the Provide Appropriate Tools Required to Intercept and Obstruct Terrorism Bill by Representative James Sensenbrenner (R—Wisconsin) (Fifarek, 2002, p. 367). Together, they number over 300 pages in length, which prompted critics to question the relatively quick Congressional approval the bill received (Coolidge, 2005, p. 8; Fifarek, p. 367; Regan, 2004, p. 482). Since the time of that passage through the period of revision in 2005 and 2006, U.S. citizens have debated the extent to which the act erodes civil liberties, and have continued to discuss in detail the elements of the USA PATRIOT Act.

Of particular importance to libraries are the changes the original act made to the Foreign Intelligence Surveillance Act (FISA), which previously maintained a "distinction between investigative conduct in domestic criminal investigations and in foreign intelligence investigations" (Jaeger, Bertot, & McClure, 2003, p. 297). Under provisions of the USA PATRIOT Act, the "wall" between foreign and domestic investigations is "dismantle[d] [..] by allowing searches when foreign intelligence gathering is a 'significant purpose' rather than 'the purpose,' and by condoning exchanges of information between intelligence officers and law enforcement officers," (Regan, 2004, p. 489). The modifications to FISA, as outlined by Jaeger, Bertot, and McClure (2003) include:

- The expansion of the circumstances under which surveillance can occur.
- The greatly expanded definition of records that can be searched and obtained in FISA investigations.
- The secrecy clause.
- The expressed ability to conduct surveillance on electronic and voice mail communications.
- The extension of the use of roving wiretaps.
- The extension of the uses of pen registers, and trap and trace devices in FISA investigations.
- The dramatic alterations to the relationships between agencies that collect intelligence information and other law enforcement organizations. (pp. 299-300)

The increased number of circumstances that can involve FISA-approved surveillance further increases the potential of abuse and may even result in "fishing expeditions" (Regan, 2004, p. 490), reminiscent of the Library Awareness Program (LAP), which "tracked the library use of people primarily of Eastern European or Russian descent" during the 1970s and 1980s (Wheeler, 2005, p. 81). However, unlike LAP, the USA PATRIOT Act "carr[ies] significant force of law," which makes if far more difficult to refuse compliance and also prevents the parties involved from discussing the investigation (Jaeger, McClure, Bertot, & Snead, 2004, p. 103). The provision is troubling to librarians who seek to create lectures and events in their libraries that spark debate and present diverse opinions. Their fear is that provisions of the USA PATRIOT Act, when married to former Attorney General Ashcroft's May 2002 "Guidelines on General Crimes, Racketeering Enterprise and Terrorism Enterprise Investigations" allowing covert surveillance of public meetings (p. 6), will create a "chilling effect" on libraries. Questions still remain on whether or not libraries self-censor their choices of speakers and programs out of fear of being investigated.

Librarians are also concerned about provisions that may allow investigations into the records of users' borrowing patterns or uses of the Internet. The USA PATRIOT Act defines a record as "any tangible thing (including books, records, papers, documents, and other items)" (H. R. 3162, section 215). Other items include computerized patron borrowing information and Internet service records. The impact information technology can have on investigations is undeniable: "When the time stamps on video surveillance tapes can be matched to web logs, the library [...] can provide police with a detailed record of an information searcher's behavior – something that was impossible in the days when all library information was located in the far corners of the stacks," (Fifarek, 2002, p. 368). Technology has not only made it easier to conduct surveillance, but it has also created new surveillance dimensions that open up different avenues of investigation, where the implications are still largely unknown.

One of the greatest causes of concern for librarians is the act's secrecy clause that prohibits libraries from acknowledging that they are or have ever been involved in a FISA investigation (H. R. 3162, section 215) or have been served National Security Letters (H. R. 3162, section 505). This so-called gag rule furthermore prohibits libraries from notifying the patron(s) potentially involved in the investigation or anyone else. The ramifications of this statute were placed in the public eye when Connecticut librarian "John Doe" refused to hand over library records despite being served a National Security Letter, which, in addition to FISA court orders, "require a library to turn over records of computer use to the government," (Mart, 2004, p. 462). The resulting Connecticut district court case found the gag rule John Doe was under that prevented him from exercising his First Amendment rights to address the rampant media speculation about the situation was unconstitutional (John Doe, et al. v. Alberto Gonzales, 2005). The case never reached the appeals court until recently, when the government issued a statement lifting the gag order (With Patriot Act debate over, government drops fight to gag librarians from discussing objections to controversial law, 2006).

By extending the uses of roving wiretaps, pen registers, and trap and trace devices, the USA PATRIOT Act enables increased surveillance on electronic and voicemail communications (H. R. 3162, sections 206, 214, 216, 218). While many researchers are alarmed by the changes, others have dismissed them as merely "technical amendments" with which "libraries had been subject to [...] prior to the enactment of the USA PATRIOT Act," and that "the library community only recently became aware of the statutory environment [...] as a result of the publicity" the USA PATRIOT Act has garnered (Pikowsky, 2002, p. 620). The greater availability of wiretaps, pen registers, and trap and trace devices have also led researchers to question just exactly what types of information will be gathered. For example, "[d]ialing, routing, and signaling information can all now be legally tracked. The law requires agents to stop short of actually reading the content of e-mail messages. However, technologically, it remains impossible to separate routing information from the e-mail message itself" (Wheeler, 2005, p. 85). With the technical advances made in pen registers and trap and trace devices, it is now possible to capture Internet addresses that someone is visiting if a pen register is connected to their computer. Mart discussed the implications in "Protecting the Lady from Toledo: Post-USA PATRIOT

Act Electronic Surveillance at the Library," saying "[w]hat section 216 did, from the librarian's perspective, is extend the reach of a pen register order, issued without any Fourth Amendment protections, to patron use at a library computer terminal. Now the government is capable of watching what patrons are reading online, while they are reading it" (p. 453).

With the increased types of information the government can collect and the increased ways in which it can collect the information, the USA PATRIOT Act also "alters FISA to allow information obtained in a FISA investigation to be shared with any government investigative agency, law enforcement agency, or attorney" (Jaeger, Bertot, & McClure, 2003, p. 300). While such a statute increases the dissemination of relevant information crucial to curtailing terrorist activities in a timely manner, it also places libraries at the mercies of the government, potentially making it difficult to report abuses of power since "[t]he lowering of judicial standards for individualized suspicion is accompanied by a weakening of judicial safeguards," (Regan, 2004, p. 489). This "lowering" "create[s] two problems: first, stripping the protection of a higher search standard from library patron records risk a chilling effect on patrons' library use. Second, the act gives the executive branch broad powers, ignoring our government's system of checks and balances" (Martin, 2003, p. 295).

Because the USA PATRIOT Act allows such surveillance, librarians have become concerned that the act will result in a chilling of reading and library activities. A chilling effect can occur "when individuals seeking to engage in activity protected by the First Amendment are deterred from doing so by governmental regulation not specifically directed at that protected activity," [emphasis omitted] (Schauer, 1978, p. 693). In practice, this chilling is manifested as "reluctance on the part of patrons to check out certain materials" and when librarians start "'screening' the purchase and availability of certain materials, not responding completely to information requests, and [having] concern about keeping certain types of patron records" (Goodrum, 2005, p. 38).

The USA PATRIOT Act has forced politicians, researchers, and the public to reexamine the Bill of Rights in the context of today's digital and political environment. For example,

...records privacy has often been located in Fourth Amendment protections against unreasonable searches and seizures. Reading privacy generally, and particularly the right to access to information [sic], and the 'chilling effects' that violations of privacy have on that right, have often been centered on First Amendment protections that guarantee a right to speech and expression. (Munoz, 2004, pp. 59-60)

When a library patron checks out a book, they are accessing material controlled by the library. Usually patron borrowing information is erased once materials are returned to the library and another patron checks it out (Fifarek, 2002, p. 367).

However, patrons' right to privacy and "library privacy is largely a matter of state law," (Munoz, 2004, p. 63) and "48 states [...] have laws protecting the confidentiality of library records, and the Attorneys General of the remaining two states, Hawaii and Kentucky, have ruled that library records are confidential and may not be disclosed under the laws governing open records," (Confidentiality and Coping with Law Enforcement Inquiries, 2002). There is also a Supreme Court precedent in *United States v. Rumely*, which protected individuals' reading habits, claiming that "[i]f the lady from Toledo can be required to disclose what she read yesterday and what she will read tomorrow, fear will take the place of freedom in the libraries, book stores, and homes of the land" (1953).

While library reading habits have historically been protected, the legal rights of users of public Internet terminals are not well defined. When library patrons use an Internet station to visit Web sites, they access Web sites and content that are not controlled by the library, generating "records of activities that occur in a public space," (Munoz, 2004, p. 69). But is the activity reading or is it Internet communication, for which "there is no reasonable expectation of privacy" (pp. 68-69)? While for some people this represents a very real difference and figures heavily in the debate surrounding the Communications Assistance for Law Enforcement Act (CALEA) and whether or not universities and public libraries must wiretap their Internet like other ISPs (McCullagh, 2006), the USA PATRIOT makes no such distinction and the act's statutes allow it to request such information from libraries nationwide.

Opposition to the USA PATRIOT Act, dismissed as "baseless hysteria" by Attorney General John Ashcroft (Coolidge, 2005, p. 7), includes First Amendment watchdog group the American Civil Liberties Union (ACLU) and the American Library Association (ALA). The ACLU provided council for Connecticut librarian John Doe (John Doe, et al. v. Alberto Gonzales, 2005) and has been very vocal in challenging USA PATRIOT Act provisions. The ALA has lent its support to the Freedom to Read Protection Act (Munoz, 2004) and has orchestrated a concerted effort among its members to lobby Congress in critique of the USA PATRIOT Act. Attorney General Ashcroft, in response to the resistance, stated during a speech in Memphis, Tennessee:

The fact is, with just over 11,000 FBI agents and over a billion visitors to America's libraries each year, the Department of Justice has neither the staffing, the time nor the inclination to monitor the reading habits of Americans. No offence to the American Library Association, but we just don't care. (Ashcroft, 2003)

The controversy between ALA and the U.S. Department of Justice's support of the USA PATRIOT Act, as depicted in the mass media, prompted one researcher following the debate to comment, that had the very public dispute been "[m]anaged in a less reactionary manner, the debate could have been an opportunity [...] to educate librarians on the process of criminal and foreign intelligence investigations, and for both librarians and law enforcement officials to find ways to work together" (p. 28).

There have been few studies attempting to measure the effects terrorism and the USA PATRIOT Act has had on libraries, no doubt due in part because of the legal and ethical issues Jaeger, McClure, Bertot, and Snead (2004) have discussed. In addition to Estabrook's (2002) analysis of Illinois public libraries' response to September 11, 2001, which found that very few libraries changed their policies in the weeks following the terrorist attacks, but that 11 libraries had been subject to information requests, another study, a joint venture between *The Sacramento Bee* and the California Library Association, found that 14 California libraries had *formal* contact with FBI agents since September 11, 2001, and that 11 complied with requests (Stanton & Bazar, 2003). Interestingly, these studies seem to call into question Ashcroft's assertion on September 18, 2003, that "[n]ot a single American's library records has been reviewed under the Patriot Act [sic]." Another report prepared for the ALA determined that law enforcement requests at both public and academic libraries totaled 137 (Goodrum, 2005, p. 36). The same report also found that 38% of public libraries and 54% of academic libraries had not been provided institutional training to help librarians handle law enforcement requests (p. 37).

It is important to remember that these studies and the studies discussed in this chapter occurred before the USA PATRIOT Act was reauthorized in March 2006. The reauthorization process modified some of the provisions that concern librarians the most. For example, section 215 was changed to make the "standards under which the FBI can obtain library records in the course of an investigation [...] slightly more stringent," in addition to allowing for disclosures of and challenges to a Section 215 orders (ALA, 2006). Section 505 was also amended so that "libraries, when functioning in their traditional roles [...] are not subject to" National Security Letters (ALA, 2006)). While these modifications do not address all of librarians' complaints of the USA PATRIOT Act, they are at least in the right direction, and continued research in this area will allow us to better assess the impact such policies have had on the library community.

Methodology

Following the events on September 11, 2001, and the subsequent passage of the USA PATRIOT Act, the Library Research Center sought to understand how national libraries were responding to new security issues in the wake of the terrorist attacks. Based on the findings from a survey assessing the impact of the terrorist attacks on Illinois libraries, the LRC administered for the Illinois State Library (Estabrook,

2002), the LRC decided to look at what was happening in libraries across the nation. On December 4, 2001, the LRC mailed surveys to a national sample of 1,503 public libraries.[1] A survey reminder was sent out on January 9, 2002. At the close of the survey in July of 2002, 1,028 out of 1,503 libraries responded, for a 68.4% response rate.

A year after the September 11 attacks, the LRC prepared a follow-up that asked whether or not libraries cooperated with law enforcement requests for information about patrons' reading habits and Internet preferences. The survey was mailed on October 14, 2002, to the directors of 1,505 public libraries, using the same national sampling procedures as the previous questionnaire.[2] The survey was closed on January 7, 2003, after a reminder was sent out. 906 libraries responded for a response rate of 60.2%.

Due to the constructs of the sampling frame that was used for both surveys, which was chosen to maximize precision of survey estimates to the library universe, all survey responses were weighted to correct for estimations made to the public library universe. The sampling procedures require a universe of all libraries serving populations over 100,000 to be surveyed, along with a sample of libraries serving populations under 100,000. If the sample had remained unweighted, the oversampling of large libraries would skew the estimations made to the library universe. In order to correct for this error, weights were used in the calculation of all statistics estimating the universe of public libraries. Weights were calculated by dividing the percentage of libraries serving populations above 100,000 in the sample into the percentage in the universe, and the same is done for libraries serving populations under 100,000.

While the September 11 survey focused on changes in the public library environment as a result of the terrorist attacks, the One Year Later survey concentrated on the awareness and impact of the USA PATRIOT Act on public libraries. Four questions were asked on both instruments to measure potential change over the year. An additional four questions were asked on both survey instruments; however, different branching structures on the instruments prohibit direct comparison. The similar questions from both surveys can be found in Table 1.

Because the Pew Internet and American Life Project (2003) had surveyed citizens about their attitudes on the anniversary of September 11, 2001, the LRC's One Year Later survey also included seven questions that were identical to those asked in that Pew survey in order to test for differences in attitudes between library directors and the public at large. Those questions can be found in Table 2.

Table 1. Similar questions on September 11 and September 11: One year later surveys

September 11	One Year Later
Question 3b: Have any staff members limited access to some Web sites? Yes/No (answered only if yes to Q3a)	**Question 2**: In response to the events of September 11, 2001, has your library restricted access to Web sites? Yes/No #2 (answered only if yes to Q1)
Question 3b: Have any staff members required the identification of patrons? Yes/No (answered only if yes to Q3a)	**Question 2**: In response to events of the September 11, 2001, has your library started to require identification from patrons to use the Internet terminals? Yes/No (answered only if yes to Q1)
Question 3b: Have any staff members monitored what patrons are doing, either visually or by reviewing the cache/history? Yes/No (answered only if yes to Q3a)	**Question 2**: In response to the events of September 11, 2001, has your library begun to monitor what patrons are doing, visually or by reviewing the cache/history? Yes/No (answered only if yes to Q1)
Question 9: Since September 11, have you voluntarily withdrawn any materials that might be used to assist terrorists, such as material on bomb making or bio-terrorism? Yes/No	**Question 3**: Since September 11, 2001, has you library voluntarily withdrawn any materials that might be used to assist terrorists, such as material on bomb making or bio-terrorism? Yes/No
The questions below cannot be directly compared due to survey branching.	
Question 3a: Due to the events of September 11, to the best of your knowledge, have staff members of your library become more restrictive regarding patron use of the Internet? Yes/No	**Question 1**: In response to events of September 11, 2001, to the best of your knowledge, has your library changed any of its policies regarding patron use of the Internet? Yes/No
Question 5b: Are any of your staff members more likely to notice the kinds of materials people are checking out? Yes/No (answered only if yes to Q5a - Would you say staff members have changed attitude toward treatment of patrons?)	**Question 4**: In response to the events of September 11, 2001, are any of your staff members more likely to monitor the kinds of materials people are checking out? Yes/No

continued on following page

Table 1. continued

Question 5b: Are any of your staff members realizing there are circumstances in which it would be necessary to compromise the privacy of patron records? Yes/No (answered only if yes to Q5a - Would you say staff members have changed attitude toward treatment of patrons?)	**Question 4**: In response to the events of September 11, 2001, are any of your staff members believing there are circumstances in which it would be necessary to compromise the privacy of patron records? Yes/No
Question 5b: Are any of your staff members having other changes in attitude or treatment of library patrons? Yes/No (answered only if yes to Q5a - Would you say staff members have changed attitude toward treatment of patrons?)	**Question 4**: In response to the events of September 11, 2001, are any of your staff members making other changes in attitude or treatment of library patrons? Yes/No

Results

The LRC analyzed responses from both surveys in three stages. To begin with, descriptive statistics and crosstabs by library size and region were generated for questions from both surveys that fell into five different categories: staff attitudes, collection development, security and policy changes, impact of the USA PATRIOT Act, and information requests. A second analysis centered on how library directors differed from the general population on questions modeled from the Pew survey, where the national public's responses serve as the baseline for comparison. Finally, data from comparable questions in both the September 11 and One Year Later surveys were analyzed using binomial regression to determine the direction and magnitude of significant differences between surveys when controlling for region and population size. We hypothesized that any significant difference would be the result of time. In all cases, significance was tested at the 0.05 level.

Statistical Overview by Question Category: LRC's September 11 and One Year Later Surveys

In analyzing the data, it was assumed that larger libraries in the North Atlantic region would be affected by the terrorist attacks and the passage of the USA PATRIOT Act thanks to their vicinity to past and potential terrorist targets more so than smaller

Table 2. Similar questions on Pew & LRC's 1 year later surveys

LRC	Pew
Question 21: Do you think the U.S. government should remove information from its Web sites that might potentially help terrorists, even if the American public has a right to know that information? Yes/No	**Question EXP 7a**: Do you think the U.S. government should remove information from its Web sites that might potentially help terrorists, even if the American public has a right to know that information? Should/Should not remove
Question 22: Do you think the U.S. government should not put information on its Web sites that might potentially help terrorists, even if the American public has a right to know that information? Yes/No	**Question EXP 7b**: Do you think the U.S. government should not put information on its Web sites that might potentially help terrorists, even if the American public has a right to know that information? Should not/ should put
Question 23: Do you think private businesses such as airlines and utility companies should remove information from their Web sites that might help terrorists, even if it limits the American public's information about this companies? Yes/No	**Question EXP 8a**: Do you think private businesses such as airlines and utility companies should remove information from their Web sites that might help terrorists, even if it limits the American public's information about this companies? Should/Should not remove
Question 24: Do you think private businesses such as airlines and utility companies should not put information on their Web sites that might help terrorists, even if it limits the American public's information about these companies? Yes/No	**Question EXP 8b**: Do you think private businesses such as airlines and utility companies should not put information on their Web sites that might help terrorists, even if it limits the American public's information about these companies? Should not/ should put
Question 25: Since 9/11/2001, have you heard or read about the government pulling information from its Web sites, fearing terrorists might make use of that information? Yes/No	**Question EXP 9**: Since 9/11/2001, have you heard or read about the government pulling information from its Web sites, fearing terrorists might make use of that information? Yes/No
Question 26: Since 9/11/2001, have YOU noticed that information that you expected to be on any government Web sites you visit was missing? Yes/No	**Question EXP 10**: Since 9/11/2001, have YOU noticed that information that you expected to be on any government Web sites you visit was missing? Yes/No

continued on following page

Table 2. continued

Question 27: Some government agencies HAVE removed information from their Web sites, saying that they are worried that the information could be useful to terrorists. Do you think that this action actually does hinder terrorists or do you think it does not make any difference? Does hinder terrorists/Does not make difference	Question EXP 11: Some government agencies HAVE removed information from their Web sites, saying that they are worried that the information could be useful to terrorists. Do you think that this action actually does hinder terrorists or do you think it does not make any difference? Does not hinder terrorists/Does not make any difference

libraries and libraries in other regions. To test this, library respondents from both surveys were placed into regional groups, which were then used for comparison. The breakdown of regional groups in Table 3 was modeled after the categories developed by the National Center for Education Statistics (1982). Libraries were also grouped according to their population service areas. Large libraries serve populations greater than 100,000; medium libraries serve populations between 15,000 and 100,000; and small libraries serve populations under 15,000. The results that follow compare libraries of different sizes in different regions and their responses to the five categories of questions in the September 11 and One Year Later surveys.

Staff Attitudes

Questions dealing with staff attitudes primarily concerned how and the degrees to which attitudes had changed given the new environment created by the terrorist attacks. These questions can be found in Table 4.

In the September 11 survey, almost one in six (19.6%) libraries indicate that staff members have changed their attitude and treatment of library patrons immediately after the terrorist attacks. This change was most often reported in libraries with large populations and in the North Atlantic and Southeastern regions of the country. Small libraries are 2.6 times less likely to report a change in staff attitude toward patrons, and medium libraries are two times less likely to report a change in staff attitude toward patrons as compared to large libraries. Almost one in four of libraries in the North Atlantic (23.4%) and libraries in the southeast (24.1%) were more likely to change their attitude and treatment of patrons after September 11. Libraries in the Midwest and Southwest were half as likely to report changes in staff attitude and treatment of patrons as compared to libraries in the North Atlantic region.

More than half (60.4%) of libraries that indicated a change in staff attitudes report that their staff is more likely to notice the kinds of materials patrons are checking out. Libraries with populations under 100,000 are about half as likely to report staff tak-

Table 3. States in four regions of the United States

North Atlantic	Great Lakes & Plains	Southeast	West & Southwest
Connecticut	Illinois	Alabama	Alaska
Delaware	Indiana	Arkansas	Arizona
District of	Iowa	Florida	California
Columbia	Kansas	Georgia	Colorado
Maine	Michigan	Kentucky	Hawaii
Maryland	Minnesota	Louisiana	Idaho
Massachusetts	Missouri	Mississippi	Montana
New	Nebraska	North Carolina	Nevada
Hampshire	North Dakota	South Carolina	New Mexico
New Jersey	Ohio	Tennessee	Oklahoma
New York	South Dakota	Virginia	Oregon
Pennsylvania	Wisconsin	West Virginia	Texas
Rhode Island			Utah
Vermont			Washington
			Wyoming

ing notice of patron materials than libraries with populations above 100,000. Almost two thirds of libraries that indicated an attitude change in staff (62.0%) realize there are circumstances where it may be necessary to compromise the privacy of patron records. Most libraries with large populations (70.3%) agree with this statement. Some small libraries with populations under 15,000 (43.2%) agree, while fewer libraries with medium-sized populations (34.2%) concur with this statement.

One year after the September 11 attacks, only 9.0% of libraries have staff that is more likely to monitor the materials people are checking out. 19.5% of libraries have staff that believes there are circumstances where it would be necessary to compromise the privacy of patron records. There were no differences by region or library size for both of these variables. Few (6%) libraries believe their staffs have made other changes in attitude or treatment of library patrons in response to the events of September 11.

Collection Development

Collection development questions were centered on whether or not libraries had used September 11 as a catalyst to add or subtract material to their collections. See Table 5 for a complete list of questions.

In the September 11 survey, 79.6% of responding libraries indicate their collection development decisions have been influenced by the terrorist attacks. It is important

Table 4. Survey questions assessing staff attitudes

Survey	Question	N	Yes	No
September 11 Survey	Since September 11, would you say staff members have changed, in any way, their attitude toward or treatment of library patrons? Yes/No	971	19.60%	80.40%
	Are any of your staff members more likely to notice the kinds of materials people are checking out? Yes/No	165	60.40%	39.60%
	Are any of your staff members realizing there are circumstances in which it would be necessary to compromise the privacy of patron records? Yes/No	163	62.00%	38.00%
One Year Later Survey	In response to the events of September 11, 2001, are any of your staff members more likely to monitor the kinds of materials people are checking out? Yes/No	830	9.00%	91.00%
	In response to the events of September 11, 2001, are any of your staff members believing there are circumstances in which it would be necessary to compromise the privacy of patron records? Yes/No	819	19.50%	80.50%
	In response to the events of September 11, 2001, have any of your staff members made other changes in attitude or treatment of library patrons? Yes/No	828	6.00%	94.00%

to note that some of the collection development choices may have been influenced by income, suggesting that larger libraries have potentially greater flexibility in their purchasing decisions due to their presumably larger budget. Of the 79.6% of libraries that indicated their collection decisions were influenced by September 11, 94.6% indicate they purchased materials related to Islam and that 92.9% added materials regarding terrorism, bioterrorism, or germ warfare. Overall, of the 79.6% of libraries who indicated their collection development decisions have been affected by September 11, 85.7% say they have added historical/political materials related to terrorist attacks. Small libraries are two times less likely to purchase historical/political materials related to September 11 for their collection, as compared to large libraries.

Table 5. Survey questions assessing collection development

Survey	Question	N	Yes	No
September 11 Survey	Have your collection purchases been influenced by the events of September 11? Yes/No	981	79.60%	20.40%
	Has your library purchased historical or political materials related to September 11? Yes/No	729	85.70%	14.30%
	Has your library purchased materials related to Islam? Yes/No	763	94.60%	5.40%
	Has your library purchased materials concerning terrorism, bioterrorism, or germ warfare? Yes/No	756	92.90%	7.10%
	Since September 11, have you voluntarily withdrawn any materials that might be used to assist terrorists, such as material on bomb making or bio-terrorism? Yes/No	944	0.10%	99.90%
One Year Later Survey	Since September 11, 2001, has your library voluntarily withdrawn any materials that might be used to assist terrorists, such as material on bomb making or bio-terrorism? Yes/No	847	1.40%	98.60%

Libraries in the West and Southwest are 1.6 times less likely to indicate their collections have been affected by the events of September 11 as compared to libraries in the North Atlantic region. Controlling for population size, libraries in the West and Southwest are still half as likely to have their collection development decisions be influenced by the events of September 11. Again controlling for population size, libraries in the Midwest are about half as likely to add historical materials related to September 11 to their collections, as compared to libraries in the North Atlantic.

In a direct response to the events of September 11, 4 libraries removed books that might aid terrorists. These libraries were located in 4 different states (California, Minnesota, Pennsylvania, and Wisconsin) and all have populations above 100,000. It is interesting to note that only one of these states was overtly affected by the terrorist attacks. In the One Year Later survey an additional 9 libraries reported to have voluntarily withdrawn library materials that could be used to assist terrorists. Due to the small numbers, tests of significance are inaccurate; however, note that 5 of the 9 libraries that removed books came from the Southeast and that 8 of the 9 libraries serve populations less than 100,000. No libraries removed materials in the states that contained the intended terrorist targets (New York, District of Columbia, Maryland, and Virginia); however, another Pennsylvania library reportedly removed books in the One Year Later survey.

Security and Policy Changes

Questions that fell into the security and policy change category dealt with how libraries had altered procedures in response to the terrorist attacks. General security changes, in addition to mail handling policies and Internet procedures, were explored. The complete list of questions is in Table 6.

Directly after September 11, 31.7% of libraries reviewed their building security. Libraries with smaller populations were significantly less likely to review building security. While only 21.3% of libraries with small legal service areas reviewed their building security, 61.1% of libraries with large legal service areas review their building security. All population groups showed significant differences in regard to reviewing building security. Libraries with legal service areas between 15,000 and 100,000 were twice as likely to review building security as libraries with populations below 15,000. Libraries with populations above 100,000 were five times as likely to review their building security when compared to libraries with legal service areas below 15,000. Correspondingly, the 11 libraries that employed additional security guards were all libraries with legal service areas above 100,000. The region of the country the libraries were located in had no effect on the likelihood to review building security once population was taken into account.

In the One Year Later survey, 55.7% of libraries have instructed their staff or board on library security. Medium-sized libraries are about half as likely to discuss library security, and small libraries are about one third as likely to discuss library security with their staff or board as compared to large libraries. There was no significant difference by region.

While mail procedures were not addressed in the One Year Later study, directly after the events of September 11, 47.2% of libraries initiated new mail handling procedures. There is a significant difference between the 77.4% of large libraries, the 53.1% of medium-sized libraries, and the 35.5% of small libraries that employ new procedures for handling mail. Regarding mailing procedures, libraries with populations over 100,000 were 6 times as likely and medium-sized libraries were 2 times as likely to employ new mail handling procedures, as compared to small libraries. 81.8% of the libraries that initiated new mail handling procedures instituted guidelines for handling suspicious mail.

Libraries located in the Southeast were half as likely to use rubber gloves when checking mail compared to those in the Northeast. Libraries with medium legal service areas were about 4 times as likely to recommend using gloves, and librar-

Table 6. Survey questions assessing security and policy changes

Survey	Question	N	Yes	No
September 11 Survey	Have the events of September 11 prompted your library to review its building security? Yes/No	952	31.70%	68.30%
	Due to the events of September 11, does your library employ (additional) security guards? Yes/No	922	0.30%	99.70%
	Since September 11, does your library follow any new procedures for handling U.S. mail? Yes/No	967	47.20%	52.80%
	Does your library recommend using rubber gloves when handling mail? Yes/No	378	42.70%	57.30%
	Does your library post USPS guidelines for handling "a suspicious letter or package?" Yes/No	418	81.80%	18.20%
	Due to the events of September 11, to the best of your knowledge, have staff members of your library become more restrictive regarding patron use of the internet? Yes/No	965	11.40%	88.60%
	Have any staff members reported patron Internet records or behaviors to outside authorities (e.g., FBI, police)? Yes/No	88	25.30%	74.70%

continued on following page

Table 6. continued

One Year Later Survey	In the past year have you instructed staff or library board regarding library security? Yes/No	841	55.70%	44.30%
	In response to events of September 11, 2001, to the best of your knowledge, has your library changed any of its policies regarding patron use of the Internet? Yes/No	853	9.80%	90.20%
	In response to events of September 11, 2001, has your library started to require identification from patrons to use the Internet terminals? Yes/No	78	41.40%	58.60%
	In response to September 11, 2001, has your library stopped requiring identification from patrons to use the Internet terminals? Yes/No	73	15.30%	84.70%
	In response to September 11, 2001, has your library begun to monitor what patrons are doing, visually or by reviewing the cache/history? Yes/No	76	35.00%	65.00%
	In response to the events of September 11, 2001, has your library installed software that erases the cache/history after each use, or at regular intervals? Yes/No	77	33.20%	66.80%
	In response to the events of September 11, 2001, has your library started keeping a sign-up sheet of users of your computer terminals? Yes/No	77	59.30%	40.70%
	In response to the events of September 11, 2001, has your library stopped keeping a sign-up sheet of users of your computer terminals? Yes/No	76	30.90%	69.10%

ies with large-sized legal service areas were 7 times as likely to recommend it as compared to small libraries. 60.0% of large libraries recommend using gloves when opening mail, while less than half of medium libraries (47.5%), and 21.1% of small libraries recommend it.

Internet policies were also explored in both surveys. Overall, 11.4% of libraries are more restrictive regarding patron use of the Internet based on responses to the September 11 survey. Controlling for population of legal service area, library staff in the Midwest are significantly less restrictive regarding patron use of the Internet directly after the terrorist attacks. There was no difference by size for increased restriction on patron use of the Internet. One in four (25.3%) of libraries that reported themselves to be more restrictive of patron Internet use were also more likely to report patron Internet records and behaviors to outside authorities. Libraries in the North Atlantic region and large libraries are 10 times more likely to report patron records or behaviors to outside authorities in regards to Internet usage when compared to smaller libraries and libraries in different regions.

In the One Year Later survey, 9.8% of libraries reportedly changed their Internet policy since the events of September 11. Libraries located in the Southeast were 2.5 times more likely to change their Internet policies as compared to the North Atlantic. Of libraries that indicated a change in their Internet policies since September 11, 41.4% of libraries have started to require identification for patrons to use the Internet terminals, while 15.3% have stopped requiring identification. Of libraries that have become more restrictive regarding patron use of the Internet, 35.0% of libraries have begun to monitor what patrons are doing visually or by reviewing the computers' cache; however, 33.2% of libraries installed software on their machines to erase the cache. More than half of libraries (59.3%) started keeping sign-up sheets for their computer terminals, while 30.9% stopped this practice. Region and population size did not affect the other variables related to Internet restriction.

Impact of the USA PATRIOT Act

Since the USA PATRIOT Act had just been passed when the September 11 survey was prepared, it included a series of questions that assessed how well responding libraries were informed about the act's provisions. Questions about the USA PATRIOT Act in the One Year Later survey were concerned with how the act impacted library policy changes. See Table 7 for the exact questions.

In response to the September 11 survey, 57.2% of libraries had heard or read about the USA PATRIOT Act. Libraries in the Southeast were approximately 1.6 times less likely to have heard about the USA PATRIOT ACT when compared with libraries in the North Atlantic. Libraries with populations under 100,000 were half as likely to have heard about the USA PATRIOT Act as compared to libraries with populations over 100,000.

Of libraries that have heard or read about the USA PATRIOT Act, 42.3% know that the act prohibits libraries from disclosing to anyone that a search warrant has been served, while 46.2% of libraries do not know. Research shows that 34.1% of libraries know that the USA PATRIOT Act does not provide procedures for quashing a search warrant. Conversely, 63.1% of libraries that have heard of the USA PATRIOT Act do not know if there are provisions for quashing a search warrant. Similarly, although 35.5% of libraries know the act allows an agent to begin the search as soon as the warrant is served, 46.0% do not know if there are any provisions regarding the

Table 7. Survey questions assessing impact of the USA PATRIOT Act

Survey	Question	N	Yes	No	Don't Know
September 11 Survey	Have you heard or read about the new antiterror law known as the "USA PATRIOT Act?" Yes/No	970	56.50%	42.40%	na
	To the best of your knowledge, is this a provision of the USA Patriot Act: It prohibits libraries from disclosing to anyone that a search warrant has been served? Yes(Correct)/ No(Incorrect)	555	42.30%	11.50%	46.20%
	To the best of your knowledge, is this a provision of the USA Patriot Act: It provides procedures for quashing a search warrant? Yes(Incorrect)/No(Correct)	555	2.80%	34.10%	63.10%
	To the best of your knowledge, is this a provision of the USA Patriot Act: It allows an agent to begin the search as soon as the warrant is served? Yes(Correct)/ No(Incorrect)	555	35.50%	18.60%	46.00%
	To the best of your knowledge, is this a provision of the USA Patriot Act: It allows for access to records without a search warrant? Yes(Incorrect)/No(Correct)	555	14.30%	47.00%	38.70%
	To the best of your knowledge, is this a provision of the USA PATRIOT Act: It allows the execution of the search warrant to be delayed until the library's legal council can be consulted? Yes(Incorrect)/No(Correct)	555	33.40%	201.00%	46.50%

continued on following page

Table 7. continued

One Year Later Survey	In the past year have you instructed staff or library board on the provisions of the USA PATRIOT Act or on what to do should a search warrant or subpoena be served? Yes/No	835	60.00%	40.00%	na
	In the past year have you instructed staff or library board regarding library policies regarding patron policy? Yes/No	841	69.60%	30.40%	na
	Has your library adopted or changed any policies in response to the passage of the USA PATRIOT Act? Yes/No/No, but in process of development	846	6.50%	79.20%	14.2% (in process)

time between search and serving of the warrant. Half of libraries (47.0%) that have heard of the USA PATRIOT Act are aware the act does not allow access to records without a search warrant, while over one third of libraries (38.7%) that have heard of the act do not know if that provision exists or not. A little more than one third of libraries that are aware of the USA PATRIOT Act (33.4%) incorrectly believe that the act allows the execution of a search warrant to be delayed until the library's legal council has been consulted, and an additional 46.5% of libraries do not know whether or not the act allows for the delayed execution of a search warrant.

Libraries that serve populations over 100,000 are 4 times as likely to have read or have heard about the act as compared to libraries serving populations below 15,000. In addition, libraries with small populations that have heard or read about it are 1.9 times as likely not to know of the provisions of delaying a search warrant for legal council as compared to libraries with populations over 100,000. While there is an association between having had an information request from authorities and having heard about the USA PATRIOT Act, there is no association between having had an information request and knowing about the provisions of the USA PATRIOT Act addressed above.

In the One Year Later survey, 60.0% of libraries have instructed their staff or library board on the provisions of the USA PATRIOT Act and what to do if a search warrant or subpoena is served. Research shows that 69.6% of libraries have instructed their library staff or board on patron privacy policies. Small libraries are about half as likely to discuss patron privacy policies with their staff or board as compared to large libraries. Libraries in the West and Southwest are half as likely to adopt or change policies in response to September 11 as compared to libraries in the North Atlantic region. Libraries serving populations between 15,000 and 100,000 are about half as likely to adopt changes to their policies, and libraries serving populations fewer than 15,000 were about a third as likely to adopt policy changes as compared to those libraries serving populations over 100,000.

Information Requests

Questions regarding information requests in the September 11 survey centered on whether or not they took place in public libraries. This questioning route was expanded in the One Year Later survey to explore not only the existence of requests, but also the request's format and frequency and if the library complied with the request. Please see Table 8 for the actual questions. It is important to note that the questions concerned information requests in general, not those specifically falling under USA PATRIOT Act jurisdiction, although the survey content included cautions about the USA PATRIOT Act's secrecy clause, which may have resulted in a context effect where respondents were primed to think of and report on USA PATRIOT Act requests over other types of information requests.[3]

Immediately after the events of September 11, 4.3% of libraries have had information requests. 80.0% of libraries with information requests had legal service areas above 100,000. Libraries serving areas with more than 100,000 people were only 10 times as likely to have had a request compared to libraries serving less than 100,000 people. Controlling for population, libraries in the Midwest are half (.478) as likely to receive an information request compared to libraries in other regions of the country.

In the One Year Later study, 10.6% of libraries have had an information request about a patron from authorities. Of the libraries that have received requests, most (79.9%) have only received one request while 19.5% received between two and

Table 8. Survey questions assessing information requests

Survey	Question	N	Yes	No
September 11 Survey	Have authorities (e.g., FBI, police) requested any information about your patrons pursuant to the events of September 11? Yes/No	977	4.30%	95.70%

continued on following page

Table 8. continued

One Year Later Survey	Have authorities (e.g., FBI, INS, police officers) requested information about any of your patrons since September 11, 2001? Yes/No	848	10.60%	89.40%
	Who requested that information?			
	FBI		32.50%	67.50%
	INS	90	0.60%	99.40%
	Police		68.30%	31.70%
	Secret Service		0.60%	99.40%
	Other		8.20%	91.80%
	What kinds of information were requested?			
	Information about specific library materials	90	5.80%	94.20%
	Information about a specific patron		74.20%	25.80%
	Other		24.00%	76.00%
	What forms did the request take?			
	Verbal request for voluntary cooperation		81.80%	18.20%
	Written request for voluntary cooperation	90	9.50%	90.50%
	Subpoena		24.00%	76.00%
	Court Order		18.70%	81.30%
	Did you cooperate?	73	49.70%	50.30%
	Have you ever sought legal advice regarding your library's obligation to respond to a request for information? Yes/No	87	63.30%	36.70%
	If law enforcement officials asked you for information about one of your patrons and ordered you not to disclose that they had asked for information, would you challenge their order by disclosing the request to anyone (e.g., the patron, the press, or a public interest organization such as the ACLU) other than your library's attorney?	86		
	Definitely would		5.40%	
	Probably would		16.00%	
	Probably would not		54.60%	
	Definitely would not		21.70%	
	Don't Know		2.30%	

five requests. Of those reporting requests, most (68.3%) came from the police while fewer (32.5%) came from the FBI. Overall, 74.2% of information requests concerned information about a specific patron, and 5.8% were information requests about a specific library material. See that 25.8% of requests concerned other issues. Also, 81.8% of requests made were verbally, 9.5% were written, 24.0% came by subpoena, and similarly 18.7% came by court order. Half of libraries that received a request asking for voluntary cooperation did cooperate (49.7%). Most libraries sought legal advice regarding the library obligation to respond to the information request (63.3%). However, 76.3% of all directors indicate that if they are presented with a request they probably would not or definitely would not challenge an information request by disclosing the information to anyone but their library's attorney. 87.9% of libraries who have a received a request indicate they probably or definitely would not challenge an information request by disclosing the information to anyone but their library's attorney. Libraries in the West and Southwest regions are about 1.6 times more likely to challenge an information request, in this manner, than those in the North Atlantic. Libraries that serve populations below 100,000 are also about 1.6 times more likely to challenge an information request in this manner, as compared to libraries serving populations above 100,000. There is a significant difference in the amount of information requests received by region. The Southeast and West and Southwest regions have seen a higher proportion of information requests with 18.6% and 20.9% respectively per regions as compared to the North Atlantic (12.2%) and Midwestern (14.4%) regions of the country.

Librarians' Views as Citizens: LRC and Pew's One Year Later Surveys

Seven questions from a Pew survey exploring national public attitudes one year after September 11 were included in the LRC's One Year Later survey. This allows us to compare library directors' responses to those of the national public since respondents to the LRC's One Year Later survey were asked to answer the Pew questions as citizens. For this analysis, we did not change the data weighting as discussed in the Methods section since we wanted to make comparisons between the general public and all library directors. Please refer back to Table 2 for a side-by-side question comparison.

Both surveys asked respondents to comment on whether or not the government should remove information that could potentially help terrorists or not post such information in the first place. While three in four persons (74.0%) in the general population think the US government should remove information from its Web sites that might potentially help terrorists, only 41.8% of library directors agree with this statement. The general population is 4.434 times more likely to agree with this statement as compared to library directors. Similarly, more than three in four persons in the general population (78.5%) think the US government should not put information on its Web sites that might potentially help terrorists, while only half (49.7%) of library directors agree. The general population is 3.91 times more likely to agree with this statement when compared to library directors.

Another set of questions found on both surveys asked respondents whether or not private businesses such as airlines or utility companies should remove potentially harmful information that could be used by terrorists or not post it in the first place on their Web sites. Research shows that 71.5% of persons in the general population think private businesses should remove information from their Web sites, even if it limits the American public's information about these companies. Fewer library directors (50.6%) agree with this statement. The general population is 2.44 times more likely to agree with this statement when compared to library directors. Correspondingly, more than three in four (77.8%) persons in the general population think private businesses should not put information on their Web sites that might help terrorists, even if it limits the American public's information about these companies. Less than half (45.2%) of library directors agree with this statement. The general population is 2.8 times more likely to agree with this statement than library directors are.

An additional question found on both surveys asked respondents whether they heard or read about the government pulling information from its Web sites in fear that terrorists might make use of that information, since September 11, 2001. About one in four (26.2%) persons in the general population have heard or read about the government pulling information from its Web sites, while more than one in three (37.3%) of library directors have heard or read of the pulling of information from government Web sites. The general population is about half (.464) as likely to have heard about the pulling of information as library directors.

Respondents on both surveys were also asked whether they had noticed that information they expected to find on a government Web site was missing since September 11, 2001. Accordingly, 4.7% of library directors, and 5.6% of the general population have noticed information that they expected to be on any government Web site they visit was missing. There is no statistical difference between library directors and the general population for this variable.

Finally, both surveys asked whether or not the removal of information from government Web sites actually hinders terrorists. One in three (31.8%) library directors believes the removal of government information from Web sites actually does hinder terrorists, while almost one in two (46.6%) persons in the general population agrees that the removal of government Web site information actually hinders terrorists. The general population is 1.79 times more likely to believe the removal of government information hinders terrorists, as compared to library directors.

Differences between LRC's September 11 and One Year Later Surveys

Comparable questions from the September 11 and One Year Later surveys were also analyzed. First, both the F-test and Chi-square were used to determine if there were any statistical differences between the surveys due to population distribution. Both tests were nonsignificant, which tells us that the two surveys have equal variance in the population of legal service areas for the responding libraries. Because there was no difference between the population distributions of the surveys and because there was no significant subsequent policy changes or terrorist attacks after September 11 and the close of the One Year Later survey, we presume the differences in survey responses were temporal in nature when we control for region.

In order to account for survey branching and small differences in question wording for the questions on both surveys dealing with patron use of the Internet as illustrated in Table 1, the following procedures were used. In the original September 11 survey, libraries were asked to indicate if they had *become more restrictive* of Internet use by patrons, while in the One Year Later survey they were asked if they had *changed* any of their Internet policies. Following this question, respondents to the One Year Later survey were asked a series of questions that were coded as restrictive or permissive. To make comparisons possible between the September 11 and One Year Later surveys, it was assumed that if a respondent in the One Year Later survey indicated they did not change their Internet policies they answered negatively to the following variables regarding specific changes to Internet policies since September 11. In addition, libraries that indicated they *changed their Internet policies* in the One Year Later survey and also indicated they *restricted access to Web sites, started to required ID from patrons to use Internet terminals, began to monitor what patrons were doing on the Internet,* or *started keeping sign-up sheets* in the One Year Later survey were recoded as being restrictive of Internet use. The answers to these restrictive questions were then compared to the September 11 question.

Using this procedure, there are significant differences between the two surveys with regard to the number of libraries who have become more restrictive about patron Internet use. Directly after September 11, 11.4% libraries indicated they had become more restrictive of patron Internet use. One year later, 9.6% of libraries indicated they had become more restrictive of Internet use since September 11. One year later, libraries are .672 times as likely to restrict patron Internet use as compared to the September 11 survey when controlling for population and region.

Questions that dealt with limited access to Web sites, patron identification, monitoring of Internet behavior, and the voluntary withdrawing of materials were similar enough from survey to survey to warrant direct comparison. Accordingly, directly after the events of September 11, 7.8% of libraries started limiting access to some

Web sites. One year later, only 3.8% of libraries reported limiting access to some Web sites. Due to the small numbers, test of significance were inappropriate. Additionally, there were not significant differences between the 39.6% of libraries that reported staff members requiring patron identification to use the Internet directly after September 11, as compared to the 40.7% of libraries that report requiring identification for patron Internet use 1 year later.

There was a significant difference between the 47.5% of libraries that reported restricting access to the Internet by monitoring what patrons were doing immediately after the events of September 11· as compared to the 34.2% of libraries that were monitoring what patrons were doing on the Internet one year later. Controlling for population and region, One Year Later libraries are 0.419 times as likely to monitor patrons as compared to libraries surveyed right after September 11. Those serving populations under 100,000 are twice as likely to monitor as compared to those serving populations over 100,000 1 year later.

Questions on the surveys that asked whether libraries had voluntarily withdrawn materials that could be used by terrorists have very few responses, which prohibited tests of significance. Directly after September 11, 0.1% of libraries indicated they withdrew materials while 1 year later, 1.2% of libraries had voluntarily withdrawn materials for the same reason.

The final 3 questions that were similar across both surveys were not directly comparable due to survey branching. In the One Year Later survey, all respondents were asked if staff members had changed their treatment of patrons in multiple ways; however, respondents of the September 11 survey were asked only if staff members changed their attitude. Then libraries that indicated no change in staff attitude toward library patrons in the September 11 survey were asked to skip questions on specific changes that corresponded to the One Year Later survey. In order to adjust for this, it was assumed that libraries that noticed no change in attitude or treatment of library patrons would have indicated negative responses to the variables regarding specific changes in staff attitude toward library patrons.

Using these procedures, there were no significant differences detected for responses between the two surveys for these questions. There was no difference detected between the 10.8% of libraries that reported staff members are more likely to notice the kinds of materials patrons are checking out compared to the 8.8% of libraries that reported this staff behavior 1 year later. Similarly, there were no significant differences between the 10.3% of libraries that report, directly after the events of September 11, staff members recognizing there are circumstances in which it would be necessary to compromise the privacy of patron records as compared the 19.1% of libraries that reported this recognition 1 year later. Again, there was no significant difference between the 7.7% of libraries that report other changes in staff attitudes and the treatment of patron directly after the events of September 11 as compared to the 5.9% who report other changes in staff attitude/patron treatment 1 year later.

Discussion and Conclusion

The responses to both the September 11 and One Year Later surveys offer us a snapshot of the library environment in the months that followed the terrorist attacks and the passage of the USA PATRIOT Act. Some of the more interesting findings include how region and size affected attitudes and policies stemming from September 11, the differences in opinions between library directors and the American public, and how some of the response frequencies for questions from the September 11 survey have or have not changed over the course of 1 year. These surveys not only demonstrate the reactionary changes libraries implemented and experienced in the immediate aftermath of the terrorist attacks, but also what some of the more lasting effects on the library environment have been.

As might be expected, libraries in the North Atlantic region of the United States were far more likely to report changes in staff attitudes, collection development, and security and policy changes that were influenced by September 11 and the passage of the USA PATRIOT Act as compared to the rest of the country. This tendency could be reflective of many issues, but the libraries' proximity to the terrorist attacks does seem to stand out. In addition to region, library size was also prognostic. Larger libraries were more likely to revise their security policies and mail-handling procedures, instruct their staff on privacy issues, add historical and political materials related to the terrorist attacks to their collections, report suspicious patron Internet behavior, and be subjected to information requests. Conversely, smaller libraries were less likely to report changes in staff attitudes, implement security changes, and instruct staff members on patron privacy. These differences attributed to library size may be indicative of library resources, staffing, and number of patrons where presumably larger libraries can command more of each. Smaller libraries may also have a localized community focus and patron base, which could potentially negate concerns about security and staff attitudes.

In addition to these generalizations, some findings by region ran counter to expectations. For instance, findings from the One Year Later survey show that over two thirds of information requests came from police vs. less than one third from the FBI. Interestingly enough, libraries in the West and Southwest, who were subjected to a high percentage of information requests according to the One Year Later survey, are also more willing to challenge information requests compared to libraries in other regions and less likely to adopt policies in direct response to September 11, which may be indicative of the social and physical space separating the West and Southwest region from the political center of the country found in Washington, DC.

When comparing library directors' responses to survey questions adapted from a national public survey developed by Pew, many differences emerged, even when the One Year Later survey instrument cautioned library directors to report as citizens. The general population was significantly more likely to feel that that the removal of information from the Internet is more likely to hinder terrorists and that the government and private businesses should remove or not post in the first place information on the Internet that terrorists could potentially use. The difference in responses between library directors and the general population potentially reflects the different values libraries vis-à-vis library directors place on the availability of information in whatever form it takes despite the potential for abuse. Additionally, the general population was half as likely to have heard about the government removing content from their Web pages as compared to library directors. This finding is not surprising given the topic's bearing on the libraries, and presumably library directors would be interested in and more likely to remember reports of the government removing information from the Internet. The number of differences and the extent to which librarians and the general public differ on issues related to information policies and other topics was outside the scope of the surveys reported here, but these findings suggest there may be some fundamental differences that further research may uncover.

In addition to exploring the differences in responses attributed to region, size, and librarian opinions, it was possible to assess the differences between surveys, and what the surveys imply about how the September 11 terrorist attacks and the passage of the USA PATRIOT Act affected the library environment. To begin with, the majority of responding libraries either did not know or incorrectly identified what the provisions of the USA PATRIOT Act were, no doubt due to the fact that the September 11 survey was mailed out to respondents only a few months after the USA PATRIOT Act has been approved. Interestingly enough, this was the case for libraries who had received information requests as well. Nevertheless, one year later, over 60% of responding libraries had instructed staff about the USA PATRIOT Act and on the privacy rights of patrons. This suggests that libraries did not understand some of the crucial provisions of the USA PATRIOT Act and how it affected libraries when it was first set in place, which suggests that the relevance of the act was not well publicized to libraries. One year later, the majority, but not overwhelmingly so, of libraries began informing staff of what to do in the event of a USA PATRIOT Act request. This suggests that over time, more libraries will issue policies that will deal with information requests, a supposition corroborated by the fact that a 2005 study found that only 38% of public libraries had not been provided with training for information requests (Goodrum, 2005, p. 37), a significant step up from the types of policy changes asked about in the September 11 and One Year Later Surveys.

Additional questions allowed us to compare responses across surveys over time. Responding libraries in the One Year Later survey were significantly less likely to be more restrictive of Internet content and less likely to monitor patron's Internet behavior than libraries responding to the September 11 survey, suggesting that these actions were more reactive in response to the terrorist attacks and the passage of the USA PATRIOT Act. However, there was no significant difference in the number of libraries in each survey that limited Internet access, requested patron identification, noticed what patrons were borrowing, or realized there were circumstances when patron privacy needed to be compromised. Because the responses to these questions suggest that whatever the immediate impact the terrorist attacks had on libraries, it has stayed roughly the same 1 year later, and perhaps demonstrates more long-term effects of September 11 and the passage of the USA PATRIOT Act.

The September 11 and One Year Later studies provide some clues as to whether or not American libraries have experienced institutional chilling on a large scale. Large libraries and libraries in the North Atlantic are more likely to report staff attitude changes and suspicious Internet behavior, and they are more likely to be aware of the USA PATRIOT Act and adopt policies to address it. North Atlantic libraries are also more likely to have their collection development choices impacted by September 11, while larger libraries are more likely to review their building security procedures. Because libraries in other regions and libraries with populations smaller than 100,000 do not exhibit the same responses suggests that a chilling effect has taken place in libraries that are geographically linked to the terrorist attacks and larger libraries, where the organizational structure requires greater oversight. The focus placed on the USA PATRIOT Act by libraries also suggests if not a chilling then an increased awareness of its impact on libraries over time. And because there were no changes in responses for questions regarding the monitoring of patron borrowing habits and staff attitudes among others across the September 11 and One Year Later surveys, we can say that the potential for chilling has not disappeared in regard to these questions.

The findings discussed in this chapter create more questions than provide answers, which only underscores the need for more research in this area. It is important to note that the September 11 and One Year Later surveys were sent to library directors. Other types of public librarians may have different perceptions of the post-September 11 library environment that may point to other changes that were not addressed in the two surveys. Also, the USA PATRIOT Act's secrecy clause makes it difficult to interpret questions dealing with information requests, since complying libraries are not allowed to report them to anyone, even well intentioned researchers. While the language in both surveys could be broadly or narrowly interpreted in regard to what type of information requests the questions were asking about, this illustrates the difficulty in interpreting the findings with any degree of specificity. Despite these limitations, the two surveys presented in this chapter clearly highlight the regional effects of the attacks over time and point to additional avenues of investigation. Continued research on library changes in response to the USA PATRIOT Act and terrorism needs to continue in order to understand better how American information habits are being both protected and compromised in today's public libraries.

References

ALA. (2006). *USA PATRIOT Act reauthorization analysis*. Retrieved July 13, 2007, from http://www.ala.org/ala/washoff/WOissues/civilliberties/theusapatriotact/usapatriotact.htm#bck

Ashcroft, J. (2002). *The attorney general's guidelines on general crimes, racketeering enterprise and terrorism enterprise investigations*. Retrieved March 16, 2006, from http://www.usdoj.gov/olp/generalcrimes2.pdf

Ashcroft, J. (2003). *Protecting life and liberty. In Speech given in Memphis, TN*. Retrieved July 13, 2007, from http://www.usdoj.gov/archive/ag/speeches/2003/091503nationalrestaurant.htm

Confidentiality and coping with law enforcement inquiries [Electronic Version] (2002). *Newsletter on Intellectual Freedom, 51*. Retrieved July 13, 2007 from https://members.ala.org/nif/v51n5/fbi.html

Coolidge, K. (2005). Baseless hysteria: The controversy between the Department of Justice and the American Library Association over the USA PATRIOT Act. *Law Library Journal, 97*(1), 7-29.

Estabrook, L. (2002). The response of public libraries to the events of September 11, 2001. *Illinois Libraries, 84*(1), 1-7.

Fifarek, A. (2002). Technology and privacy in the academic library. *Online Information Review, 26*(6), 366-374.

Goodrum, A. (2005). *Impact and analysis of law enforcement activity in academic and public libraries*. American Library Association. Retrieved April 11, 2006, from http://www.ala.org/washoff/contactwo/oitp/LawRptFinal.pdf

Jaeger, P., Bertot, J., & McClure, C. (2003). The impact of the USA Patriot Act on collection and analysis of personal information under the Foreign Intelligence Surveillance Act. *Government Information Quarterly, 20*(3), 295-314.

Jaeger, P., McClure, C., Bertot, J., & Snead, J. (2004). The USA PATRIOT Act, the Foreign Intelligence Surveillance Act, and information policy research in libraries: Issues, impacts, and questions for libraries and researchers. *Library Quarterly, 74*(2), 99-121.

John Doe, et al. v. Alberto Gonzales (Connecticut District Court, 2005).

Kronholz, J. (2003, October 28). Reader beware: Patriot Act riles an unlikely group: Nation's Librarians; Fears about terrorism clash with principles of privacy as online searches surge; FBI: "Bad Guys" use Web, too. *Wall Street Journal*, p. A1.

Lakner, E. (1998). Optimizing samples for surveys of public libraries: Alternatives and compromises. *Library and Information Science Research, 20*(4), 321-342.

Mart, S. (2004). Protecting the lady from Toledo: Post-USA PATRIOT Act electronic surveillance at the library. *Law Library Journal, 96*(3), 499-473.

Martin, K. (2003). The USA PATRIOT Act's application to library patron records. *Journal of Legislation, 29*(2), 283-306.

Matthews, J., & Wiggins, R. (2001). Libraries, the Internet and September 11 [Electronic Version]. *First Monday,* 6. Retrieved July 13, 2007, from http://www.firstmonday.org/issues/issue6_12/matthews/index.html

McCullagh, D. (2006). Appeals court takes dim view of Net-tapping rules [Electronic Version]. *CNET News.com.* Retrieved July 13, 2007, from http://news.com.com/Appeals+court+takes+dim+view+of+Net-tapping+rules/2100-1028_3-6069105.html

Munoz, R. (2004). A legal analysis of the ALA's support of the Freedom to Read Protection Act. *Journal of Information Ethics, 13*(2).

NCES. (1982). Statistics of public libraries, 1977-78. In J. Grady and D. Davis (Project Directors), *ALA Survey of Librarian Salaries 2005* (57). USA: American Library Association.

NCES. (2002a). *Public libraries survey, fiscal year 1999.* Retrieved July 13, 2007, from http://nces.ed.gov/surveys/libraries/DataFiles.asp#Pub

NCES. (2002b). *Public libraries survey, fiscal year 2000.* Retrieved July 13, 2007, from http://nces.ed.gov/surveys/libraries/DataFiles.asp#Pub

Pew. (2003). *September 11 anniversary 2002 data set.* Retrieved July 13, 2007, from http://www.pewinternet.org/PPF/r/29/dataset_display.asp

Pikowsky, R. (2002). An overview of the law of electronic surveillance post September 11, 2001. *Law Library Journal, 94*(4), 601-620.

Pressley, S., & Blum, J. (2001, September 17). Hijackers may have accessed computers at public libraries. *The Washington Post,* p. A4.

Regan, P. (2004). Old issues, new context: Privacy, information collection, and homeland security. *Government Information Quarterly, 21*(4), 481-497.

Schauer, F. (1978). Fear, risk, and the First Amendment: Unraveling the "Chilling Effect." *Boston University Law Review, 58,* 685-732.

Stanton, S., & Bazar, E. (2003, September 22). Defying a key part of the Patriot Act as they fight for reader's rights... Librarians step up... They prepare for "knock on the door." *The Sacramento Bee,* p. A1.

Sudman, S., Bradburn, N., & Schwarz, N. (1996). *Thinking about answers: The application of cognitive processes to survey methodology.* San Francisco: Jossey-Bass.

United States v. Rumely, 345 U.S 41 (Supreme Court, 1953).

Uniting and Strengthening America by Providing Appropriate Tools Required to Intercept and Obstruct Terrorism (USA PATRIOT) Act of 2001, 107th Congress H. R. 3162 Cong. Rec.(2001).

Wheeler, M. (2005). The Politics of access: Libraries and the fight for civil liberties in post-9/11 America. *Radical History Review, 93*, 79-95.

With Patriot Act debate over, government drops fight to gag librarians from discussing objections to controversial law [Electronic Version] (2006). *ACLU Press Release*. Retrieved July 13, 2007, from http://www.aclu.org/natsec/gen/24995prs20060412.html

Endnotes

[1] The sample was chosen out of 5,055 U.S. public libraries serving populations of over 5,000 in 49 states, excluding Illinois. The LRC wanted a response rate of at least 60% to achieve adequate precision for whole-universe estimates and subgroup analyses. The universe sampling frame was the FY1999 Federal-State Cooperative System (FSCS) annual directory published by the National Center for Education Statistics (NCES, 2002a). The survey was mailed out to all libraries serving populations over 100,000 and a random (proportionately stratified by population served) sample of libraries serving populations between 5,000 and 99,999 (Lakner, 1998).

[2] The sample was chosen out of 5,094 public libraries serving populations of over 5,000 in all 50 states. The universe sampling frame was the FY2000 FSCS annual directory (NCES, 2002b).

[3] For a discussion of context effects, see Chapter 5 in Sudman, Bradburn, and Schwartz (1996).

Chapter V

Watching What We Read:
Implications of Law Enforcement Activity in Libraries Since 9/11

Abby A. Goodrum, School of Journalism at Ryerson University, Canada

Abstract

Libraries in the U.S. have long been places of interest to government law enforce-ment agencies, and academic and public librarians have long sought to balance their commitment to the protection of privacy and intellectual freedom, with their desire to support legitimate requests for assistance from the government (Foerstel, 1991; Starr, 2004). In some instances, librarians have even gone to jail to protect the privacy of their patron's records (Horn, 1994). To better understand the nature of this contact and its impact on the public's privacy and access to information, the American Library Association's Office of Information Technology Policy (ALA OITP) funded a study which included a nationwide survey of public and academic libraries and structured interviews with librarians and library leaders. The study confirms that federal, state, and local law enforcement have been visiting libraries as part of their investigations and that law enforcement activity has precipitated change in the policies and practices of public and academic libraries. Finally, the data from this study suggest that overall, the Patriot Act and similar legislation passed as a result of the September 11 terrorists attacks have had limited or very limited direct impact on academic and public library activities. Most libraries have not changed policies related to the retention of patron information, use of library materials including government information, or removed material from the library, nor has there been any significant change in library material usage. In those instances when changes did occur, reasons appear to be due to budget and financial matters rather than concern over requirements of the Patriot Act or other similar legislation. Another issue central to this discussion has been the degree to which the ALA should engage in significant lobbying efforts to change or modify the Patriot Act and related terrorist laws. The general sense that one receives is that the Patriot Act is "awful" from an abstract perspective, but "it doesn't really affect my library or patrons as directly as budget cuts and other day to day concerns." Librarians can't afford to lose local support, so they do not become politicized over legal issues that may be quite abstract in the minds of their patrons or staff.

Introduction

In a library (physical or virtual), the right to privacy is the right to open inquiry without having the subject of one's interest examined or scrutinized by others. Confidentiality exists when a library is in possession of personally identifiable information about users and keeps that information private on their behalf. (Privacy: An Interpretation of the Library Bill of Rights. ALA, 2002)

This chapter provides a summary of the first comprehensive study of the impact of law enforcement activity in America's libraries since 9/11.

Libraries in the U.S. have long been places of interest to government law enforcement agencies, and academic and public librarians have long sought to balance their commitment to the protection of privacy and intellectual freedom, with their desire to support legitimate requests for assistance from the government (Foerstel, 1991; Starr, 2004). In some instances, librarians have even gone to jail to protect the privacy of their patron's records (Horn, 1994).

After 9/11, there were accounts from libraries across the United States that law enforcement activity in libraries had increased at the same time that access to certain governmental information (formerly available publicly through the library depository program) was diminishing. Additional concern about law enforcement contact with libraries also occurred as a result of the passage of the USA PATRIOT Act (P.L. 107-56). To better understand the nature of this contact and its impact on the public's privacy and access to information, the American Library Association's Office of Information Technology Policy (ALA OITP) funded a study which included a nationwide survey of public and academic libraries and structured interviews with librarians and library leaders. The purpose of the study was to obtain descriptive information regarding the type of contact academic and public librarians have had with law enforcement agencies, and to obtain information about how the potential for law enforcement contact and contact itself has affected library systems, processes, management, and the overall operation of the library.

The study was comprised of a double-blind online survey of public and academic libraries and in-depth structured interviews of librarians and library leaders. The study drew a representative sample of 1,536 public libraries and contacted all 4,008 U.S. academic libraries for the survey. Over 1,400 libraries participated in the study (33% of public library sample and 23% of academic libraries). Of the 400 librarians invited to take part in the follow-up interviews, 50 agreed to do so. In analyzing the data and discussing study findings it should be kept in mind that the limited number of respondents should caution readers against generalizing the data to the larger population. This being said, however, the data and findings point to a number of key findings and issues requiring additional attention.

The study confirms that federal, state, and local law enforcement have been visiting libraries as part of their investigations. Survey results indicate at least a total of 137 legally executed requests by federal and state/local law enforcement in both academic and public libraries have taken place since October 2001, 63 legally executed requests for records in public libraries and 74 legally executed requests in academic libraries. The study also finds that law enforcement activity has precipitated change in the policies and practices of public and academic libraries since the September 11, 2001, terrorist attacks in the United States.

The next section of this chapter provides a brief overview of the study methodology. Then, data from the national surveys of academic and public libraries and a summary of the interviews with academic and public librarians and library leaders. The chapter closes with a brief discussion of the data and conclusions from the study.

Methodology

The study sought to obtain descriptive information regarding the type of contact academic and public librarians have had with law enforcement agencies, and to obtain information about how the potential for law enforcement contact and contact itself has affected the management and operation of libraries in the United States recently. The study utilized a national survey distributed to academic and public librarians over the Web, as well as in-depth interviews with librarians and library leaders conducted between January and April of 2005. This section will describe the sampling procedures, the survey instrument, and interview protocol development, procedures used to distribute surveys and conduct the interviews, and information regarding the response rate.

Sampling Procedures

The researchers drew a sample of public libraries, academic libraries, and key opinion leaders to obtain data. The manner in which these various samples were developed is described below.

Public Library Survey Sample

With assistance from the National Center for Educational Statistics (NCES), the study drew a sample of 1,536 public library administrative units. The sample was selected from the Public Library Data 2001 Universe File of public libraries maintained by NCES (NCES, 2001).[1] According to the Universe File, there are 8,974 public library systems in the United States.

In drawing the sample, the public library Universe File was stratified by library legal service population class (the legal service population classes were as follows: million+, 500,000-999,999, 100,000-499,999, 25,000-99,999, 5,000-24,999, and less than 5,000) and, within legal service population class, by three metropolitan status codes (the metropolitan status groupings were as follows: CC=Central City [Urban], NC=Metropolitan Area, but not within central city limits [Suburban], NO=Not in a Metropolitan Area [Rural]). Figure 1 describes this sampling process.

Requests for participation were extended to additional public libraries as replacements for nonrespondents.

Academic Library Survey Census

The academic participant list was developed using the 2004 Integrated Postsecondary Education Data System (IPEDS) academic file.[2] This file lists 4200 entries for academic institutions, including community colleges, four-year colleges, and universities (not all of which have libraries). Duplicate addresses and non-U.S. institutional listings were removed, leaving a list of 4,008 libraries. All 4,008 were contacted to request participation.

Interview Sample

Participants were sought to represent both library opinion leaders (library professionals with knowledge of the national scene with respect to library policy and

*Figure 1. U.S. public library systems by metropolitan status and population of legal service area**

Metropolitan Status**					
Population of Legal Service Area	URBAN	SUBURBAN	RURAL	MISSING	TOTAL
<25,000	51	1,821	5,212	57	7,141
25,000-49,999	56	409	421	9	895
50,000-99,999	121	201	193	4	519
100,000-249,999	143	85	53	3	284
250,000-499,999	59	13	4	1	77
500,000-999,999	31	8		1	40
MILLION+	16	1	1		18
TOTAL	477	2,538	5,884	75	8,974

* The numbers in this table are based on FY 2001 public library data, the latest available national figures (NCES, 2003). The "missing" column indicates public library systems for which metropolitan status codes are not available/designated. Should NCES release the FY 2002 data during the initial phases of the study, the study team will use the 2002 data to develop the sampling frame.
** The actual metropolitan status designations provided in the NCES database (2003) uses the categories of Central City (Urban); Metropolitan Area, but not Central City (Suburban); and Not in a Metropolitan Area (Rural). The labels of Urban, Suburban, and Rural are used to facilitate reading. The table uses the metropolitan status designation of the administrative entity; branches will differ for the approximately 16% of library systems with branches.

practices) as well as librarians from library settings that included a balance between public and academic libraries. A list of participants was developed from the ALA membership directory. Members holding office in one of ALA's governing bodies (roundtables, committees, etc.) were selected at random as library leaders, and all other members were categorized as either public or academic librarians before a random draw from each category. In total, 400 librarians were e-mailed requesting a telephone interview.

Survey Instrument Development and Administration

The study team conducted a pilot study to develop and test the survey instrument in 2004. Based on comments provided by survey reviewers, the team developed two final versions of the survey form: one for public libraries and one for academic libraries.

Due to concerns about the gag order provision of the Patriot Act (Section 215) the survey was examined by legal counsel for the Office of Information Technology Policy (OITP) and approval for the study questions was sought from the Department of Justice.

The survey was developed as a Web-based instrument and was mounted on a secure server at the University of Waterloo. The majority of data collection (with a few exceptions) occurred via Web survey form. In order to ensure anonymity and validity of participants, each library was assigned a unique ID number and password for access to either the Academic Library survey of the Public Library survey. In a few instances (less than five) libraries requested to have a paper copy of the survey mailed to them and Web data entry was completed by a member of the research team. Web survey collection occurred from January-April 2005. Once the data were received and downloaded into a separate data file the actual responses were destroyed to further ensure the anonymity of respondents.

Letters were mailed at the end of December 2004 to all library directors selected to participate in the study. The letter identified the purpose of the study, instructions for accessing the survey Web site and contact information for the principal investigator. These instructions also appeared on the Web-based version of the survey. Of the 5,544 letters mailed out in the first announcement, 61 were returned by the post office, and we were able to correct the addresses for 48 of these.

A second follow up letter was sent in February 2005 as a reminder. To boost the survey response rate, the study team also contacted nonresponding libraries vie e-mail and telephone. A small sample of public libraries was selected for demographic characteristics, and was contacted to complete the survey over the telephone.

The study was also promoted at the 2005 ALA Midwinter Meeting and through library mailing lists, and state library networks.

Interview Protocol Development and Administration

A preliminary interview protocol was developed in 2004 and pilot tested on five library respondents. Information from these interactions was used to refine the protocol and extend the pilot test to 12 librarians and library leaders, resulting in a semistructured series of questions and probes.

The participants comprised both library opinion leaders (individuals with knowledge of the national scene with respect to library policy and practices) as well as librarians from settings that included public and academic libraries. Participants were contacted by e-mail and a telephone interview was scheduled. The interviews were conducted through a third party conferencing system that provided secure and anonymous 800 number access, and transcripts of the interviews.

Data analysis began as data were collected and these were used to refine the line of questioning for subsequent data collection. Data collection continued until a saturation point was reached, that is, a point of redundancy where new information did not emerge.

Response Rate

Although there were 1,354 responses to the surveys, this represents approximately 33% of public libraries in the sample, and 23% of academic libraries. Similarly, of the 400 librarians who were contacted, only 50 agreed to take part in the interviews.

This study employed a number of techniques to increase the likelihood of response from libraries including:

- Sending an initial letter requesting participation and explaining the purpose of the survey and stressing the importance of prompt response
- Promoting the study at the Midwinter Meeting of the American Library Association
- Providing notices in pertinent ALA, and PLA literature to announce the conduct of the survey
- Performing a second mailing of the request for participation to all nonresponding libraries
- Contacting state library agencies for assistance in increasing the response rate
- Making the survey available on a Web site, and providing mailed copies for those libraries without Web access
- Returning all respondent phone call and e-mail queries concerning survey questions and procedures within 48 hours of receipt
- Providing reminder e-mails and telephone calls to nonrespondents
- Contacting a set of 568 public libraries by telephone and offering to complete the survey over the phone with assistance

While conducting the study, many librarians and library directors provided reasons for not participating. The researchers found that the vast majority of people who declined to participate in the study indicated that they simply did not have the time and had too many other pressing items on their agenda. There were other reasons that contributed to nonresponse, but lack of time and other more pressing demands was the primary reason:

"Due to a lack of staff support we are unable to comply with your request to complete the survey....The time we devote to the various ARL and SPEC surveys is all that we can contribute in responses at this time."

"We get a lot of these types of requests and can't answer all of them. We are a small library with little support, sorry."

Another fairly common reason given for nonparticipation was the library's lack of Patriot Act or other official law enforcement requests. As one librarian stated:

"I feel quite strongly that the Patriot Act needs to be abolished, but we've had no requests here in our library. I don't want to fill out the survey and skew your results."

"I've worked in three large library systems since 9/11 and not had a single request at any of them."

A very few librarians contacted the researchers for more information about the legality of the survey questions and indicated that they had not yet taken the survey out of fear of violating the gag order. Finally, there may have been some reluctance to participate due to an e-mail (undocumented) that reported the study to be a hoax:

"...it was because there was e-mails going around saying it (the study) was just a hoax."

The next section presents results of both the public and academic surveys and of the interview protocols.

National Survey Results

Law Enforcement Visits to Public Libraries

A key question this study addressed was the degree to which there have been law enforcement visits to public libraries. Overwhelmingly, most respondents indicated

Figure 2. Public library respondent and population breakdowns by population of legal service area

Population of Legal Service Area	Population	Respondents (n=470)
<25,000	79.5%	82.0%
25,000-49,999	10.0%	7.9%
50,000-99,999	5.7%	3.9%
100,000-249,999	3.2%	3.0%
250,000-499,999	0.9%	1.1%
500,000-999,999	0.4%	1.7%
Million +	0.2%	0.4%

that their libraries have not been visited since September 11 by either federal or state/local law enforcement officials. For public libraries responding, however, there were 16 instances of legally executed requests for information from federal agencies and 47 instances when state/local law enforcement officials brought a legally executed request for one or more types of records.

While contacts with law enforcement presenting official legal orders represent one aspect of library contact with law enforcement, library staff giving law enforcement information without a court order represents another. Once again, the vast majority of respondents indicated that they had not voluntarily reported information to law enforcement officials. In public libraries, 14 respondents indicated that the library had given information about certain patrons once or more often without a legally executed law enforcement request. Forty-eight respondents indicated that the library had given information about certain patrons once or more often without proper documentation from state or local law enforcement officials asking them to do so.

Since a number of demographic characteristics of both the sample and the population for public libraries are known, a comparison between the nature of the respondents and the population can be made. Figure 2 shows that generally, the respondents to the survey are similar to the population in terms of population of legal service area. Figure 3 also shows that in terms of metropolitan status, that is, rural, suburban, and urban, responses are similar to the actual population, although the respondents are slightly weighted to more suburban responses and less rural responses.

Library Policies and Practices

This section of the survey asked respondents to discuss library policies and practices. Figure 4 shows that some 64% of respondents have established policies and

Figure 3. Public library respondent and population breakdowns by metropolitan status

Metropolitan Status	Population	Respondents (n=470)
Rural	62.6%	58.0%
Suburban	30.5%	37.1%
Urban	6.9%	4.9%

procedures for dealing with requests from law enforcement agencies and 36% do not. Figure 5 suggests that for those libraries that have developed policies and procedures, the greatest level of involvement in that development has come from library board members. A distant second and third level of involvement, respectively, came from other public libraries and the state library.

With regard to library training for the handling of requests or orders for information by law enforcement agencies or officials, Figure 6 shows that 62% of respondents indicated library staff have been trained to do this, but 38% have not been trained.

The survey also explored public library changes to a number of library policies. Figure 7 indicates that 64% of respondents have not changed any policies regarding the collection and retention of patron information. But it is interesting to note that some 32% of respondents indicated that they now collect less information about patrons than before the Patriot Act.

Figure 8 shows that the majority of respondents (65%) indicated that the library does not attempt to make patrons aware of the existence of the Patriot Act and its possible implications for patron activities in the library. In addition, Figure 9 suggests that 95% of public library staff have not altered their professional activities in reaction to the Patriot Act and other antiterrorism measures. Figure 15 also gives examples of some of the changes in behavior that the other 5% reported.

The survey also explored the degree to which patrons inquired to library staff regarding library policies or practices in relation to the Patriot Act. Figure 10 summarizes responses to this topic and shows that 55% indicated there had been no patron inquires and 31% indicated that the library had received fewer than 10 such responses. Nonetheless, Figure 10 also shows that 179 respondents reported that the library had received at least one or more inquires regarding library policies or practices in relation to the Patriot Act.

Contact with Law Enforcement Agencies

Figure 11 shows that overwhelmingly, respondents indicated that the library has not volunteered information about certain patrons to federal and state/local law enforce-

Figure 4. Public library policies or procedures for requests for information

Yes, the library has established policies or procedures for dealing with requests for information from law enforcement agencies or officials	63.8% (n=298)
No, the library does not have established policies or procedures for dealing with requests for information from law enforcement agencies or officials	36.2% (n=169)

Figure 5. Public library policies or procedures development

Local government agencies or officials	17.4% (n=82)
Library board members	53.2% (n=250)
Representatives members of the community	4.5% (n=21)
Law enforcement agencies or officials	8.3% (n=39)
State library	22.6% (n=106)
Other public libraries	24.0% (n=113)
Library consortia	14.7% (n=69)
Other	11.7% (n=55)
Other Identified Individuals/Agencies	• American Library Association Web site • County, city, town, board, or library attorney • State library association (e.g., Florida Library Association) • Professional workshop
* May not total to 100.0% as respondents could select more than one option.	

Figure 6. Public library librarian training for handling requests for information

Yes, the library trains library staff on how to handle requests or orders for information by law enforcement agencies or officials	62.0% (n=289)
No, the library does not train library staff on how to handle requests or orders for information by law enforcement agencies or officials	38.0% (n=177)

Figure 7. Public library changes to policies regarding the collection and retention of patron information since passage of the USA PATRIOT Act

Yes, the library collects and retains *more* information about patrons than before the act	3.4% (n=16)
Yes, the library collects and retains *less* information about patrons than before the act	32.1% (n=150)
No, we have not changed any policies regarding the collection and retention of patron information	64.5% (n=302)

ment officials. On the other hand, it is also interesting to note that 14 respondents indicated that the library had volunteered information about certain patrons one or more times without federal law enforcement officials asking them to do so. And, 48 respondents indicated that the library had volunteered information one or more times about certain patrons without state or local law enforcement officials asking them to do so.

With regard to the number of instances of requests for records and other items by law enforcement officials, Figure 12 shows that the vast majority of respondents indicated that no such requests had been received. There were, however, 16 instances of requests for such information of at least one or more types from federal agencies and 47 instances when state/local law enforcement officials requested one or more types of such records. Of these, 10 instances were requests for electronic records or inspection of computer hard drives.

Overview

The data from the public library survey suggest that overall there has been limited impact on public libraries as a result of law enforcement activities since October 2001.

Figure 8. Public library patron awareness of the existence of the USA PATRIOT Act

Yes, the library attempts to make patrons aware of the existence of the USA PATRIOT Act of its possible implications for patron activities in the library	34.8% (n=160)
No, the library does not attempt to make patrons aware of the existence of the USA PATRIOT Act of its possible implications for patron activities in the library	65.2% (n=300)

Figure 9. Public library staff alterations in professional behavior in reaction to the USA PATRIOT Act

Yes, members of the library staff have altered their professional activities in reaction to the USA PATRIOT Act and other antiterrorism measures	5.3% (n=24)
No, members of the library staff have not altered their professional activities in reaction to the USA PATRIOT Act and other antiterrorism measures	94.7% (n=432)
Sample Changes in Behavior	

1. Small library, used to call patron to let them know book available, but not anymore.
2. Staff have been careful to keep fewer records relating to computer use and Interlibrary Loan requests. Computer vendors and technicians have been asked to recommend methods to erase records of Web sites visited by library customers.
3. We do not keep log of dates and times of Internet patron users as we did in the past.
4. Records are kept for materials that are currently out to patrons, as soon as materials are returned the record is no longer necessary and is removed. We still operate on a manual circulation system so there is no computer record.
5. We give more vague and generalized answers to questions rather than being specific about anything. We try not to "point fingers" or "name drop" about anything if possible.
6. Spoken at public on the implications of the act for library use, privacy, etc.

Figure 10. Public library number of patron inquiries to library staff regarding library policies or practices in relation to the USA PATRIOT Act

Number of Patron Inquiries	
None	55.3% (n=256)
<10	31.3% (n=145)
10-25	4.8% (n=22)
26-50	1.5% (n=7)
>50	1.1% (n=5)
Don't Know	6.0% (n=28)

Clearly, there are some instances where policies have been changed, collections have been modified, and some libraries have been contacted by law enforcement agencies/officials. But interestingly, some 36% of respondents indicated that they have no policies for dealing with requests from law enforcement agencies. In addition, almost 40% of respondents indicated that in their library training for the handling of requests or orders for information by law enforcement agencies or officials had not occurred. Thus, for some public libraries changes and impacts have occurred after October 2001 related to law enforcement activities. But for the majority of respondents there has only been very limited, if any, impacts or changes.

Law Enforcement Visits to Academic Libraries

Similar to public libraries, most academic libraries that responded indicated that they have not been presented with official legal orders from law enforcement since October 2001. For academic libraries that responded, there were 33 instances of requests for information from federal agencies and 41 instances when state/local law enforcement officials brought a legally executed request for one or more types of records.

Turning over information to law enforcement without proper documentation is also a slight factor for academic libraries. In academic libraries, 24 respondents indicated that the library had given information about certain patrons to federal law enforcement officials once or more often and 45 respondents indicated that the library had

Figure 11. Public library number of instances of voluntarily providing information about the activities of patrons

Number of Instances	Federal Contact		State/Local Contact	
	The library has volunteered information about certain patrons to federal law enforcement officials upon the informal request of federal law enforcement officials	The library has provided information about certain patrons without law enforcement officials asking us to do so	The library has volunteered information about certain patrons to state and local law enforcement officials upon the informal request of state/local law enforcement officials	The library has provided information about certain patrons without state or local law enforcement officials asking us to do so
0 Times	98.3% (n=451)	98.7% (n=453)	96.5% (n=441)	95.6% (n=434)
1 Time	1.5% (n=7)	1.1% (n=5)	2.2% (n=10)	3.3% (n=15)
2 Times	0.2% (n=1)	0.2% (n=1)	0.9% (n=4)	0.9% (n=4)
3 Times	-	-	0.2% (n=1)	-
4 Times	-	-		-
5 Times	-	-	0.2% (n=1)	-
6 Times	-	-	-	-
7 Times	-	-	-	-
8 Times	-	-	-	-
9 Times	-	-	-	-
10 Times	-	-	-	0.2% (n=1)

Figure 12. Public library number of instances of requests for records and other items by law enforcement agencies

Number of Instances	Federal agency served the library with an official legal order for library records, materials, or other content	Official federal legal order to produce paper records	Official federal legal order to produce electronic records or inspection of computer hard drives	State or local law enforcement official legal order for library records, materials, or other content	Official state/local agency legal order to produce paper records	Official state/local agency legal order to produce electronic records or inspection of computer hard drives
0 Times	97.8% (n=447)	98.0% (n=448)	98.5% (n=450)	95.4% (n=435)	96.5% (n=441)	94.3% (n=443)
1 Time	2.0% (n=9)	1.8% (n=8)	1.3% (n=6)	3.3% (n=15)	2.6% (n=12)	1.3% (n=6)
2 Times	0.2% (n=1)	0.2% (n=1)	0.2% (n=1)	0.7% (n=3)	0.7% (n=3)	0.4% (n=2)
3 Times	-	-	-	0.2% (n=1)	-	0.4% (n=2)
4 Times	-	-	-	0.2% (n=1)	-	
5 Times	-	-	-	-	-	-
6 Times	-	-	-	-	-	-
7 Times	-	-	-	0.2% (n=1)	0.2% (n=1)	-

given information about certain patrons to state or local law enforcement officials with only an informal law enforcement request.

Figure 13 shows that 73% of respondents to the survey are serving institutions with enrollments of 5,000 or smaller. Some 27% of the respondents serve institutions with enrollments larger than 5,000. Figure 14 shows that respondents were almost exactly split between being in private vs. public institutions.

Library Policies and Practices

This section of the survey asked respondents to discuss library policies and practices. Figure 15 shows that 48% of respondents have established policies and procedures for dealing with requests for information from law enforcement agencies and 52% do not. Figure 16 suggests that for those libraries that have developed policies and procedures, the greatest level of involvement in that development has come from college legal counsel (21%) and from library committee members (17%). The data also show that there are a range of other stakeholders that may have participated in the development of policies and procedures.

Figure 17 finds that 46% of respondents are in libraries that have provided training in how to handle requests or orders for information by law enforcement agencies and 54% have not provided such training.

The survey also explored academic library changes to a number of library policies. Figure 18 indicates that 76% of respondents have not changed any policies regarding the collection and retention of patron information since passage of the Patriot Act. But it is interesting to note that some 23% of respondents indicated that they now collect less information about patrons than before the Patriot Act.

In terms of the library attempting to make patrons aware of the existence of the Patriot Act and its possible implications for patron activities in the library (see Figure 19), 77% of respondents indicated that the library did not make such efforts, whereas 23% did attempt to make patrons aware of the Patriot Act and its implications. Figure 20 suggests that 96% of academic library staff have not altered their professional activities in reaction to the Patriot Act and other antiterrorism measures. Figure 20 also gives examples of some of the changes in behavior that the other 4% reported.

Figure 13. Academic library respondents by institution enrollment

Enrollment	Respondents (n=884)
<1,000	27.3%
1,000-5,000	46.1%
5,000-7,500	8.5%
7,500-15,000	10.4%
15,000-45,000	7.1%
45,000 +	0.6%

Figure 14. Academic library respondents by private/public institution designation

Public/Private Designation	Respondents (n=884)
Public	49.9%
Private	50.1%

Figure 15. Academic library established policies or procedures for requests for information

Yes, the library has established policies or procedures for dealing with requests for information from law enforcement agencies or officials	47.9% (n=416)
No, the library does not have established policies or procedures for dealing with requests for information from law enforcement agencies or officials	52.1% (n=452)

Figure 16. Academic library established policies or procedures development*

No policies developed as a result of the USA PATRIOT Act	16.6% (n=147)
Provost	14.5% (n=128)
Higher Education Administrators	15.5% (n=137)
Board of Regents/Board of Governors	3.6% (n=32)
Faculty Senate	2.6% (n=23)
College Legal Counsel	21.3% (n=188)
Library Committee Members	16.7% (n=148)
Law Enforcement Agencies/ Officials	3.5% (n=31)
State Library	1.7% (n=15)
Other Academic Libraries	9.8% (n=87)
Library Association, such as ALA or ARL	5.9% (n=52)
Library Consortia	3.5% (n=31)
Other	5.8% (n=51)
Other Identified Individuals/ Agencies	• Office of the State Attorney General • Academic Technology Committee • Dean of Libraries & Media Services Human Resources
* May not total to 100.0% as respondents could select more than one option.	

The survey also explored the degree to which patrons inquired to library staff regarding library policies or practices in relation to the Patriot Act. Figure 21 summarizes responses to this topic and shows that 59% indicated there had been no patron inquires and 24% indicated that the library had received fewer than 10 such responses. Nonetheless, Figure 21 also shows that 239 respondents reported that the library had received at least one or more inquires regarding library policies or practices in relation to the Patriot Act.

Contact with Law Enforcement Agencies

Figure 22 shows that overwhelmingly, respondents indicated that the library has not volunteered information about certain patrons to federal and state/local law enforcement officials. On the other hand, it is also interesting to note that 24 respondents indicated that the library had volunteered information about certain patrons without federal law enforcement officials asking them to do so at least once or more often.

Figure 17. Academic library librarian training for handling requests for information

Yes, the library trains library staff on how to handle requests or orders for information by law enforcement agencies or officials	45.8% (n=395)
No, the library does not train library staff on how to handle requests or orders for information by law enforcement agencies or officials	54.2% (n=468)

Figure 18. Academic library changes to policies regarding the collection and retention of patron information since passage of the USA PATRIOT Act

Yes, the library collects and retains *more* information about patrons than before the act	1.3% (n=11)
Yes, the library collects and retains *less* information about patrons than before the act	23.1% (n=199)
No, we have not changed any policies regarding the collection and retention of patron information	75.6% (n=651)

Figure 19. Academic library patron awareness of the existence of the USA PATRIOT Act

Yes, the library attempts to make patrons aware of the existence of the USA PATRIOT Act of its possible implications for patron activities in the library	22.6% (n=190)
No, the library does not attempt to make patrons aware of the existence of the USA PATRIOT Act of its possible implications for patron activities in the library	77.4% (n=651)

Figure 20. Academic library staff alterations in professional behavior in reaction to the USA PATRIOT Act

Yes, members of the library staff have altered their professional activities in reaction to the USA PATRIOT Act and other antiterrorism measures	4.1% (n=34)
No, members of the library staff have not altered their professional activities in reaction to the USA PATRIOT Act and other antiterrorism measures	95.9% (n=796)
Sample Changes in Behavior	

7. More careful. More involvement in professional organization workshops and training.
8. No longer maintain usage statistics.
9. Destroyed/erased patron records upon return of library materials; set computers to delete visited pages ASAP.
10. We now include it as part of our curriculum in our library research methods courses.

11. We have mounted several displays, included Patriot Act as a search in our library instruction sessions and worked on a policy to handle any Patriot Act requests.
12. We have added many titles to our collection concerning many aspects of the subjects regarding or changed by the events occurring on September 11.
13. Many external links from our Web site have been removed when the information was removed from the Internet by federal and other Web sites.
14. More willing to help authorities and more disgusted with ALA's antigovernment agenda.

Figure 21. Academic library number of patron inquiries to library staff regarding library policies or practices in relation to the USA PATRIOT Act

Number of Patron Inquiries	
None	59.0% (n=497)
<10	24.3% (n=205)
10-25	3.1% (n=26)
26-50	0.8% (n=7)
>50	0.1% (n=1)
Don't Know	12.6% (n=106)

And, 45 respondents indicated that the library had volunteered information about certain patrons without state or local law enforcement officials asking them to do so at least once or more often.

With regard to the number of instances of requests for records and other items by law enforcement officials, Figure 23 shows that the vast majority of respondents indicated that no such requests had been received. There were, however, 33 instances of requests for such information from federal agencies and 41 instances when state/local law enforcement officials requested one or more types of such records.

Overview

The data from the academic library survey suggest that overall there has been limited impact on public libraries as a result of law enforcement activities since October 2001. Clearly, there are some instances where policies have been changed, collections have been modified, and some libraries have been contacted by law enforcement agencies/officials. But interestingly, some 52% of respondents indicated that they have no policies for dealing with requests from law enforcement agencies. In addition, almost 54% of respondents indicated that in their library training for the handling of requests or orders for information by law enforcement agencies or officials had not occurred. Thus, for some academic libraries changes and impacts have occurred after October 2001 related to law enforcement activities. But for the majority of respondents, there has only been very limited, if any, impacts or changes.

Figure 22. Academic library number of instances of voluntarily providing information about the activities of patrons

Number of Instances	Federal Contact		State/Local Contact	
	The library has volunteered information about certain patrons to federal law enforcement officials upon the informal request of federal law enforcement officials	The library has provided information about certain patrons without law enforcement officials asking us to do so	The library has volunteered information about certain patrons to state and local law enforcement officials upon the informal request of state/local law enforcement officials	The library has provided information about certain patrons without state or local law enforcement officials asking us to do so
0 Times	98.0% (n=804)	98.8% (n=805)	96.8% (n=792)	97.7% (n=795)
1 Time	1.5% (n=12)	0.9% (n=7)	2.3% (n=19)	1.6% (n=13)
2 Times	0.2% (n=2)	0.1% (n=1)	0.4% (n=3)	0.5% (n=4)
3 Times	0.1% (n=1)	0.1% (n=1)	0.4% (n=3)	0.2% (n=2)
4 Times	-	-	-	-
5 Times	-	-	0.1% (n=1)	-
6 Times	-	-	-	-
7 Times	-	-	-	-
8 Times	-	-	-	-
9 Times	-	-	-	-
10 Times	-	0.1% (n=1)	-	-
35 Times	0.1% (n=1)	-	-	-

Figure 23. Academic library number of instances of requests for records and other items by law enforcement agencies

Number of Instances	Federal agency served the library with an official legal order for library records, materials, or other content	Official federal legal order to produce paper records	Official federal legal order to produce electronic records or inspection of computer hard drives	State or local law enforcement official legal order for library records, materials, or other content	Official state/local agency legal order to produce paper records	Official state/local agency legal order to produce electronic records or inspection of computer hard drives
0 Times	98.2% (n=806)	99.4% (n=816)	98.4% (n=807)	98.0% (n=801)	99.1% (n=810)	97.8% (n=801)
1 Time	1.6% (n=13)	0.6% (n=5)	1.3% (n=11)	1.8% (n=15)	0.9% (n=7)	2.0% (n=16)
2 Times	0.2% (n=2)	-	0.2% (n=2)	0.1% (n=1)	-	0.1% (n=1)
3 Times	-	-	-	-	-	0.1% (n=1)
4 Times	-	-	-	-	-	-
5 Times	-	-	-	-	-	-
6 Times	-	-	-	-	-	-
7 Times	-	-	-	-	-	-

Interview Results

This section of the report provides a summary of findings from semistructured interviews conducted between February and April 2005. The respondents comprised both library opinion leaders (individuals with knowledge of the national scene with respect to library policy and practices), as well as librarians from library settings that included public and academic libraries.

Figures 24, 25, and 26 provide an overview of the respondents, their organizations, and their broad geographic regions. In order to protect the anonymity of respondents, specific institutional and geographic place names have been omitted.=

The following section provides a set of verbatim quotations from the interviews with librarians and library leaders. These responses have been grouped according to recurring themes that emerged from the analysis.

Overview of Library Responses

Although the size of our respondent sample limits broad generalization, the interviews clearly document a high level of concern about contemporary legal impacts on libraries. Most of the respondents were concerned specifically with the impact on patron privacy and on the library's responsibility in protecting patron records. We also noted that librarians expressed distinctive concerns about the level of awareness possessed by library patrons regarding current legislation's impact on library use and patron's lack of familiarity with current legislation's impact on the confidentiality of their records. Although respondents shared a strong sense of the library's role in providing education on these issues, there was some disagreement

Figure 24. Frequency of interviewees by organization

Academic	19 (38%)
Public	15 (30%)
Library Leader	13 (26 %)
Regional Consortia	3 (6%)

Figure 25. Frequency of interviewees by region[3]

Midwest	10 (20%)
Northeast	9 (18%)
West	7 (14%)
National	6 (12%0
South	6 (12%)
Northwest	5 (10%)
Southeast	3 (6%)
Southwest	2 (4%)
North	2 (4%)

Figure 26. Interviewees by type of organization and region

Title	Type of Organization	Region
Instruction/reference	Public university	Northeast
Library Leader	Professional association	National
Collection Librarian	Private university	Northwest
Reference	Suburban public library	West
Reference/Public Services	Suburban public library	South
Library Leader	Professional association	South
Reference	Mid-sized public library	Northwest
Chief Librarian	Public college	Northwest
Systems librarian	Metropolitan public library	Southeast
Library Leader	Professional association	National
Reference Librarian	Public college	Midwest
Curator	Large public university	Northeast
Science librarian	Large public university	Midwest
Technical services	Central public library	Northeast
Library Leader	Professional association	Midwest
Deputy Director	Suburban public library	North
Cataloging services	Regional library system	Southwest
Library Leader	Professional association	Midwest
Catalog and metadata	Private college	Northeast
Database Acquisitions	County library system	Midwest
Technical services	Metropolitan public library	West
Librarian	Small town public library	Southeast
Library Leader	Professional association	West
Reference	Private college	Midwest
Director outreach	Public library	Northeast
Library Leader	Professional association	Northeast
Librarian	Suburban public library	West
Reference Librarian	Small business school	Southwest
Library Leader	Professional association	National
Dean of learning resources	Private college	Northeast
Archivist	Private college	Midwest
Librarian	Small town public library	Northeast
Administrator	Public university	Northeast

continued on following page

Figure 26. continued

Library Leader	Professional association	National
Access services	Public library	Midwest
Government documents	Public University	Northwest
Head of Reference	Urban public library	South
Library Leader	Professional association	West
Director	Public library	Midwest
Director	Community college	Northwest
Library Leader	Professional association	National
Library Leader	Professional association	Southeast
Librarian	Regional consortium	West
Digital Reference Librarian	Large public university	Midwest
Director	Christian College	South
Reference	Metropolitan public library	West
Associate librarian	Private university	North
Library Leader	Professional association	National
Reference	Small public college	South
Director	Community college	South

about how politicized a library should be. Most pointed to library policies and training efforts—particularly those governing staff responses to external requests for information –as appropriate library responses to recent legislation, but some librarians urged caution and balance in addressing the Patriot Act publicly.

From conducting the interviews, we identified several important points that influenced the course of our work on this project. First, the interviews clearly document a level of concern and awareness about contemporary legal issues among the respondents questioned. For example, respondents made the following statements:

"There are just any number of basic rights that are at risk here. And given the role of the library in a democracy to provide information so people can make informed decisions about the issues that face them, number one, they're going to be concerned about having a record extant that would in some way implicate or compromise their anonymity in reviewing this information, for whatever reason—material about terrorists, about political bodies of various sorts."

"But I think it's going to have rising impact on America itself, and that will certainly be true of American institutions. And the libraries I think—whether academic or

public or even special for that matter—are among the ranking democratic institutions because they are free and open to the public for reasons that are specified in the Constitution and the Declaration of Independence."

"We are a mining community, and I buy material on explosives regularly, because I think it's important people have access to current, accurate information, not only on how to handle explosives safely, but for people who are affected by these materials being transported through the community and used nearby can assess whether the commercial enterprises are, in fact, following adequate safety procedures. Those sorts of inquiries are going to be distinctly chilled, because people are going to be afraid to check out materials that might help them answer and ask the questions that need to be addressed."

"I feel that one of the most important things that a public library can do is to provide a patron with access to information, to help them or at least give them the possibility of making good choices that they need to make in their lives. And what I think the reaction or the culture or whatever we want to call it from the Patriot Act and 9/11 is to start narrowing down that universe of resources that people are—they want to restrict what people have access to and I think the moment you start restricting, you start hurting people's ability to make good choices for their lives and I just find that a horrible shame."

"I think overall, librarians have always had a concern about confidentiality or privacy. I personally suspect it may be higher than some of the individuals who use the library. But I think the recent legislation has really brought an awareness, not only to librarians, as to how they handle the data we collect, but also to our customers. We're hearing more from our customer's about what do you do with the information that you have. Do you keep it for ever, that kind of thing, which, you know, 20 years ago we would not have heard. So I think it has raised awareness both on our customer's part, and on ours. "

"Even if [Section 215] is not being used, if it's never been used, if they never plan to use it, it creates this whole chilling effect on people's assumption that their intellectual interests (what they read, what they do, in terms of borrowing books, buying books, those kinds of things) is private. It makes you start wondering whether it is or it isn't. That in itself, even if it's never used, goes against the grain of democracy."

We also observed information from respondents suggesting that organizational policies and training affecting staff members were the library's primary means of addressing concerns about recent legislation. Librarians spoke of the protection afforded by existing polices, as well as the need to craft new policy. Consider the following statements:

"Well, we tightened up our procedures internally. We probably have had more discussions with our attorney than we've had, you know, in my 20 years. We had long discussions about the U.S.A. Patriot Act and you know what our responsibilities and the roles were. You know and obligation to the public, how do we deal with as a staff? What procedures do we have in place? You know and our library advisory board was very concerned about that and wanted a statement, you know, in our policy saying that we could not always protect them, so we've -- those things have impacted us. I think we've probably been more careful about not keeping any logs of user data around."

"I think prior to the legislation, I don't know if we had any kind of written policies as to what we did with patron records. I think we just took whatever was happening with the automation system and accepted that default status. I think what we did was after that legislation was passed, we looked at what type of information we archived and clarified what it was that we were archiving and made sure that we had policies in place that remove that information, anything that we didn't need to keep beyond, you know, obviously keeping track of materials that are currently out. We, also, wrote up a policy statement that we communicated with the students and the faculty that that information could be shared with law enforcement, if it was subpoenaed or requested and I don't know if we have anything currently out there that says that but I know, at that time, you know, a couple of years ago we did do that."

"We don't do enough in terms of educating new librarians, and all staff...the person who's going to be approached in one of these cases is the clerk at the front desk. We need to make sure that every person who works in a library really understands what's going on and why these things are important..."

"Because my experience has been, and it could be just coincidence, but the four or five times the FBI has come into our library, they have been here during lunch hour. Or they have been here right after six o'clock. And in my mind, I think, are they assuming there's no supervision here and they can approach the most gullible employee and get whatever information they want?"

We noted that librarians expressed distinctive concerns about the level of awareness possessed by library patrons. On several occasions, librarians noted their beliefs that most patrons had minimal awareness of the legal climate surrounding libraries or the effects that climate might have on the disposal of their patron records. Here are a few relevant comments:

"The average person somehow doesn't worry about it…they feel they're not criminals, not terrorists, so therefore what do they have to worry about."

"I think most of them have heard the name. I do not think most of them really understand that their library records could be read by Homeland Security. So, I don't think the average person really understands that their privacy could be an issue."

"We did have—oh, maybe half a dozen patrons come into the library and specifically ask what we were doing to try to protect their privacy, in view of the privacy—the Patriot Act."

"No, I think people are aware of it to the extent they want to be. I just don't think they, you know—I don't think they lay awake nights worrying about it. Again, I think they think the legislation is aimed at processes that can protect them from being victims of terrorist behavior, and they're pretty much in favor of that."

"Well, I think the public's going to have to get a little hotter under the collar than they are now. As I said before, we have lots and lots of library users who could not care any less."

Parallel to suggestions that patrons were lacking in a complete understanding of the law, some respondents also made comments suggesting a lack of information or misinformation at a personal, institutional, or state level:

"No, we had a pretty strong privacy policy in the library prior to the Patriot Act, if that's what you mean by recent legislation, and the state here has written into the code that there are protections for privacy, as far as borrowing records go. So, you know, the state hasn't done anything differently and our policies remain the same."

"And honestly I don't keep real close track, so I mean I don't know what the very latest is. I would say that there is—over the last few years there is a general concern about the issue of privacy in the libraries. And actually, to some extent, I see this concern as having gone down, I think like two years ago, I think it was a much hotter topic, I think right now it's a little bit more in the back burner. I don't think

there's been a lot of actual cases put in front of the library community where it would get people upset. And that's not to say that there aren't problems, it's just that I haven't—you know, there hasn't been anything yet to bring to my attention, and I don't pay attention to the little things, it would have to be something significant for me to really pay attention to."

"I don't believe that anything has really changed…I mean we always have had to comply with requests from law enforcement agencies—whether local or state or federal—and this is nothing different. Maybe I'm just not aware of what's changed in this."

"We tried to educate our board of trustees about the Patriot Act and its effect on privacy of patron records about a year ago and it was just so incredibly frustrating. They acted like we were either hysterical or like we were just creating a tempest in a teapot. Then about six months after that, some other group got together with the city council and passed a city resolution condemning the act. So why didn't they listen to the librarians?"

A related theme focused on librarians and libraries in an activist role with respect to public education. For example, some libraries have taken an active role—using posters and other techniques—in letting patrons know about the conditions pertaining to privacy of their circulation records. Without such measures, and in the absence of a library records privacy case with national notoriety, it seems unlikely that library patrons will get "up in arms" about possible government intrusions into their patron records.

"I think that public libraries and the American Library Association would do well to have public forums, you know, just as a library might have a forum on any number of issues—topics—or to invite the League of Women Voters, or other nonpartisan organizations to come and have an open discussion and let citizens judge for themselves, and invite an FBI agent to come and talk the legitimate—why they believe the Patriot Act is legitimate, or an attorney who supports the Patriot Act, or an elected official who supports the Patriot Act, and also someone perhaps from the ACLU, or American Library Association, or public librarian, to talk about their concerns about it."

"There are just too many people who aren't paying attention. So I think public education is probably the most important piece, whatever way that works, either bookmarks at the library, letters to the editor, speaking to groups."

"Making people aware so that people who wouldn't have thought of it before, or wouldn't have thought of it in terms of yeah, it could be you instead of them always thinking well, they wouldn't come for me because I'm obviously not a terrorist, but putting it in terms of it happening to every man."

These quotes suggest a belief among these librarians that they see activism as an important part of the role of librarians and libraries. These sentiments magnify the notion of libraries as a locus of activism and education for privacy, free speech, and related access issues. Librarians did not consistently share this view, however, and several librarians called for caution and a more balanced response to recent legislation:

"We're also publicly funded institutions and you know, we have patrons that feel that we should be collecting this data, you know and it's hard to walk that line and sometimes, of course, the ALA line is, you know, all or nothing and in the real world sometimes we have to, you know, answer our political fathers, sometimes report to the police on certain things just to operate, so it's not a black and white issue."

"I don't think that our library is a place to take that kind of stand, you know."

"I mean we're very much about representing both sides of an issue, in terms of our collection and information we provide to our patrons. And, you know, I think that mounting a poster on the wall is a veiled attempt at informing people when, in a way, it's taking a political position."

"But then, again, you know, you don't wear political buttons in the library either. When you're working at a public library, you're essentially content-neutral while you're there."

"I think historians will look at this as a time we were under attack, much like Pearl Harbor, and realize that we're in a war and it will be viewed as a war. Probably with—the Patriot Act is an attempt to take necessary precautions."

"If those people, you know, the political fathers are in charge right now, depending on the political persuasion I mean that can impact budgets and if they see the library as promoting or even providing information about a view that isn't popular, I think that can end up impacting your budget. Like I say, we're in a fairly liberal community here but our state, overall, is very conservative and so—I mean I know for a fact that our legislatures, you know, many of them just say, why do we even

have the Internet, you know, because it's evil. So, you know, to this—even after all this time that's out there, so you know, we just have to be—you know, you have to get the word out to the public I think because if you just let it filter through some political groups or special interest groups, you know, it can really—you know, your users are your best advocates, I guess, is what I'd say."

"So I guess you can say, to some extent I think the Patriot Act works, I think it's there to protect the American citizens from terrorists who want to kill them. And so I don't see this as big of an issue as some people do. Some people sit there and say, we're opening the door a lot, we're setting a precedent so that anybody can come in now with very little cause and, you know, look for lots of library records. And my attitude is, let's deal with that when we come to it."

The data from the interviews suggest that overall there has been limited impact on libraries as a direct result of law enforcement activities since October 2001. While many librarians have been concerned about the potential for patron privacy violations, most felt that the patrons themselves were not concerned. Several librarians mentioned extensive efforts to revise policy, conduct privacy audits, and train staff to deal with law enforcement requests. However, this was not consistently voiced by all respondents. Librarians were unified in their desires to provide their patrons with access to diverse information in a safe environment, but were less cohesive in terms of how active or politicized their libraries should become.

Discussions and Conclusion

This chapter summarizes some 1,404 responses from academic and public librarians, including interviews with librarians and leaders in the library community regarding the impact of law enforcement activities in academic and public libraries since 9/11. As such, it represents the first national and examination of librarians' perceptions of law enforcement activity in academic and public libraries since the September 11, 2001, terrorist attacks.

In analyzing the data and discussing study findings it should be kept in mind that the limited number of respondents should caution readers against generalizing the data to the larger population. This being said, however, the data and findings point to a number of key findings and issues requiring additional attention.

Law Enforcement Visits to Academic and Public Libraries

A key question this study addressed was the degree to which there have been law enforcement visits to academic and public libraries requesting various types of information. Overwhelmingly, most respondents indicated that their libraries have not been visited since the September 11 attacks by law enforcement officials, either from the federal or state/local officials.

For public libraries, however, there were 16 instances of requests for such information from federal agencies and 47 instances when state/local law enforcement officials requested one or more types of such records. For academic libraries, there were 33 instances of requests for such information from federal agencies and 41 instances when state/local law enforcement officials requested one or more types of such records.[4] It should be noted that each request might represent a call for the records of a single individual or the records for all members of the library's community.

Because of the nondisclosure requirements in section 215 of the Patriot Act, it is difficult to ascribe the above instances of visits specifically to the Patriot Act. Nonetheless, the study found that respondents reported a total of 137 instances where law enforcement officials had visited the library and requested information. It seems quite likely that at least *some* of these visits were implemented under the guidelines of the Patriot Act, despite former U.S. Attorney General Ashcroft's assertion that no federal agents had visited libraries requesting information as a result of the Patriot Act.[5]

Voluntary Reporting of Information to Law Enforcement Officials

Once again, the vast majority of respondents indicated that they had not voluntarily reported information to law enforcement officials. In public libraries 14 respondents indicated that the library had volunteered information about certain patrons at least once or more often without federal law enforcement officials asking them to do so. And, 48 respondents indicated that the library had volunteered information about certain patrons at least once or more often without state or local law enforcement officials asking them to do so. In academic libraries, 24 respondents indicated that the library had volunteered information about certain patrons without federal law enforcement officials asking them to do so at least once or more often, and 45 respondents indicated that the library had volunteered information about certain patrons without state or local law enforcement officials asking them to do so at least once or more often.

Thus, the study identified some 131 instances where at least once or more often, without law enforcement officials asking them to do so, respondents indicated that they had volunteered information regarding specific patrons to federal and state/local law enforcement officials. Depending on one's political point-of-view, this finding may be somewhat unsettling and may seriously injure patrons' trust in the privacy of their activities in academic and public libraries.

Awareness and Importance of Law Enforcement Acts

The study suggests that patrons have limited awareness of or knowledge about specific provisions of the Patriot Act or other related laws, such as the Foreign Intelligence Surveillance Act (FISA), that may affect patrons' privacy in academic and public libraries. Indeed, many librarians feel that the general public doesn't know or care about privacy of library records, although some librarians feel it is their duty to provide education to remedy this situation.

Responses to the interviewers' attempts to encourage librarians to participate in the study also indicates some lack of understanding about the implications of the Patriot Act. To some degree, the sense of the respondents is that the Patriot Act and other related laws, in a number of instances, do not change "how we always have done things in my library."

Training and Education

A key question to consider is the degree to which it is the responsibility of the library community to educate both staff and users as to the issues and requirements that result from the Patriot Act and other recent terrorist-related laws and regulations. In public libraries, respondents indicated that 38% of their institutions had not provided training to staff in how to handle law enforcement requests for information, and in academic libraries some 54% of the respondents replied that their institution had not provided training.

This finding reinforces the notion that a significant number of academic and public libraries either are not aware of the potential impacts from the Patriot Act in their library, do not consider these potential impacts important, or otherwise have other more pressing priorities and concerns. During the interviews, a number of participants suggested that training and education would be a "good thing to do," but they had not implemented it as yet. Thus, training of staff or educating community members regarding the act appears to be a low priority for many librarians.

Chilling Effect on the Library?

The data suggest that at some libraries, there may be a chilling effect on the potential use and credibility of the degree to which librarians can protect patron information from requests from law enforcement agencies. The "chilling effect" can be best thought of as a reluctance on the part of patrons to check out certain material, ask certain types of questions, or concern about the privacy of their records. For the librarian's part this "chilling effect" manifests itself in "screening" the purchase and availability of certain materials, not responding completely to information requests, and concern about keeping certain types of patron records.

Some 5% of public library respondents and 4% of academic library respondents indicated that library staff have altered their professional activities in reaction to the Patriot Act and other antiterrorism measures. Almost 10% of academic library respondents indicated that at least once or more often patrons indicated to library staff that the Patriot Act had caused changes in library services. But more striking is that in public libraries, almost 40% of respondents indicated that patrons had inquired to library staff one or more times about policies or practices related to the Patriot Act. These data could suggest a "chilling" effect on libraries as a result of the Patriot Act.

Loss of Patron Data

A significant number of librarians indicted that they had, or were contemplating, erasing all patron records on a daily basis. This is problematic for a number of reasons: library circulation records are used for justifying expenditures, applying for funding, and improving services to the community. Many of the librarians interviewed indicated that they were unsure of how the integrated library systems such as GEAC, SIRSI, and Innovative Interfaces actually stored and backed up patron records, and vendors had been slow to respond to library concerns about the Patriot Act and patron privacy. As one librarian described the situation: "Libraries are dumping their usage data indiscriminately. We will look back on these years as a black hole for library statistics. The only source for what people read in the early years of this century will be Amazon.com."

Politicization of the Library

An interesting theme uncovered during the interviews was librarians' sense that they are walking a fine line between the needs of law enforcement and the rights of their patrons. Librarians' shared concern was that, given the need for national security and the fact that many Americans felt that steps should be taken to help secure the country from terrorist attacks, this perceived need must be balanced with the professional obligation to protect patrons. The sense of walking a fine line is complicated by respondents' obvious confusion about the responsibilities of libraries under the Patriot Act. Indeed, 65% of respondents in public libraries and 77% of academic librarians indicated that they do not inform patrons about the existence of the Patriot Act and of its possible implications for patron activities in the library.

The findings also indicate that libraries struggle to balance their responsibility regarding national, large-scale issues like USA PATRIOT with pressing day-to-day responsibilities.

The general sense that one receives is that the Patriot Act is "awful" from an abstract perspective, but "it doesn't really affect my library or patrons as directly as budget cuts and other day to day concerns." Librarians can't afford to lose local support, so they do not become politicized over legal issues that may be quite abstract in the minds of their patrons or staff. Personally, some librarians might feel very strongly about the potential for privacy loss, but professionally they feel more a compelling responsibility to deal with daily practical issues and problems.

Final Thoughts

Requests by law enforcement agencies for patron records and surveillance of patron activities in libraries have a long history in the United States. The response from libraries to such requests during the first and second world wars was enthusiastically supportive. The FBI's Library Awareness Program during the Cold War era was met with much more resistance from individual librarians and from the library profession as a whole. In the current post 9/11 environment, many librarians seem torn between their commitment to intellectual freedom and their commitment to national security.

The data from this study suggest that overall, the Patriot Act and similar legislation passed as a result of the September 11 terrorists attacks have had limited or very limited direct impact on academic and public library activities. Most libraries have not changed policies related to the retention of patron information, use of library materials including government information, or removed material from the library, nor has there been any significant change in library material usage. In those instances when changes did occur, reasons appear to be due to budget and financial matters rather than concern over requirements of the Patriot Act or other similar legislation.

In addition, it was pointed out that the September 11 terrorist acts and the resultant Patriot Act occurred years ago and no terrorist activities had happened in the country since. Indeed, one may wonder if the study had been administered early in 2002 instead of Spring 2005 if the responses might have been significantly different than what has been reported here.

In addition, despite the ALA's efforts to inform libraries of the need for specific policies and procedures for handling law enforcement requests for various types of information, a number of libraries have not, as yet, made such changes.

Another issue central to this discussion has been the degree to which the ALA should engage in significant lobbying efforts to change or modify the Patriot Act and related terrorist laws. Such lobbying efforts might be a relatively low priority for some librarians and at least one respondent stated that he or she was, "more willing to help authorities and more disgusted with ALA's antigovernment agenda."

The general sense that one receives is that the Patriot Act is "awful" from an abstract perspective, but "it doesn't really affect my library or patrons as directly as budget cuts and other day to day concerns." Librarians can't afford to lose local support, so they do not become politicized over legal issues that may be quite abstract in the minds of their patrons or staff. Personally, some librarians might feel very strongly about the potential for privacy loss, but professionally they feel more a compelling responsibility to deal with daily practical issues and problems.

References

Foerstel, H.N. (1991). *Surveillance in the stacks: The FBI's Library Awareness Program*. Greenwood Press.

Horn, Z. (1994). *ZOIA! Memoirs of Zoia Horn: Battler for the people's right to know*. McFarland & Co.

Starr, J. (2004). Libraries and national security: An historical review. *First Monday, 9*(12).

Endnotes

[1]   See: http://nces.ed.gov/

[2]   See: http://nces.ed.gov/ipeds/

[3]   Northeast: CT, DE, DC, ME, MA, MD, NY, NH, NJ, PA, RI, VT, Southeast: FL, GA, LA, NC, SC, South: AR, AL, MS, TN, WV Southwest: AZ, NM, OK, TX, Midwest: IL, IN, IA, KS, MO, NE, OH, West: AK, CA, HI, MT, NE, UT, WA WY Northwest: ID, OR, North: MI, MN. ND, SD, WI

[4]   Readers should recall that these numbers are based on a sample of roughly 25% of public and academic libraries: thus the actual numbers of law enforcement visits may be higher.

[5]   Eggen, D. (2003, September 18). Ashcroft: Patriot Act provision unused. *The Washington Post*, p. A.13.

Section III

Security, Technology, and Democracy

Chapter VI

Resisting Government Internet Surveillance by Participating in Politics Online and Offline

Brian S. Krueger, University of Rhode Island, USA

Abstract

While more is probably known about the causes of political participation than any other political behavior, the research program suffers in that it generally assumes citizens operate within an unproblematic surveillance context. This chapter argues that the growing use of the Internet for political participation and the government's expanded electronic surveillance capacities make this assumption increasingly dubious. Drawing on Michel Foucault's insights concerning surveillance and resistance, I develop empirical hypotheses related to surveillance and Internet political participation. Testing these hypotheses using data derived from a unique probability sample survey of U.S. Internet users, surveillance is shown to influence online political activity. Those who oppose the current administration, and who perceive the government monitors their Internet behavior, participate in politics online at the highest rates. Next, I test whether perceptions of online surveillance lead to a similar higher probability of conventional offline political activity. The results suggest that for those opposed to the regime's policies, online surveillance increases the likelihood of engagement in offline political participation.

Introduction

Political participation plays a well-understood role in various theories of democratic politics. Participation is said to promote system stability by legitimizing the current regime (e.g., Salisbury, 1975), facilitate the moral development of individuals (e.g., Mill, 1991; Pateman, 1970) and determine who governs and receives policy benefits (e.g., Key, 1949; Radcliff, 1994). Given the importance of political participation across a diverse range of democratic theories, a persistent question for empirical political scientists has been, "why do people participate?" Broadly considered, the factors found to facilitate individual political participation commonly fall into four categories: socioeconomic (e.g., Milbrath, 1965), psychological (e.g., Miller & Shanks, 1996), civic resources (e.g., Verba & Nie, 1972), and mobilization (e.g., Rosenstone & Hansen, 1993). Yet, while scholars probably know more about the causes of political participation than any other political behavior, the research program suffers in that it generally assumes ordinary citizens operate within an unproblematic surveillance context.

Typically, when scholars do consider the impact of surveillance on political participation, they focus on narrowly defined targets such as Black Panther, Communist, or Native American activists rather than on citizens in general (e.g., Churchill & Vander Wall 1990; Cunningham 2004; Donner, 1980; Rogin, 1987). Even those who do include ordinary individuals' privacy concerns as a determinant of political participation (completion of the U.S. Census) argue explicitly that these concerns likely do not extend to other forms of political participation (Couper, Singer, & Kulka, 1998; Singer, Mathiowetz, & Couper, 1993).

Although the political participation literature's neglect of surveillance was perhaps reasonable a decade ago, three developing conditions render it questionable. First, the Internet has become a mainstream avenue for political participation in the United States. Over 60% of the U.S. adult population now connects to the Internet. Of those who do connect, two-thirds engage in some type of online political activity (CSRA, 2003). This worldwide network of computers provides the technological infrastructure that makes the widespread surveillance of mass activity feasible for the first time in U.S. history (Nehf, 2003; Schwartz, 1999; Westin, 2003).[1]

Second, the September 2001 attacks on the World Trade Center and Pentagon provided justification for the passage of several new "antiterrorism" laws that expand the government's surveillance powers (for reviews, see Nelson, 2002; Pikowsky, 2002; Solove, 2004). Many of the key provisions of the central piece of antiterrorism legislation, the USA PATRIOT Act (Uniting and Strengthening America by Providing Appropriate Tools Required to Intercept and Obstruct Terrorism), focus directly on electronic surveillance. Lower barriers now exist for the government to intercept electronic mail transmissions and monitor Web surfing, all without necessarily informing the individual of this surveillance (Berkowitz, 2002; Nelson, 2002).

Other initiatives have been proposed, but delayed, that would further expand the state's surveillance capacity (e.g., Operation TIPS, Total Information Awareness, Patriot Act II). Taken together, even these already passed provisions harness much of the surveillance potential latent in the technological design of the Internet. Of course, for the purposes of this chapter, these new surveillance capacities mean little if ordinary citizens escape from their gaze.

Some suggest that whatever the terrorism prevention benefits of these surveillance techniques, one side effect will be the increased monitoring of ordinary citizens' Internet activity (Lyon, 2001). Lower barriers now exist for the government to intercept citizens' phone and electronic mail transmissions, all without necessarily informing the individual of this surveillance (Berkowitz, 2002; Nelson, 2002). As important, in a "with us or against us" environment where reminders are given "to all Americans that they need to watch what they say, watch what they do," those wishing to do the U.S. harm may be synonymous with those criticizing the government's policies (Fleischer, 2001, p. 11; see also Blanchard, 2002; Gould, 2002; Williams, 2003). For example, the USA PATRIOT Act's new definition of domestic terrorism, which includes "acts dangerous to human life that are a violation of the criminal laws of the U.S. or of any state, that appear to be intended...to influence the policy of a government by intimidation or coercion," requires only a small leap to approximate many classic definitions of political participation (e.g., Pateman, 1970). Accordingly, recent revelations indicate that the FBI has created new domestic terrorism files of peaceful antiwar demonstrators (Lichtblau, 2005) and that the Bush administration's NSA has and continues to monitor the phone and e-mail communications of U.S. citizens without judicial oversight (Risen & Lichtblau, 2005). Because the media have exposed these government activities, citizens opposed to the current administration's policies may wonder to what extent their political activity may increase their likelihood of becoming a target of governmental surveillance.

Others go further, plainly arguing that the recent history of government surveillance suggests that these electronic surveillance tools, at least in part, were designed to monitor and stifle legitimate political dissent (Shehadeh, 2002; Troyer, 2003). They note that most of the individuals with a Hoover era Counter Intelligence Program (Cointelpro) file had no connection to foreign subversives or any history of violence but were monitored simply because of their political beliefs or affiliation (e.g., Donner, 1980; Solove, 2004). The FBI used surveillance as an end in itself to interfere with political expression, "A secret political file serves up a banquet of fears. Do they have a 'file' on me? What could they possibly have found out about my past? Is there any derogatory information in my record?" (Donner, 1980, p. 172). To be sure, how closely current government electronic surveillance practices correspond to the Cointelpro era remains open to debate. Whatever the validity of these claims, many now believe that the government uses these surveillance powers to monitor ordinary citizens' Internet activity.

Despite the growing use of the Internet for political activity, the government's expanded electronic surveillance capacities, and the belief by many that the government monitors ordinary citizens, empirical studies do not incorporate surveillance into political participation models. This chapter seeks to integrate this compelling factor by using Michel Foucault's well-developed insights on surveillance to generate empirical hypotheses involving Internet political participation.[2] Using Foucault has distinct advantages. Not only does Foucault place surveillance at the center of his theory of disciplinary society, but also, his imagery offers a framework for understanding how the architectural characteristics of the Internet likely impact individuals' reaction to online surveillance.[3]

Surveillance, Social Control, and Resistance

In perhaps his best known work, Surveiller et Punir (Discipline and Punish), Foucault uses Jeremy Bentham's Panopticon as a fundamental metaphor for his conception of modern society that seeks to produce normal, useful, and docile subjects out of deviants[4] who depart as much from society's norms as its laws (1979). Surveillance lies at the heart of techniques of normalization in modern society. To condition subjects requires "a whole set of techniques and institutions for measuring, supervising and correcting the abnormal…which, even today, are disposed around the abnormal individual, to brand him and to alter him" (Foucault, 1979, p. 199).

The specific mechanisms of surveillance's power are best expressed through the architectural characteristics of the Panopticon. The circular prison, with its central observation tower, uses both light and blinds to completely monitor inmates while eliminating the visibility of the guards. The inmates, unsure of the direction of the guards' gaze, imagine the guards view their actions at all times, and act as if they are watched so as to avoid punishment. Because the watchers remain hidden from the prisoners, the Panopticon requires few real guards. Though actual punishment is unlikely due to the small number of real guards, inmates internalize the prison's rules by imagining the ersatz surveillance and gradually condition themselves through the repetition of normal behavior. To keep this facade of constant surveillance also requires the isolation of inmates. "The isolation of the convicts guarantees that it is possible to exercise over them, with maximum intensity, a power that will not be overthrown by any other influence; solitude is the primary condition of total submission" (Foucault, 1979, p. 237).

Given a perfect panoptic surveillance system, where individuals are categorized (as deviant), blinded (from the watcher), and isolated (from each other), we generally would expect deviants to condition themselves into normal, or at least docile, subjects. Yet, Foucault only uses the idealized Panopticon as a metaphor for modern disciplinary techniques. Surveillance never conditions subjects absolutely (for a discussion, see Digeser, 1992).

Resistance to the conditioning effects of surveillance is not only possible but is inadvertently encouraged by the very process of conditioning (Dumm, 1996; Foucault, 1982; Pickett, 1996). For Foucault, individuals only accept surveillance's normalizing influence to the degree that it remains hidden (1978). And it cannot be hidden completely. Because the Panopticon's surveillance techniques only condition when the inmates conjure the image of a watchful guard, this necessary aspect of control also dialectically produces the possibility of resistance (Digeser, 1992; Gordon, 2002). When surveillance is recognized, resistance can occur by specifically rejecting these normalizing forces (the micropolitics of resistance). Because resistance is localized, the forces it works against, in part, shape it. For example, Orwell reminds us that simply writing in a personal journal can become an act of resistance; Winston Smith's realization that Big Brother wants to control his very thoughts prompts his journal entries, shaping the form of his resistance (Grant, 2003).

Consequently, for the context considered in this chapter, one must focus on the specific type of conditioning encouraged by the surveillance system to understand the form that resistance may take. Government Internet surveillance works to create docility among those most opposed to the regime by creating anxiety about whether dissenting online political activity may make them more of a focus of observation, perhaps by the government opening a file on them (Digeser, 1992; Foucualt, 1979). Accordingly, resistance to the docility encouraged by government Internet surveillance would take the form of political activity. This notion of political participation as resistance against the forces of docility coincides with the conceptualization of "postmodern participation" developed explicitly by Jessica Kulynych. "A concept of performative resistance sees tactics and strategies that resist not only the global strategies of economic domination, but also the construction of apathetic, quiescent citizens. When power is such that it can create quiescence, the definition of political participation must include those forms of political action that disrupt and counter quiescence" (1997, p. 338). Moreover, while Kulynych's notion of political participation moves beyond conventional conceptualizations to include a number of "ordinary activities," she also recognizes that depending on the context, "conventional political activities may also take on the character of resistance" (p. 341). Clearly, in an environment where surveillance works to create docile subjects out of political dissidents, resistance may take the form of conventional political activity.

Applying the Internet

While disciplinary power alone implies the possibility of resistance, as discussed, the structure of the surveillance environment can serve to facilitate or stifle resistance. Actual surveillance systems never fully recreate the idealized Panopticon.

In view of this, Gary Marx observes, "control systems are not usually as effective and efficient as their advocates claim and they often have a variety of unintended consequences" (2003, p. 371; see also Marx, 1988). If a surveillance system allows the watched to view the watcher, then power becomes exposed even further, increasing the likelihood of resistance. Surveillance systems also seldom achieve complete isolation. While the isolation of deviant influences tends to produce docility and the acceptance of conditioning, horizontal communication breeds resistance. Alternative conceptions of acceptable behavior, communicated across individuals, expose the synthetic norms encouraged by the disciplinary surveillance.

The Internet surveillance techniques at the disposal of the federal government conform to some aspects of the idealized panoptic model. Certainly, these techniques create uncertainty regarding whether the government monitors individuals' (especially those critical of the regime) Internet activity. Yet, many argue that the structure of the Internet provides a poor fit for an effective disciplinary Panopticon. Whereas a crucial component of effective disciplinary surveillance requires the few to watch the many, while preventing the many from watching the few, modern information technologies also reverse these relations (Boyne, 2000; Green, 1999; Lim, 2002; Staples, 1997). Internet users can watch their watcher.[5] Boyne suggests "the machinery of surveillance is now always potentially in the service of the crowd as much as the executive," refining the notion of a Synopticon (Boyne, 2000).

For surveillance to discipline its subjects also requires the lack of horizontal communication between subjects. Yet, the decentralized information and communication network enhances one-to-one (e.g., electronic mail, instant messaging), many-to-many (e.g., chatrooms, Web pages), and one-to-many (e.g., listservs, blogs) forms of communication. Describing this nonconforming feature of the technological environment Munro suggests that, "the network promotes lateral communication and 'informates' those who are under surveillance" (Munro, 2000, p. 690). By allowing the watched to view the watcher as well as communicate horizontally with others that may offer subversive perspectives, the Internet conforms poorly to the idealized Panopticon. Therefore, Internet surveillance should perform poorly as an instrument of social control, with many individuals resisting the docility encouraged by this surveillance by participating in politics.

Hypothesis

Taken as a whole, Foucault and his followers offer a useful framework for considering the impact of perceived government surveillance on political activity. First, the framework identifies political deviants as the primary targets of government surveillance. Second, the perspective offers two possible reactions to this surveillance, docility or political resistance. Third, by focusing on the structure of the surveillance environment, the framework is particularly helpful identifying the conditions under which these two potential reactions most likely occur. Docility occurs most often when the surveillance system isolates individuals from each other, as well as blinds individuals from surveillance and those conducting the surveillance. Political resistance occurs most often when individuals are aware of surveillance, can watch their watcher, and can communicate horizontally with others. Therefore, given the Internet's structure, I expect that for those who disagree with dominant political opinion, perceptions that the government monitors citizens' Internet activity should result in higher levels of Internet political activity. Also, because they are not the focus of government surveillance, the political activity levels of citizens who agree with dominant opinion should not be affected by perceived surveillance. The remainder of the chapter tests these hypotheses about online political activity and Internet surveillance, considers whether online surveillance influences conventional offline political activity, and discusses the implications of the results.

Data

As part of a larger project, the Center for Survey Research Analysis (CSRA) at the University of Connecticut generated a probabilistic telephone sample of U.S. Internet users commencing in April 2003. The timing of the interviews, begun after U.S. military forces took control of Tikrit and the Pentagon declared an end to the major fighting, allows for evaluations of political behavior during the diplomatic phase and offensive period of the Iraq War.

Measurement

One of the dramatic findings from studies of the FBI's Cointelpro period was that most of the content in the FBI's files pertained to nonviolent, conventional, political activity (Donner, 1980).[6] Given this past focus on conventional political activity, I sought to measure similar Internet activity over the past 12 months with affirmative answers to the following questions: Have you used the Internet to contact an elected representative, government official, or candidate for office to express your opinion about a local, national, or international issue [19.0% of Internet users]? Have you contributed money to a political party, candidate, organization, or some other political cause over the Internet? [3.2%] Have you signed an Internet petition about a local, national, or international issue [13.7%]? Have you used the Internet to look for information about a local, national, or international issue? [34.1%] Have you used the Internet to try to persuade another person about your view on a local, national, or international issue [12.7%]? This sample of Internet political acts is summed to produce a scale of overall online political participation [alpha = .67].

To test the hypotheses, two key explanatory variables need measurement, perceived government Internet surveillance and support for the war in Iraq. Government Internet surveillance is measured by assessing whether respondents strongly disagree, disagree, neither agree nor disagree, agree, or strongly agree with the following statement, "The government monitors citizens' electronic mail and web surfing." Nearly 52% of Internet users agree or strongly agree with this statement. Support for the war in Iraq is measured by answers to the following question, "Would you say that you oppose or support the war in Iraq? [probe strongly or somewhat]" This indicator of support or opposition to the war in Iraq most directly identifies political deviants. Blanchard (2002), outlining the administration's expectations of citizens during an international crisis, suggests that responsible citizens do not dissent; and most do not, as 71% of the sample indicate support for the war in Iraq. Moreover, because the new electronic surveillance capacities of the federal government focus on terrorism, and the war in Iraq was packaged as part of the war on terrorism, I expect that those unsupportive of the war effort would become sensitive to this potential gaze.

I also sought to measure the customary explanatory factors theorized to influence political participation in general (Verba, Schlozman, & Brady, 1995) as well as medium specific explanations of Internet political activity (Best & Krueger, 2005). I measure respondent's level of interest in politics using an 11-point scale anchored by 0 (a total lack of interest) and 10 (a great deal of interest). The number of hours reported free from work, home, and school responsibilities measures respondents' free time. To measure civic skills I create a scale giving one point for every activity engaged in the last 12 months as part of their job, church, or other organization. The activities include: writing a letter, took part in making a group decision at a meeting, planning or chairing a meeting, and giving a presentation or speech [alpha = .78].

The effective use of the Internet requires technical sophistication. Online skills should help an individual overcome the technical hurdles associated with navigating the Internet, just as civic skills help individuals act in a complex social and political world (e.g., Krueger, 2002). To create the online skills scale I sum four items: designed a Web page, sent an attachment via e-mail, posted a file to the Internet, and downloaded a program from the Internet [alpha = .75]. I also include an Internet specific physical resource. A broadband connection may enhance the likelihood of engaging in a variety of online activities (e.g., Grubesic & Murray, 2002). To measure this physical resource, I create a broadband dummy variable.

Finally, I use a two-step procedure to measure mobilization. Individuals initially respond to the question, "Did anyone from a political party, campaign, or political organization contact you over the Internet about a local, national, or international issue?" Those answering affirmatively receive a follow-up question, "Prior to being contacted, did you ever provide the political party, candidate for public office, or political interest group your e-mail address"? Those contacted without providing their contacting information are scored 1, while all others are scored 0.

Methods

I estimate an ordered probit model of the online participation scale using government Internet surveillance and support for the war in Iraq, as well as an interaction term of these two variables. A statistically significant interaction term would suggest that support for the Iraq war moderates the effect of government Internet surveillance. The model also includes controls for political interest, mobilization, civic resources, Internet resources, and demographics.[7] After estimating the model, I calculate the change in the probability of participating in three or more political acts[8] caused by moving from a variable's minimum to maximum value while keeping all other variables set to their mean (or zero category for dichotomous variables). This technique allows for effective comparisons of magnitude across explanatory variables. Finally, to protect against spurious findings resulting from specification and estimation, I re-run the analysis using alternate models.

Results

Table 1, column 1 displays the results from the ordered probit model of online political activity. The pattern of coefficients conforms to past studies of political participation on the Internet. Political interest, resources, mobilization, and socioeconomic factors all significantly predict the likelihood of online political activity. Even age's negative coefficient, suggesting that younger individuals are more likely to act politically online, parallels previous online participation models (e.g., Krueger, 2002). Crucially, to test the hypotheses, the interaction term needs examination. The statistically significant interaction term (War Support * Surveillance) suggests that individuals' level of support for the war moderates perceived surveillance's influence on the probability of participating in politics via the Internet.

Figure 1 graphically represents the pattern of moderation. For those who strongly oppose the war, I calculate the predicted probabilities of engaging in high levels of online political activity by the level of imagined government surveillance. Of those who strongly oppose the war, those who most agree that the government monitors citizens' Internet activity possess the highest likelihood of engaging in online political activity. Everything else equal, those who strongly oppose the war and strongly feel the government does not monitor citizens' online activity posses a 4.7% chance of engaging in three or more online political acts, whereas those who strongly oppose the war and strongly feel the government monitors citizens' Internet activity possess a 19.4% chance. For those who strongly support the war, I also calculate the predicted probabilities of engaging in high levels of online political activity by the level of imagined government surveillance. Everything else equal, those who strongly support the war and strongly feel that the government does not monitor citizens possess a 7.1% chance of engaging in three or more online acts. Those strong

Table 1. Models of online political participation

	Model 1	Model 2	Model 3
Age	-.010 ** (.004)	-.009 ** (.004)	-.011 ** (.005)
Gender (male)	-.077 (.112)	-.053 (.113)	-.296 ** (.143)
Race (white)	.538 *** (.164)	.542 *** (.162)	.297 (.227)
Education	.325 *** (.067)	.323 *** (.068)	.182 ** (.088)
Income	.033 (.050)	.029 (.050)	-.009 (.058)
Mobilization	.596 *** (.152)	.587 *** (.155)	.563 *** (.214)
Political Interest	.190 *** (.029)	.204 *** (.031)	.229 *** (.077)
Free-time	.028 (.017)	.031 * (.017)	.005 (.037)
Civic Skills	.066 * (.036)	.059 (.037)	.143 (.116)
Internet Skills	.266 *** (.048)	.274 *** (.047)	.296 *** (.099)
Broadband	.226 * (.116)	.234 ** (.119)	.216 (.140)
Surveillance	.278 ** (.116)	.208 * (.111)	1.021 *** (.387)
War Support	.125 (.104)	.107 (.100)	.921 *** (.355)
Surveillance*War	-.069 *** (.027)	-.055 ** (.026)	-.302 *** (.097)
Trust Internet		.044 (.045)	
Ideology		-.084 (.057)	
Trust Government		-.051 (.078)	
Pseudo R-Square	.350	.357	N/A
Chi-Square	199.84 ***	221.70 ***	N/A
N	580	572	573

continued on following page

Table 1. continued

> Note on Table 1:
>
> *Significant at p < .10, two-tailed test; ** Significant at p < .05, two-tailed test;*
>
> **** Significant at p < .01, two-tailed test.*
>
> *Model 1: Baseline Ordered Probit; Model 2: Inclusion of "Third" Variables;*
>
> *Model 3: Instrumental Variable Model.*

Figure 1. War support's moderating effect on surveillance (online political participation)

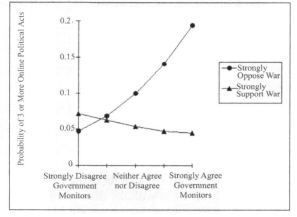

war supporters who strongly feel that the government monitors citizens engage in high levels of online political activity at marginally lower rates (4.5% likelihood).[9] Taken together, these results tend to confirm the hypotheses regarding the influence of surveillance on individual online political activity.

To comprehend the relative importance of surveillance for online political participation requires comparison to other predictors of online participation. Table 2 displays the changes in the probability of participating in three or more online political acts caused by moving from each statistically significant variable's minimum to maximum value. Considering only the control variables, political interest (.213 change), Internet skills (.198 change), and mobilization (.108 change) rank as the three most powerful predictors of online activity. Five variables exert less influence (≤.100 change), while three other variables' coefficients cannot be differentiated confidently from zero. These results suggest that for political deviants the magnitude of the relationship between surveillance and online political participation (.147 change) compares favorably to the most powerful predictors of online participation.[10]

Although these results seem clear, I also consider some potential criticisms. The classic "third variable" problem may threaten this analysis. Some might argue that

Table 2. Change in predicted probabilities of engaging in three or more online political acts

	Minimum to Maximum
Political Interest	.213
Internet Skills	.198
Surveillance*	.147
Mobilization	.108
Education	.100
Age	-.073
Race	.055
Broadband	.036
Civic Skills	.032

Note on Table 2:

*Change in probability for those who strongly oppose war. For all those who oppose war, the change in probability equals .117.

the interaction term simply represents some other variable that is missing from the model that also independently covaries with the dependent variable. Although the baseline model does include most of the major previously demonstrated explanations of participation, and the threats posed by excluded variables never can be removed fully from multivariate models, three such "third variables" seem particularly compelling in this context. First, the interaction term may simply capture some underlying dimension of trust in the Internet. Second, the interaction term may simply capture an underlying dimension of trust in the government. And finally, the interaction term may simply represent those most ideologically opposed to the current regime.[11] If these third variables are responsible for the results, then presumably the magnitude and significance of the interaction term would disappear if I include more direct indicators of these three concepts in the model. To test this supposition, I respecify the model including an indicator of trust in Internet users, trust in government, and an ideology measure.[12] The fourth column of Table 1 reports the results from this model. None of the new variables' coefficients can be distinguished from zero. More importantly, the interaction term remains significant, of the correct sign, and of the same general magnitude.

Finally, these results may confuse cause with effect. Just as participating in politics may increase political interest or civic skills, participation also could increase perceptions of surveillance among those opposed to the regime's policies. To account for this potential endogeneity and purge any reciprocal effects from the estimates,

I use an instrumental variable model. In the first stage models, estimates for each potentially endogenous variable (Freetime, Civic Skills, Internet Skills, Political Interest, Surveillance, War Support, and Surveillance*War) are obtained using instruments that are correlated with the endogenous variables but not with the second stage model's error. The fifth column of Table 1 reports the second stage estimates.[13] Again, the results do not differ markedly in terms of substance or significance.

The Offline Implications of Online Surveillance

The above results clearly suggest that perceiving that the government monitors citizens' Internet activity encourages those opposed to the Bush Administration to resist the normalizing forces of government surveillance by participating online. The theoretical framework suggests that the ability to monitor the government's actions online and horizontally communicate online with others who may hold nonconforming perspectives helps individuals resist political quiescence. Although individuals may monitor the government and communicate with others on the Internet, there is little reason to expect that their higher levels of political activity would be restricted to the Internet. In other words, applying the framework to the offline world of politics suggests that those who oppose the administration's policies and perceive the government monitors ordinary citizens' Internet activity would also engage in offline politics at higher rates compared to those opposed to the administration but do not perceive government monitoring.

To test the proposition that online surveillance may stimulate offline political activity, the same independent variables and model specifications are used to predict parallel forms of offline political activity.[14] The following questions are combined in an index to comprise the new dependent variable (offline political participation): Have you personally gone to see, made a phone call to, or sent a postal letter to an elected representative, government official, or candidate for office to express your opinion about a local, national, or international issue [20.4% of Internet users]? Have you contributed money to a political party, candidate, organization, or some other political cause over the telephone, by postal mail, or in person? [21.2%] Have you signed a written petition about a local, national, or international issue [20.8%]? Have you telephoned, written a postal mail letter, or spoken with someone in an effort to persuade that person about your view on a local, national, or international issue [16.2%]? This sample of offline political acts is summed to produce a scale of overall offline political participation [alpha = .63].

Table 3, column 1 displays the results from the ordered probit model of offline political activity. The pattern of coefficients conforms to past studies of political participation. Just as in the online model, political interest and civic skills predict the likelihood of offline political activity. Whereas Internet skills predicts online political activity, consistent with past studies comparing online and offline participa-

Table 3. Models of online political participation

	Model 1	Model 2	Model 3
Age	.019 *** (.004)	.018 *** (.004)	.009 * (.005)
Gender (male)	.054 (.118)	.031 (.117)	-.141 (.161)
Race (white)	.264 (.171)	.317 * (.177)	.136 (.206)
Education	.041 (.073)	.067 (.071)	.003 (.090)
Income	.067 (.046)	.079 * (.047)	.036 (.051)
Mobilization	.085 (.189)	.094 (.192)	.222 (.219)
Political Interest	.177 *** (.029)	.173 (.029)	.269 *** (.084)
Free-time	-.006 (.018)	-.003 (.108)	-.021 (.039)
Civic Skills	.122 *** (.041)	.122 *** (.041)	.160 (.114)
Internet Skills	.020 (.047)	.018 (.048)	-.013 (.089)
Broadband	.039 (.120)	.046 (.125)	.108 (.145)
Surveillance	.169 (.105)	.174 (.109)	.696 * (.367)
War Support	.077 (.096)	.030 (.097)	.761 ** (.357)
Surveillance*War	-.049 ** (.025)	-.049 * (.026)	-.247 *** (.095)
Trust Internet		-.024 (.046)	
Ideology		.131 ** (.058)	
Trust Government		-.041 (.117)	
Pseudo R-Square	.259	.273	n/a
Chi-Square	106.60	119.01	n/a
N	580	573	573

continued on following page

Table 3. continued

Note on Table 3:
Significant at p < .10, two-tailed test; ** Significant at p < .05, two-tailed test; *** Significant at p < .01, two-tailed test.
Model 1: Baseline Ordered Probit; Model 2: Inclusion of "Third" Variables; Model 3: Instrumental Variable Model.

tion, Internet skills fails to predict offline participation. Similarly, consistent with past research, age negatively predicts online political participation but positively predicts offline participation (e.g., Best & Krueger, 2005).

To test the hypothesis that perceived online surveillance stimulates offline political activity for those opposed to the regime, the interaction term needs examination. The statistically significant interaction term (War Support * Surveillance) suggests that individuals' level of support for the war moderates perceived surveillance's influence on the probability of participating in offline politics. This interaction term retains the same sign and general significance in the alternative model that includes additional independent variables (Table 3, column 2). Finally, in the instrumental variable model (Table 3 column 3), the interaction term continues to be confidently distinguishable from zero and again displays a negative coefficient.[15] Because the magnitude and significance of the interaction term remains stable across these various specifications and estimation procedures, the relationship between perceived government online surveillance and offline political participation appears robust.

Figure 2 graphically displays how support for the Iraq War moderates the relationship between online surveillance and offline participation. For those who strongly oppose the war, I calculate the predicted probabilities of engaging in high levels of offline political activity by the level of imagined government surveillance. Of those who strongly oppose the war, those who most agree that the government monitors citizens' Internet activity possess the highest likelihood of engaging in online political activity. Everything else equal, those who strongly oppose the war and strongly feel the government monitors citizens' online activity posses a 19.1 % chance of engaging in three or more offline political acts, whereas those who strongly oppose the war and strongly feel the government does not monitor citizens' Internet activity possess a 8.6% chance. I also calculate the predicted probabilities of engaging in high levels of offline political activity by the level of perceived government surveillance for those who strongly support the war. Everything else equal, those who strongly support the war and strongly feel that the government monitors citizens possess a 4.2% chance of engaging in three or more offline political acts. Those strong war supporters who strongly feel that the government does not monitor citizens engage in high levels of offline political activity at marginally higher rates (7.3% likelihood). Taken together, these results confirm the secondary hypothesis regarding the impact of surveillance on individual offline political activity.

Figure 2. War support's moderating effect on surveillance (off-line political participation)

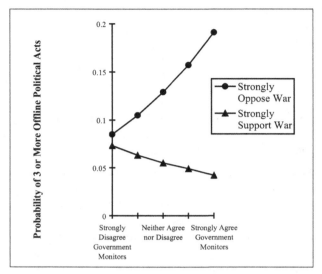

Finally, to understand the relative importance of online surveillance for offline political participation requires comparison to other predictors of online participation. Table 4 displays the changes in the probability of participating in three or more offline political acts caused by moving from each statistically significant variable's minimum to maximum value.[16] Age (.242 change) and political interest (.213 change) clearly rank as the two most powerful predictors of offline activity. Five additional variables also influence the likelihood of offline political activity, with perceived surveillance exerting the greatest impact of these additional variables (.106). These results suggest that for political deviants the magnitude of the relationship between surveillance and offline political participation (.106 change) does not quite approach the most powerful predictors of offline political participation, but does compare favorably to many longstanding predictors of participation such as civic skills, income, and race.

Discussion

Although political participation scholars typically assume an unproblematic surveillance context for ordinary citizens, the results from this analysis suggest that this assumption may be unwarranted in the contemporary technological and political environment. Over 50% of U.S. Internet users feel the government monitors ordinary citizens' Internet activity. More importantly, the results from this analysis suggest that the surveillance context influences online and offline political participation; and, the magnitude of this influence rivals other longstanding explanatory factors. To be sure, this evidence does little to diminish the importance of classic predictors of participation such as mobilization, resources, psychological engagement, and socioeconomic factors. Even so, if the determination of the relative importance of explanatory factors is the primary goal of the empirical study of political participation, then these initial analyses make clear that the surveillance context deserves serious consideration.

The specific nature of the relationship between governmental Internet surveillance and online political participation has implications for the ongoing debate about whether the Internet and associated technologies will become a means of social control or citizen empowerment (e.g., Lim, 2002; Lowi, 1975; Staples, 1997). While individuals do perceive that the government uses the Internet to monitor citizens, this gaze does not attenuate politically unorthodox individual's participation. Instead, it seems that the structure of the Internet promotes political resistance, at least within the context considered in this analysis. Those most out of step with dominant opinion, who also feel that the government monitors citizens' Internet activity, participate in politics both online and offline at the highest rates. The Internet appears to be an unwieldy instrument of social control.

These results underscore the utility of the Foucauldian imagery for understanding individual political behavior and parallels research from other disciplines such as sociology, health, education, and labor studies that routinely use this theoretical

Table 4. Change in predicted probabilities of engaging in three or more off-line political acts

	Minimum to Maximum
Age	.242
Political Interest	.212
Surveillance*	.106
Civic Skills	.070
Ideology	.068
Income	.045
Race (white)	.039

Note on Table 4:

*Change in probability for those who strongly oppose war. For all those who oppose war, the change in probability equals .089.

lens to comprehend individual behavior (e.g., Button, Mason, & Sharrock, 2003; Gastaldo & Holmes, 1999; May, 1999; Troman, 1997). Yet, to date no empirical studies of political participation rely on these insights. Of course, the results from this one analysis should not be overgeneralized. Future efforts to assess the impact of surveillance on individual political behavior should consider if and how perceived surveillance influences behavior in other contexts. Do individuals react to surveillance similarly outside of a war setting? To what extent do individuals actively resist surveillance by employing avoidance tactics such as using code words within or encrypting electronic mail messages? And, do individuals perceive the government monitors all types of Internet activity, or only those focused on issues related to terrorism or political dissent?

Finally, the overwhelming Congressional re-authorization of the Patriot Act in early 2006 and the recent revelations that the Bush Administration has monitored and continues to monitor citizens Internet activity suggests that increased government surveillance should not be seen as a temporary reaction to 9/11, but rather a durable part of the early 21st century. Clearly, more work is needed to link major longstanding theories concerned with surveillance and privacy (such as Liberalism and Postmodernism) with the specific nature of the contemporary environment so that scholars can better comprehend the empirical participatory implications of government surveillance in societies that rely heavily on citizen political engagement for the health of the polity.

References

Bartels, L. (1991). Instrumental and quasi-instrumental variables. *American Journal of Political Science, 35*, 777-800.

Berkowitz, R. (2002). Packet sniffers and privacy: Why the no-suspicion-required standard in the USA Patriot Act is unconstitutional. *Computer Law Review and Technology Journal, 7*, 1-21.

Best, S., & Krueger, B. (2005). Analyzing the representativeness of Internet political participation. *Political Behavior, 27*, 183-216.

Blanchard, M. (2002). Why can't we ever learn: Cycles of stability, stress, and freedom of expression in United States history. *Communication Law and Policy, 7*, 347-378.

Boyne, R. (2000). Post-panopticism. *Economy and Society, 29*, 285-307.

Button, G., Mason, D., & Sharrock, W. (2003). Disempowerment and resistance in the print industry? Reactions to surveillance–capable technology. *New Technology, Work and Employment, 18*, 50-61.

Center for Survey Research & Analysis (CRSA). (2003). *Data obtained from the survey center at the University of Connecticut.*

Churchill, W., & Vander Wall, J. (1990). *Agents of repression.* Boston: South End Press.

Couper, M., Singer, E., & Kulka, R. (1998). Participation in the 1990 decennial census: Politics, privacy, pressures. *American Politics Quarterly, 26,* 59-80.

Cunningham, D. (2004). *There's something happening here: The new left, the klan, and FBI counterintelligence.* Berkeley: University of California Press.

Digeser, P. (1992). The fourth face of power. *The Journal of Politics, 54,* 977-1007.

Donner, F. (1980). *The age of surveillance.* New York: Knopf.

Dumm, T. (1996). *Michael Foucault and the politics of freedom.* Thousand Oaks, CA: Sage.

Fleischer, A. (2001). *Press briefing by Ari Fleischer on September 26.* Transcript retrieved from http://www.whitehouse.gov/news/releases/2001/09/20010926-5.html

Foucault, M. (1978). *The history of sexuality.* New York: Pantheon Books.

Foucault, M. (1979). *Discipline and punish: The birth of the prison.* New York: Vintage.

Foucault, M. (1980). *Power/knowledge.* New York: Pantheon Books.

Foucault, M. (1982). The subject and power. In H. Dreyfus & P. Rabinow (Eds.), *Michel Foucault: Beyond structuralism and hermeneutics.* Chicago: University of Chicago Press.

Foucault, M. (1988). *Truth, power, self.* In L. Martin, H. Gutman, & P. Hutton (Eds.), *Technologies of the self: A seminar with Michel Foucault.* London: Tavistock.

Gastaldo, D., & Holmes, D. (1999). Foucault and nursing: A history of the present. *Nursing Inquiry, 6,* 231-240.

Gordon, N. (2002). On visibility and power: An Arendtian corrective of Foucault. *Human Studies, 25,* 125-145.

Gould, J. (2002). Playing with fire: The civil liberties implications of September 11. *Public Administration Review, 62,* 74-79.

Grant, J. (2003, April 11). Uncle Sam over my shoulder. *The Chronicle of Higher Education,* B9-B10.

Green, S. (1999). A plague on the panopticon: Surveillance and power in the global information economy. *Information, Communication & Society, 2,* 26-44.

Grubesic, T., & Murray, A. (2002). Constructing the divide: Spatial disparities in broadband access. *Chapters in Regional Science, 81,* 197-221.

Key, V.O. (1949). *Southern politics in state and nation.* New York: Knopf.

Krueger, B. (2002). Assessing the potential of Internet political participation in the United States: A resource approach. *American Politics Research, 30,* 476-498.

Kulynych, J. (1997). Performing politics: Foucault, Habermas and postmodern participation. *Polity, 30,* 315-346.

Lau, R., & Pomper, G. (2002). Effectiveness of negative campaigning in U.S. Senate elections. *American Journal of Political Science, 46,* 47-67.

Lichtblau, E. (2005, July 18). Large Volume of FBI Files Alarms US Activist Groups. *New York Times.* p. A12.

Lim, M. (2002). Cyber-civic space in Indonesia: From panopticon to pandemonium? *International Development and Planning Review, 24,* 383-400.

Lowi, T. (1975). The third revolution, politics, and the prospect for an open society. *IEEE Transactions on Communications, 23,* 1019-1027.

Lyon, D. (2001). Surveillance after September 11. *Sociological Research Online, 6,* 1-27.

May, T. (1999). From banana time to just-in-time: Power and resistance at work. *Sociology, 33,* 767-783.

Marx, G. (1988). *Undercover: Police surveillance in America.* Berkeley: University of California Press.

Marx, G. (2003). A tack in the shoe: Neutralizing and resisting the new surveillance. *Journal of Social Issues, 59,* 369-390.

Milbrath, L. (1965). *Political participation.* Chicago: Rand McNally.

Mill, J.S. (1991). *On liberty and other essays.* Oxford University Press.

Miller, W., & Shanks, J. M. (1996). *The New American Voter.* Cambridge, MA: Harvard University Press.

Munro, I. (2000). Non-disciplinary power and the network society. *Organization, 7,* 679-695.

Nehf, J. (2003). Recognizing the societal value in information privacy. *Washington Law Review, 78:* 1-92.

Nelson, L. (2002). Protecting the common good: Technology, objectivity, and privacy. *Public Administration Review, 62,* 69-73.

Pateman, C. (1970). *Participation and democratic theory.* Cambridge University Press.

Pickett, B. (1996). Foucault and politics of resistance. *Polity, 28,* 445-466.

Pikowsky, R. (2002). An overview of the law of electronic surveillance post September 11, 2001. *Law Library Journal, 94,* 601-620.

Radcliff, B. (1994). Turnout and the Democratic vote. *American Politics Quarterly, 22*, 259-76.

Risen, J. and Lichtblau, E. (2005, December 16). Bush Lets U.S. Spy on Callers Without Courts. *New York Times*. p. A1.

Rogin, M. (1987). *Ronald Reagan, the movie*. Berkeley: University of California Press.

Rosenstone, S., & Hanson, J. (1993). *Mobilization, participation and democracy in America*. New York: Macmillan.

Salisbury, R. (1975). Research on political participation. *American Journal of Political Science, 19*, 323-41.

Schwartz, P. (1999). Privacy and democracy in cyberspace. *Vanderbilt Law Review, 52*, 1609-1701.

Shehadeh, M. (2002, December 3). The latest new "war on terrorism." *CounterPunch*. Retrieved from http://www.counterpunch.org/shehadeh1203.html.

Singer, E., Mathiowetz, N., & Couper, M. (1993). The impact of privacy and confidentiality concerns on survey participation. *Public Opinion Quarterly, 57*, 465-482.

Solove, D. (2004). Reconstructing electronic surveillance law. *George Washington Law Review, 72*, 1264-1305.

Staples, W. (1997). *The culture of surveillance: Discipline and social control in the United States*. New York: St. Martins Press.

Troman, G. (1997). Self management and school inspection. *Oxford Review of Education, 23*, 345-365.

Troyer, L. (2003). Counterterrorism: Sovereignty, law, subjectivity. *Critical Asian Studies, 35*, 259-276.

Vavreck, L., Spiliotes, C., & Fowler, L. (2002). The effects of retail politics in the New Hampshire primary. *American Journal of Political Science, 46*, 595-611.

Verba, S., & Nie, N. (1972). *Participation in America: Political democracy and social equality*. New York: Harper.

Verba, S., Schlozman, K.L., & Brady, B. (1995). *Voice and equality*. Cambridge, MA: Harvard University Press.

Warren, S., & Brandeis, L. (1890). The right to privacy [the implicit made explicit]. In F.D. Schoeman (Ed.), *Philosophical dimensions of privacy: An anthology*. Cambridge University Press.

Westin, A. (1967). *Privacy and freedom*. New York: Antheneum.

Westin, A. (2003). Social and political dimensions of privacy. *Journal of Social Issues, 59*, 431-453.

Williams, P. (2003). Loose lips and other ships. *The Nation, 276*, 10.

Endnotes

[1] Although Westin is not concerned only with state Internet surveillance, Lyon (2001) reminds us that particularly after September 11, the state also can exploit the surveillance capacity of various commercial networks and databases when needed (e.g., the surveillance assemblage).

[2] A potential criticism of the use of Foucault in this context needs consideration. Some may suggest that using Foucault to develop empirical hypotheses runs counter to his "post-structuralist" imagery. Yet, it is not the methods of science as a way of knowing that bothers Foucault, but instead the privileged position of science that excludes nonscientific ways of knowing and claims neutrality. Methods and theories (even science or Marxism) can be used, as a toolkit, if they are useful in a particular context (1980). Foucault does not "esteem the virtues of direct cognition and base their [his] practice upon an immediate experience that escapes encapsulation in knowledge. It is not that which we are concerned. We are concerned, rather, with the insurrection of knowledges that are opposed primarily not to the contents, methods or concepts of science, but to the effects of the centralizing powers which are linked to the institution and functioning of an organized scientific discourse" (1980, p. 84).

[3] The liberal tradition offers a competing framework for understanding the influence of surveillance on political participation. Liberal theorists, from John Stuart Mill (1991), to Samuel Warren and Louis Brandeis (1890), to Alan Westin (1967) all note the lack of privacy's chilling effect on free expression. Using this framework, Paul Schwartz directly argues that in the absence of electronic privacy, "Americans will hesitate to engage in cyberspace activities—including those that are most likely to promote democratic self rule" (1999, p. 1650).

[4] Importantly, political deviants rank as one of the first groups of abnormal individuals monitored by the state (Foucault, 1979, p. 215). Less well known is that Foucault cites the imprisonment of Tunisian political dissidents as one of two major impetuses for his writing Discipline and Punish (1988).

[5] Stephen Green discusses the use of new information technologies to watch the state, "The profound decentralization of new-gathering, its informality at point of production and the global audiences that can be assessed, all dramatically reshape notions of power and protest. The video—and television—camera have proved dynamic as a catalyst for social change—used in televising state violence in Eastern Europe, in capturing human rights offences on film or to immortalize brutality against animals, these 'electronic eyes' offer a new perspective on the discourse of surveillance and power. Relations are reversed and the public becomes the informed audience, while authority suffers the

inspecting gaze…[and this] information (the product of others' surveillance) is available en masse online" (1999, pp. 38-39).

[6]   Donner explains how the FBI made a credible threat of domestic subversion from ordinary political activity, "[t]he sheer accumulation of items—a signature on a peace petition, presence at a demonstration, receipt of left-wing literature, a speech at a conference on police brutality—each innocuous in itself, invites the inference that the subject is subversive" (1980, p. 171).

[7]   These demographic variables include: age, gender, race, education, and income. I measure age with an interval level variable, gender with a dummy variable (male=1), race with a dummy variable (white=1), education with a 4-point variable ranging from "less than high school" to "college graduate," and income with a 5-point variable ($25,000 increments).

[8]   I chose three or more online political acts to represent a "high" level of activity because only 18.2% of Internet users engage in three or more online acts.

[9]   Because the margins of error overlap for the strongly agree the government monitors predicted probability and the strongly disagree predicted probability, surveillance does not exert a significant impact on the likelihood of political activity for strong war supporters.

[10]   As Kulynych (1997) notes, all conventional political activity cannot be considered resistance. This chapter does not argue that all online political activity, even by those opposed to the regime, should be conceived as resistance. Instead, in this nonlinear model that predicts the likelihood of participation, for those strongly opposed to the regime the amount of political activity considered resistance is best expressed as the increase in the probability of participating in online politics caused by surveillance (.147 change).

[11]   Without running the new model, a descriptive analysis of the data led me to doubt the ideology explanation. While 54.4% of those who oppose the war feel that the government monitors citizens' Internet activity, 50.0% of those who support the war also feel the government monitors citizens' activity. This wide distribution indicates that feelings about government monitoring do not simply reside among those opposed to the Bush administration.

[12]   Agreement with the following statement measures Internet trust, "Generally speaking, most people on the Internet can be trusted." Government trust is measured with the following question, "How much of the time do you think you can trust the government to do what is right?" Ideology is measured using the following question, "In politics today, do you consider yourself a liberal, moderate, or conservative [probe would that be strong or not so strong]?"

[13]   I also ran a two-stage ordered probit model that produces similar results. However, because few statistical packages include diagnostics for two-stage probit models, and others have used two-stage least squares to estimate political

participation scales (Verba, Schlozman, & Brady, 1995), I report the two-stage OLS model.

Instrumental variable models require reasonably robust first stage estimates. However, no accepted standard seems to exist regarding the level of robustness; two recent articles using an instrumental variable approach report a wide range of first stage R-squares—from .05 to .47 (Lau & Pomper, 2002; Vavreck, Spiliotes, & Fowler, 2002). The first stage models fall safely within this range (.12 to .37). Within the first stage models, the excluded instruments should contribute a large percentage to the model's R-square (Bartels, 1991). Again, no standard percentage contribution to the R-square exists, though the same recent articles report percentages between 14 and 45. In this chapter's model, the percent contributions from the excluded instruments range from 48 to 84, suggesting that the excluded instruments strongly predict the endogenous variables relative to the other independent variables.

I also assess the validity of the instruments using a Sargan exogeneity test. This tests the null hypothesis that the excluded instruments are uncorrelated with the error term in the second stage participation model. The Sargan statistic fails to achieve even a liberal level of statistical significance (p = .69); therefore the null hypotheses cannot be rejected. This suggests that the chosen instruments are exogenous and can be confidently excluded from the second stage model. The instruments are as follows: Marital status, region, home ownership, parental status, adults in residence, population density, employment status, years in the community, foreign travel, club involvement, church involvement, recreational involvement, 2000 election turnout, high school governance, high school newspaper, parental political discussion, high school computer course, high school typing course, officer in high school club, violent crime victim, television viewership, programmed a VCR, years using the Internet, use Internet from work, use Internet from home, and family members who use the Internet.

[14] The data set includes parallel offline indicators for four of the five online acts of participation. Accordingly, the offline dependent variable ranges from zero to four, whereas the online dependent variable ranges from zero to five.

[15] The robustness of the first stage estimates (R-squares from .12 to .37), the percent contribution to the first stage R-squares by the excluded instruments (48% to 84%), and the exogeneity of the excluded instruments tested by the Sargan statistic (p = .74) all reach conventional thresholds for two-stage least squares.

[16] Because the ideology variable is statistically significant, I use model 2 (Table 3, column 2) to calculate the predicted probabilities.

An earlier version of this chapter appeared in Social Science Computer Review, 23(4), pp. 439-452, copyright 2005 by Sage Publications. Reprinted by permission of Sage Publications Inc.

Chapter VII

Security, Sovereignty, and Continental Interoperability:
Canada's Elusive Balance

Jeffrey Roy, Dalhousie University, Canada

Abstract

In an era of digital government, citizen-centric governance is a central aim, one that is often predicated on more efficient and responsive service owed, in large part, to greater digital connectivity internally (i.e., to share information in new manners), as well as externally (i.e., to gather information and reach out to citizens and stakeholders). Antiterrorism efforts accentuate this focus, albeit with a very different set of aims. Governments have been quick to establish new antiterrorism and homeland security measures that create new and expanded capacities for gathering, analyzing, and sharing information, both within governments and across governments and other sectors, notably the private sector.

Introduction

In an era of digital government, citizen-centric governance is a central aim, one that is often predicated on more efficient and responsive service owed, in large part, to greater digital connectivity internally (i.e., to share information in new manners), as well as externally (i.e., to gather information and reach out to citizens and stakeholders). Antiterrorism efforts accentuate this focus, albeit with a very different set of aims. Governments have been quick to establish new antiterrorism and homeland security measures that create new and expanded capacities for gathering, analyzing, and sharing information, both within governments and across governments and other sectors, notably the private sector.

In doing so, tensions have arisen with respect to both the appropriate scope of governmental action, as well as the proper mix of secrecy and transparency within a security apparatus operating under a unique and delicate balance between autonomy and accountability. Such tensions also extend beyond borders. In Canada, for example, not only is there a set of debates and concerns about public sector action within the county that closely resembles that of the United States, but there is growing awareness about technological and political interdependence on a continental scale. As a result, North American governance faces new and rising pressures to adapt to a post-9/11 nexus of security, technology, and democracy that carries implications for governance both within and across national borders.

Following this introduction, the second section examines the evolving nexus between homeland security efforts and digital infrastructure, as well as the central themes of information management and identity. The Canadian security response to 9/11 is then reviewed in the next section, drawing parallels and pressures for convergence between Canada and the United States. Then the fourth section further explores quandaries of continental governance from the Canadian perspective, and followed by an examination of two specific illustrations of such quandaries: the plight of Maher Arar tied to bilateral information sharing, and proposed new ID requirements for border crossings. The final section offers a brief conclusion.

Antiterrorism's Digital Infrastructure

Although there are many dimensions and meanings of "security," we invoke the term here with respect to two, partially distinct areas. First, cyber-security and online reliability represent important foundational platforms necessary to underpin the sustained expansion of e-commerce, e-government, and all forms of online activity. Secondly, homeland or domestic security strategies devised to both respond to and proactively thwart criminal and terrorist threats are based upon information management capacities and a widening digital infrastructure in order to plan, coordinate, and conduct action. Our focus is very much on the latter, albeit with recognition of the close ties between both dimensions.

September 11, 2001, marks a critical turning point. Prior to then, digital security could arguably have been presented as primarily an extension of e-commerce and e-government in terms of technologically enabled service delivery. Indeed, security remains central as companies and governments devote considerable attention to encryption, information management systems, and related elements that underpin online transactions (Holden, 2004). The overarching aim is to design technical systems and organizational channels to bolster confidence among Internet users while spoiling the intentions of would-be commercial criminals or thrill seeking hackers (Clifford, 2004; Joshi, Ghafoor, & Aref, 2002; Nugent & Raisinghani, 2002). The details of such efforts often remained shielded from widespread political and consumer debate: for most observers and users of digital systems, technical intricacies remained hidden (Bryant & College, 2002; Demchak, 1999). What mattered were outcomes for users such as convenience or cost (Hart-Teeter, 2003; Ronchi 2003).

Since 9/11 the mindset of many governments has shifted (Barber, 2003; Brenner, 2004; Waugh, 2003). The American fixation on homeland security, for example, denotes an important new face of e-government in terms of resources and priorities (Pavlichev & Garson, 2004). Governments now seek new and expanded antiterrorism measures that are premised on new or expanded capacities for coordinated information sharing, planning, and responding on a government-wide scale (Fitzgerald, 2004; Henrich & Link, 2003; Roy, 2005a). Interoperability has become a guiding principle: often viewed in a technical or digital manner (i.e., computers, networks, and databases being able to communicate with one another), in any organizational environment the human and managerial layers to such connectedness are as complex (Allen, Juillet, Paquet, & Roy, 2001, 2005; Fountain, 2001; Gill 2004; Scholl, 2005). Moreover, interoperability across sectors (notably private industry) also becomes important (Dutta & McCrohan, 2002).

Central to this security apparatus are information flows and identities. With respect to information, the challenge is not generating more of it but rather making sense of it. An increasingly common example is data mining that, much like the term implies, involves digitally and virtually trolling through massive amounts of information gathered in raw form, and then analyzing it for meaningful patterns or events (Sirmakessis, 2004). Cyber-security and information management systems are not only crucial to gathering and processing information, but also safeguarding it against accidental or malicious threats. Such issues are now viewed through a national security lens as the potential for threats against critical infrastructure components that include information databanks, defence operations, and energy and environmental management systems that all rely increasingly on computer systems and connectivity (Denning, 2003).

For public sector security authorities expanding their digital capacities there are three sets of factors, each comprising a partially distinct set of risks, uncertainties, and controversy. The first set is the significant financial investments now flowing into an expanded digital infrastructure for information analysis, communications, research, and development, and new screening and surveillance systems. Some industry estimates point to homeland security spending levels in the United States to surpass $180 billion by 2008, including all levels of government and the private sector (an amount rivalling the total annual budget of the Government of Canada).[1]

Clearly, future spending is subject to numerous uncertainties, not the least of which being the occurrence and scale of any future terrorist attacks. Current spending levels have generally received little political opposition in the shadow of 9/11. However, such massive injections of public funds face growing questions about the extent to which managerial, accountability, and oversight capacities are sufficient for such resource injections. Therefore, the second and quite related set of factors is the size and complexity of deployment. Difficulties that plague the U.S. Department of Homeland Security are a case in point: the department has been unable to fulfil its role in effectively consolidating and coordinating the formation and usage of terrorist watch lists from its various subunits, a deficiency ascribed by officials to an insufficiently developed infrastructure for doing so.[2]

The third set of factors, the most politically contentious, is the appropriate scope of objectives and means by democratically accountable governments. Tensions in the U.S. between a traditional mindset of limited government and the post-9/11 jump in support for an expansion of state activity are thus central in shaping political debate, particularly in the spring of 2005 (when the Patriot Act underwent a Congressional review under the guise of a sunset clause). Despite some Congressional resistance and debate, the main legislative pillars of the Patriot Act remain in place.

A key issue in such an environment is concern about insufficient openness on the part of public authorities (Reid, 2004). U.S. government watchers, for instance, claim that over the past 4 years, in particular, the culture of secrecy has been reinforced at the expense of transparency and public accountability.[c] Another, related dimension to such concern that secrecy is becoming the norm in security matters—due in part to covert activity, but also the extraordinary level of complexities that permeate an increasingly ubiquitous and invisible infrastructure:

Law enforcement and intelligence services don't need to design their own surveillance systems from scratch. They only have to reach out to the companies that already track us so well, while promising better service, security, efficiency, and perhaps most of all, convenience...More than ever before, the details of our lives are no longer our own. (O'Harrow, 2005, p. 300)

Such concerns about surveillance tie information and identity (De Rosa, 2003). In order to learn anything specific about an individual or group of individuals, there must be reliable identifier, or critical enablers of digital systems (Heymann, 2002). An example is the deployment of biometric tools on passports and other forms of identification.[4] Importantly, biometric devices not only allow for national authorities to screen incoming visitors, but they also enable authorities to monitor the movements of their own citizens abroad, provided there is interoperability on a transnational scale (Su et al., 2005).[5] This pressure for more coordination across borders underscores a key challenge to traditional notions of national sovereignty and power and drives more distributed governance patterns (Bennett & Raab, 2003; Giddens, 2002; Hayden, 2005; Ougaard & Higgott, 2002; Paquet, 1997). A paradox of antiterrorism is the reassertion of national authority in an environment nonetheless dependent on transnational governance. Security, mobility, and commerce thus become co-evolving agendas cross-border relations, particularly with neighbouring countries (Ferguson & Jones, 2002; Jorgensen & Rosamond, 2002; Salter, 2004).

The Canadian Response

For Canadians, the tragic impacts of 9/11 were felt first and foremost in terms of the loss of human life, indirectly via American neighbours and more directly through the loss of 24 Canadian citizens killed. In other ways, responses to the initial attacks also underscored the closeness of the two neighbouring countries.[6]

In the days that would follow, an additional and hugely significant collateral threat to Canada took shape, albeit one economically oriented. The threat was underscored by two occurrences: first, stories circulating in the American media that at least some of the hijackers entered the U.S. by way of the Canadian—U.S. border (a theory that would prove unfounded); and secondly, the seemingly endless line of trucks extending back some 36 kilometres from the Windsor—Detroit border crossing (joining Ontario and Michigan). The first point threatened to expose Canada as a weak link in U.S. security, whereas the second image underscored the economic catastrophe that could result from being cast in this manner.[7]

Accordingly, it is difficult to overstate the sensitivity of Canadian authorities to American views and actions. According to Meyers (2003), the U.S. forged ahead with the securitization of its borders and "dragged" Canada along with it. In the aftermath of 9/11, plans that had already been underway were fast-tracked to create a "smart border" accord of some 30 points to reinforce security while facilitating mobility, a balance facilitated in large part through technological innovation, bilateral interoperability, and biometric potential.[8] The Government of Canada reinforced this focus with a major financial commitment to border security in late 2001.[9]

Within the country, the legislative centrepiece of Canada's response to 9/11 case with Bill C-36, the country's first official Anti-Terrorism Act, thereby defining terrorism legislatively for the first time and expanding the powers and means of federal authorities to combat such activities.[10] Underwriting this expansion is also an enhanced degree of secrecy in many aspects of law enforcement and legal proceedings, the focus of which has been the subject of much debate in a manner not unlike debates surrounding the USA Patriot Act (Allman & Barrette, 2004). Complementing this legal extension is wider recognition of the importance of digital security in order to underpin organizational interoperability, ensure the resilience and integrity of government information holdings, and also address the risks and realities associated with the transnational scope of terrorist activity (Brown, 2003; Preyer & Bos, 2002). In short, digital security would serve as central tenant in the war on terror (Hart-Teeter, 2004).

As in the U.S., however, the technical and organizational capacities of the Canadian government for doing so were quickly shown to be suspect, and greatly in need of overhaul (Kernaghan & Gunraj, 2004; Roy, 2005a). For instance, with respect to IT security generally across government, there is evidence of long-time neglect. In a 2002 audit of government IT security, the Auditor General reported that "little baseline information existed in the state of IT security across government." A follow up audit in 2004 described progress as "unsatisfactory."[11]

Along with these technical difficulties are challenges for better coordination across government. The Auditor General again concludes that horizontal efforts have fallen short: "gaps and deficiencies point to a requirement to strengthen the management framework of issues that cross agency boundaries, such as information systems, watch lists, and personnel screening" (Auditor General of Canada, 2004, p. 39). In one effort to create an Integrated National Security Assessment Centre in 2003 to "use intelligence from many sources to produce timely analyses and assessment of threats to Canada", the difficulties of establishing a collaborative mechanism overrode the importance of its role (ibid.). In a separate study, the Senate Standing Committee of National Security and Defence reported similar findings—quoting one assessment of what is required—namely, "an unprecedented level of cooperation inside and outside of government" (Standing Senate Committee, 2004, p.14).[12]

A holistic response to such problems came in 2004 via Canada's first ever National Security Policy that featured a more integrated framework: antiterrorism, policing, border control, and cyber-security are the purview of a single Minister.[13] The U.S. Department of Homeland Security served as inspiration for Canada's Department of Public Safety and Emergency Preparedness Canada (PSEPC):

(PSEPC) was created to secure the safety of Canadians while maintaining the benefits of an open society. It integrates under one minister the core activities of the previous

Department of the Solicitor General, the Office of Critical Infrastructure Protection and Emergency Preparedness and the National Crime Prevention Center.[14]

Cyber-security and informational strategies have been greatly bolstered: indicative of new approaches is the Advance Passenger Information/Passenger Name Record (API/PNR) program is designed "to protect Canadians by helping to identify high-risk, would-be travellers:

The Canada Border Services Agency (CBSA) is authorized to collect and retain information on travellers and to keep it for customs purposes under section 107.1 of the Customs Act. API is basic data that identifies a traveller and is collected at the time of check-in.[15]

While the Canadian government points to 9/11 as reason enough for such measures, four important concerns have been presented by critics. They are: (1) infringement on the privacy rights of Canadians; (2) the secrecy surrounding government operations managing such initiatives (and by extension the related information sources); (3) the potential for "function creep" where information gathered by one part of government for one purpose (in this case antiterrorism) invariably finds its way into other processes tied to other purposes; and (4) the possibility for errors or mishaps due to mismanagement of information and identities in particular.

The interplay of these four sets of concerns has shaped much of the debate. For example, although the first point is partially mitigated by a variety of legislative safeguards addressing privacy concerns, as well as the independent Privacy Commissioner (reporting to Parliament rather than the Government), these same Commissioners are often among the most active critics of government action, underscoring problems associated with secrecy, function creep, and identity management (Loukidelis, 2004).[16] The potential for error and mismanagement within the security apparatus is also a prevalent theme of the most recent Auditor General findings (Auditor General of Canada, 2005a, 2005b).

Continental Interoperability
and Governance Quandaries

Security concerns now predominantly shape relations between Canada and the U.S. (as well as those between U.S. and Mexico[17]). Moreover, the pursuit of this common security agenda is increasingly informational and digital and a level of interoperability between authorities must be achieved in order to facilitate a collective sense of confidence in one another, and a basis for joint action. From the Canadian perspective, historical concerns about U.S. dependency (and dominance) remain a major political issue and as a result, interoperability is a term often interchanged with integration in political debate.

For some, wider collaboration therefore requires a continental "community" that embraces many shared interests while respecting national differences and independence (Pastor, 2001, 2004). Pastor's efforts underpin the trilateral vision endorsed by prominent representatives of Canada, the U.S., and Mexico and released by the Council of Foreign Relations (at a time chosen in part to coincide with the North American Leaders Summit in Waco, Texas, in March 2005).

The trilateral initiative is bold, albeit incrementally so, in proposing to complement more integrative security measures with a new political dialogue and shared economic investment aimed at the collective prosperity of all parts of the continent.[18] Such a vision is predicated in part on an optimistic interpretation of public opinion data that suggests sufficient support in all three countries to underpin a more unified continental ethos to complement national affiliations.

Without referring to this blueprint itself, the leaders drew from it in pledging to create a trilateral framework, the Security and Prosperity Partnership for North America. Such a commitment is consistent with the trilateral aspirations of the Mexican President who has been the most aggressive in calling for the pursuit of stronger governance ties in a manner akin to the model of Europe. The significance of the participation of Canada's Prime Minister in this joint pledge was notably tempered by commercial tensions between the two countries (in particular, lumber and beef) and the decision announced just days before the Summit that Canada would not partake in the U.S.-led initiative for ballistic missile defence. Moreover, trilateral relations involving Mexico are far less visible in Canada than bilateral coverage: Mexico and Canada are in some respects separated by a similar fixation with the U.S. from their own vantage point. While some Canadians may be open to the notion of a Mexican ally in trilateral negotiations, thereby blunting U.S. power to some degree, others take the view that such a 3rd party can only dilute progress that could otherwise be made on a bilateral basis.[19]

Yet, nowhere is the absence of a stronger basis for continentalism more apparent than in the U.S.: terrorism concerns and homeland security efforts joining an expanded and often contentious U.S. focus around the world limit the room for more politically integrative approaches to North American governance. Moreover, for many elected representatives in federal and state legislators, differences between southern and northern bilateral agendas merit incremental and distinct responses more than committing to a trilateral community. In short, there is little indication that 9/11 will play a similarly catalytic role toward continental integration as WWII did in kick-starting the construction of a more integrationist and unified European agenda. As all proponents of strengthened North American governance acknowledge, comparisons with the European Union (EU) must be sensitive to the unique time durations of each continent (and the near half century since the Treaty of Rome vs. the formation of NAFTA in 1992), the EU's ever-expanding membership that now stands at 25 (vs. 3 North American countries), and the U.S.'s unique presence not only continentally, but globally as well.

Recent evolutions in EU governance and security may be further revealing in two respects. First, early indicators suggest that the e-government project in Europe has done more to assert national level authority and visibility than any corresponding European dimension (EGovernment Observatory, 2002; Roy, 2005b). Secondly, the recent elevation of security and safety issues within the EU political agenda has exposed the absence of sufficient continental capacities for interoperability and collaboration across member states (Grabbe, 2005; Henderson, 2005; Smith, 2004). The inherent secrecy of this sector, both nationally and at the level of the EU, may very well impede stronger European efforts as public mistrust limits the willingness of countries to relinquish resources and responsibilities to this upper governance tier (Shearman & Sussex, 2004). In North American, in the absence of political institutions, it is reasonable to presume that such secrecy would be compounded.

One can expect that the U.S. model of homeland security will continue to serve as an important reference point for Canadian-U.S. relations. For the Canadian government such a path risks relying on deception or at best, something less than full candour in publicly asserting independence while privately pursuing interdependence with U.S. authorities wherever practically possible.[20] Moreover, this incremental approach to continental interoperability aligns itself rather well with the already secretive nature of domestic security within each country. The danger of such a path lies in both the expanded realm of secrecy across many aspects of public sector operations pertaining to security that will grow to include a wider set of trans-border provisions, but also that the resulting governance apparatus will become insular and unaccountable, provoking either dangerous overextensions of authority or unintended consequences from mismanagement or error.[21]

The Canadian government is not without some understanding of these pressures, particularly, widening calls for more openness and accountability in security matters. Accordingly, a new joint Parliamentary Committee is being established to for the first time in Canadian history, provide a mechanism of political review over the security community.[22] In addition, the government has created a new body, a Cross-Cultural Roundtable, as well as an external advisory board on national security.

What remains suspect, however, is the extent to which this new political forum can challenge the traditional culture of secrecy surrounding security operations. Although the new Parliamentary Committee is meant to transcend overt partisanship in Canada (with representation from all political parties in Parliament), members will be sworn to secrecy under existing legislative rules severely limiting the public release of information (in many cases rules have been strengthened under recent antiterrorism legislation). Accordingly, it is unclear the extent to which this new body will serve as a vehicle for expanding public awareness and involvement in security matters, and thus a basis for strengthened accountability. New tensions may also arise in devising workable relationship and a division of duties between the new Parliamentary Committee and other review bodies in place, particularly as all of these actors adjust and adapt to the ongoing and potential changes to the security apparatus.[23]

With respect to continental security, there is clearly no reason to expect a new Parliamentary structure to have more success in engaging American stakeholders in such a political review mechanism. The risks for Canada in this type of setting are many. First, in bilateral (and now trilateral) trilateral discussions, the negotiating power of Canadian authorities is likely to be weakened by the backdrop of a public viewed as inherently unaware, suspicious, or even hostile to most options entailing closer and more overt forms of collaborative action. Secondly, the citizenry in turn is likely to become cynical as evidence emerges (most often through errors or contentious incidents exposed in an after the fact manner) that demonstrates the pursuit of such collaboration though more backhanded channels. Thirdly, in such an environment the growing digital component to security efforts will unfold in a largely insular and hidden fashion. In the context of North American relations, this latter point is central: the consequence is that rather than engage in an open dialogue (that would in turn help facilitate a basis of public learning to guide future decisions), simplified political debates and the more complex realities of governing face a widening gap.

Illustrative of such risks is the foreign policy statement in Canada released in April 2005. At one time billed as an important rethinking of Canada's role in the world (and within it, the continent), the initiative became tightly managed by the government of the day, sensitive to its minority status in Parliament and ongoing bilateral sensitivities with the U.S. Accordingly, the statement reinforces the familiar rhetoric of close bilateral collaboration with a safeguarding of distinct national interests and outlooks. Although there acknowledgement of plans to "strengthen coordination of cross-border law enforcement and counterterrorism programs," there is little discussion of either the political or digital mechanisms that are envisioned for doing so. Moreover, the lack of public consultation and the absence of any formal political discussion upon its release (along with ongoing coverage of a widening corruption scandal) ensure a minimal impact, reinforcing present contours of secrecy (and by extension for many, indifference) and suspicion (on the part of those already hostile to closer continental ties) shaping continental security matters.

The Arar Inquiry and New ID Requirements

Maher Arar is a Syrian-born Canadian citizen who came to Canada in 1987, subsequently earning a Master's Degree and finding employment as a telecommunications engineer for an Ottawa-based company. In September 2002, returning from a trip to Tunisia on a stop-over in New York, he was detained by U.S. security officials, questioned, and eventually deported from the United States to Jordan and then to Syria where he would be interrogated, imprisoned and tortured for more than 1 year.

Upon his eventual return to Canada in late 2003, his crusade to shed light on what he alleged to be a groundless campaign resulted in the formation by the Canadian government of an independent public inquiry (or Commission of Inquiry) to examine this affair.[24] The inquiry was established to not only determine what happened to Mr. Arar and why, but also review the appropriateness of the actions of Canadian officials in the case, as well provide recommendations on a new oversight mechanism for the security related actions of the Royal Canadian Mounted Police (the federal police service with certain responsibilities pertaining to domestic security).

Secrecy provisions of Canada's national security apparatus (closely modeled, as discussed, after the U.S.) proved to be the source of what remains ongoing legal battles between various stakeholders in the camp of Mr. Arar and the Government of Canada. On repeated occasions, significant portions of government submissions and testimony have been censored for "national security reasons." Moreover, the government overruled decisions by the judge leading the inquiry, who argued for the release of information to the public (in some cases the government chose to black out portions of the judge's rulings pertaining to the information in question).

After prolonged legal disagreements (delaying the proceedings of the inquiry) the main parties came to an agreement in late March 2005 that would seem to significantly relent to the government view by temporarily agreeing to no longer seek public release of the details in question.[25] Similarly, in the spring of 2005, government lawyers argued that RCMP officers should not be compelled to testify (due to national security provisions), and at least one notable stakeholder involved in the process went so far to suggest that the Inquiry's findings may never be fully released due to the government's "culture of secrecy" strengthened under the guise of security.[26]

On September 18th, 2006, less than a year since the arrival to power of a new Conservative-led minority government, the Inquiry released its first of two reports, detailing Arar's treatment and the actions of Canadian government officials and stakeholders. Most centrally, the inquiry provided complete exoneration of Mr. Arar himself with respect to terrorist activities and affiliations. Justice O'Connor concluded that: "I have heard evidence concerning all of the information collected about Mr. Arar in Canadian investigations, and there is nothing to indicate that Mr.

Arar committed an offence or that his activities constitute a threat to the security of Canada (O'Connor, 2006, p. 9).

With respect to the legal battles pertaining to significant amounts of information not released to the public purview, the Inquiry effectively agreed to release what it could for the time being (i.e., what the government was prepared to allow) and continue its legal challenge in federal courts to eventually override national security provisions that have acted as a shield against full disclosure. Despite this ongoing issue, the report's exhaustive findings proved enough to spark a major political debate about the actions of the RCMP, seemingly responsible for providing inaccurate and inflammatory information about Arar to U.S. authorities (information that likely resulted in Mr. Arar's deportation from the U.S.).

Though invited, U.S. authorities declined any participation in the Arar inquiry, and it emerged that the decision to deport Arar came as a great surprise to Canadian officials (who were kept in the dark for many days as to his whereabouts and who were accordingly not consulted prior to the decision to send Arar to Jordan for transfer to the Syrian prison). The Inquiry further confirmed that since 9/11, security agencies in Canada and the U.S. have routinely and more aggressively shared information, in many cases ignoring procedures for verification and prior approval before doing so. Defenders of such actions invoke the heightened terrorist threat as reason enough for such action, though a troubling aspect of the Arar Commission's findings is that while his case proved the most extreme, there may well be other examples of false or incomplete information flows that could prove consequential.

The information sharing practises reveal the extent to which security actors on both sides of the border view interoperability (i.e., greater information sharing and co-ordination action) as an important aspect of the war on terror. Yet, they also reveal the present absence of political accountability and oversight in the Canadian polity to determine appropriate mechanisms and protocols for doing so.

Border Crossings and Identification

Soon after becoming Canada's new Minister of Public Safety in early 2006, Stockwell Day let it be known that he was quite open-minded about the prospects for a new national identification (i.d.) card. Pointing to new U.S. entry requirements, concerns about terrorism, and recent initiatives in other countries, notably Great Britain, the Minister expressed the certain inevitably of Canada following suit. The only constant throughout 2006 from political pronouncements and bilateral meetings has been uncertainty that pervades U.S. plans pertaining to border identification and control. With every high level meeting subtleties change, and the uncertainty is unnerving for many citizens, businesses, and border towns, and indeed for the country as a whole.

What is known is that the U.S. Congress has passed a law imposing new identification requirements for border crossings that will take effect at airports next year and all land crossings the year following. For Americans, a new national i.d. card will be introduced as an alternative to a passport, but a necessary supplement to existing forms of identification. For those seeking entry into the U.S., including visa-exempt countries, new restrictions will apply. For a time, it seemed a passport would be obligatory, although Mr. Day's recent pronouncements suggest otherwise.

Without question, beginning in 2008 it is going to be more difficult for Canadians to cross into the U.S. without a passport. Minister Day's optimistic portrayal of this situation cannot mask the emergence of a two-tiered border, one for passport holders and the other for the rest. As the Minister acknowledged, those in the latter queue will need an extra dose of patience and politeness to endure a more probing and formal process of validation than has typically been the case to date.

Terrorism and illegal immigration are hot button political issues as Congressional elections approach. Despite such resolve, uncertainty pertaining to Canadians and other foreigners also extends to what the specifics of new laws will mean for traveling Americans. Less than one quarter of all Americans currently possess a passport, and few people in Washington are in the know as to what the U.S. federal government has in mind for a new identification scheme. Some observers, and many lobbyists from the business community, clearly hope that with elections over in 2007 (albeit temporarily, as Presidential campaigns take shape), the current confusion may actually yield additional breathing room before new restrictions are fully enforced. The notion of a "pilot project" is thrown about, leading to an extended transition period that will allow plenty of time for Canada to adjust.

Minister Day's apparent willingness to watch and learn from the American experience may well reflect this sentiment, perhaps one that is being reinforced through internal, bilateral channels between governments. It may also reflect the fact that a new national i.d. card for Canadians is not one of the five core priorities of the Harper minority government (elected in January 2006), and as the Liberals discovered when they broached the issue a few years ago, opinions can quickly polarize.

As discussed, the political context has shifted dramatically since 2001, and many public opinion surveys show widespread support for new i.d. schemes, including those based on biometrics. From the government standpoint, interoperability is now not only a foundational aspect of service transformation, but it is a critical element of national security. New legislation in both Canada and the U.S. has enabled government-wide restructuring organizationally and a much greater ability on the part of public agencies to extract and process information from both internal and external sources.

This determination to cast an antiterrorism network both physically and virtually within bolstered national borders is a powerful driver of the need to create new i.d. mechanisms. Along with the UK plan, the U.S. federal government recently passed

legislation requiring states to adhere to new technological standards for the issuance of driver's licenses, a step likely to be followed by a national database of such
registrations that will most certainly be accessible to security agencies.

The lessons for Canada are twofold. First, and the one most readily acknowledged by
Minister Day, is the growing peer pressure on Canada to act, particularly as continental
interoperability tied to border management hovers over this country's trade access
to the world's largest open market. Although Minister Day is certainly not wrong to
avoid specific proposals for a new national i.d. card in his initial pronouncements,
a key lesson of his predecessors is the failure of the previous Liberal Government
to move beyond the purview of a Parliamentary Committee and facilitate broader
public debate and engagement.

This failure stems partly from the culture of secrecy that traditionally pervades
the national security apparatus, becoming even more firmly entrenched since
9/11. Former Deputy Prime Minister Ann McLellan confessed to being frustrated
by the engrained levels of resistance to more openness, a sentiment echoed by
several Senate Committee reports in recent years. A long-delayed plan for a new
Parliamentary Committee of National Security to provide, for the first time in this
country's history, some degree of direct political monitoring of security agencies,
continues to languish.

The findings from the Arar Inquiry may help to illuminate these issues in the near
future, as might Conservatives pledge to broaden access to information provisions.
Yet, the Conservatives have also promised to augment the resources of the highly
secretive Canada Borders Services Agency, create a new foreign spy agency, and
expand the country's military and law enforcement capabilities.

For the time being, then, there remains an implied notion of deferential trust that
has characterized the very limited relations between the public and elected officials
on the one hand and security and intelligence agencies on the other hand. This relationship lies at the heart of any new i.d. plan, not only because it is the Minister
responsible for security that is seemingly intent on leading this file, but also because
the engrained secrecy of national security and intelligence bodies may be fertile
ground for internal mismanagement, function creep, civil rights abuses, and the
diminishment of privacy.

Such arguments will be only too quickly exploited by sceptics of any new i.d.
scheme, unless the government demonstrates a genuine commitment to cultivating
trust through direct political and public engagement. Such a commitment begins
during the consultative phase, but it extends equally to implementation and the need
for new oversight mechanisms beyond the usual sort of reactionary, after-the-fact
investigations routinely undertaken by Parliamentary Officers and judicial inquiries.
In short, public opinion is not overtly hostile to the prospect of government action
on the matter of identification—nor can support merely be taken for granted—especially in the aftermath of the Arar affair.

Conclusion

The evolution of Canadian security policy over the past few years reveals three major lessons for both Canadian democratic governance and Canada's participation in continental governance relations. First, the U.S. reaction to 9/11 has been the predominant factor shaping Canadian policy and governmental structure. Secondly, the inherently secretive nature of security policy and the national security apparatus is gradually and incrementally being extended to the continental realm. Thirdly, the governing style and structures of Westminster Parliamentary government may well be particularly conducive to reinforcing this second point, limiting the public discourse on both current domestic matters and prospective continental choices.

The fact that there is little indication of more formalized continental governance in the short term nonetheless provides some time for reflection. As a result, there may be an opportunity for a new National Security Committee of Parliamentarians to think outside the box with respect to its role in not only reviewing existing national security arrangements but also preparing, in concert with the public at large, the ground work for future reforms. There are many high level and important issues that will crowd the work of this new body, issues rooted in fundamental concepts such as freedom, rights, terrorism, and domestic and international law. At the same time, the Committee would be well advised to tackle two themes explicitly and innovatively: the continental dimension to "national security" and the growing prominence of digital technology within and between governments.

In terms of an explicit continental focus, the Committee should seek to forge new and direct political ties between elected officials in Canada, the U.S., and Mexico. Although any such mechanism would undoubtedly begin with a limited, consultative role, at the very least the formation of a publicly recognized and regularized vehicle for political dialogue would begin to lay the groundwork to better integrate continental interdependence and trilateral political review. The sketching of a modest agenda for trilateral action and institutional building offered by Pastor, provides, if nothing more, an open and useful starting point for political dialogue and an exchange of views.

With respect to digital technologies, the main challenge is twofold. First, the new National Security Committee must be equipped with the resources and the will to foster expertise in the intricacies of technological and political interoperability and its impacts on a changing organizational security apparatus both domestically and continentally (and undoubtedly globally to some degree as well). Not only is this investment crucial to shaping the continental dimension to its work, it is equally central to understanding and contributing to national security domestically.

The Committee can, for example, provide a tangibly visible and political dimension to the issue of managerial horizontality that permeates national security and information technology efforts in practise, but is all but ignored in public (replaced instead, in the former case, by an overtly simplistic assigning authority to a single Minister for the entire portfolio of agencies, departments, and cross-governmental processes[27]). The second and final report of the Arar Inquiry, expected in late 2006, will help facilitate such a dialogue by proposing new mechanisms for RCMP oversight.

The final thematic dimension then is Canada-U.S. relations and whether the Conservatives are likely to embrace closer ties with the U.S. on key matters of trade, defence, and security. Regarding the latter realm of security there is pressure from the private sector in Canada to more aggressively pursue what may be termed a form of political interoperability via more integrated governance mechanisms (despite little evidence that such an agenda would gather traction in Washington[28]). There is some tension here between the common Conservative orientations of President Bush and Prime Minister Harper (and the feeling in both countries that relations have deteriorated in recent years under Liberal rule, a dynamic not limited to Canada of course) and the latter's calls for the bolstering of Canadian defence forces and more assertions of Canadian sovereignty (particularly in the Arctic where Canadian claims are resisted by the U.S. and indeed, many other countries).

On the whole, however, there is little reason to expect a departure from the trend of this decade of U.S.-led security efforts shaping Canadian policy and governmental organization. While the previous government pursued continental alignment and interoperability in a largely reactionary manner, often disconnected from the more contentious political discourse of trade disputes and sovereignty assertions, the Conservative Government will need to reconcile both continental and domestic pressures in balancing openness and democratic accountability with ongoing pressures for secrecy that are prevalent in the realm of security.

References

Allen, B., Juillet, L., Paquet, G., & Roy, J. (2001). E-government in Canada: People, partnerships and prospects. *Government Information Quarterly, 30*(1), 36-47.

Allen, B.A., Paquet, G., Juillet, L., & Roy, J. (2005). E-government and collaboration: Structural, accountability and cultural reform. In M. Khosrow-Pour (Ed.), *Practising e-government: A global perspective* (pp. 1-15). Hershey, PA: Idea Group.

Allman, W., & Barrette, D. (2004). *Opening submission of the International Civil Liberties Monitoring Group*. Ottawa, Canada: Commission of Inquiry into the Actions of Canadian Officials in Relation to Maher Arar.

Auditor General of Canada. (2004). *National security in Canada—the 2001 Anti-Terrorism Initiative*. Ottawa, Canada: Government of Canada, www.oag-bvg. gc.ca

Auditor General of Canada. (2005a). *National security in Canada—the 2001 Anti-Terrorism Initiative*. Ottawa, Canada: Government of Canada, www.oag-bvg.gc.ca

Auditor General of Canada. (2005b). *Passport services*. Ottawa, Canada: Government of Canada, www.oag-bvg.gc.ca

Barber, B. (2003). *Fear's empire: War, terrorism and democracy*. New York: W.W. Norton.

Batini, C., Cappadozzi, E., Mecella, M., & Talamo, M. (2002). Cooperative architectures. In W.J. McIver & A.K. Elmagarmid (Eds.), *Advances in digital government —Technology, human factors and policy*. Boston: Kluwer Academic.

Barry, D. (2004). Managing Canada—US relations in the post-9/11 era—Do we need a big idea? *Policy Paper on the Americas V XIV* (11): Center for Strategic and International Studies.

Bennett, C.J., & Raab, C. (2003). *The governance of privacy*. Burlington: Ashgate.

Brenner, S.W. (2004). U.S. cybercrime laws: Defining offences. *Information Systems Frontiers*, *6*(2), 115-132.

Brown, M. (Ed.). (2003). *Grave new world—Security challenges in the 21ˢᵗ century*. Washington, DC: Georgetown University Press.

Bryant, A., & Colledge, B. (2002). Trust in electronic commerce business relationships. *Journal of Electronic Commerce Research*, *3*(2), 32-39.

Clifford, M. (2004*). Identifying and exploring security essentials*. Upper Saddle River, NJ: Pearson Prentice Hall.

Courtois, B. (2005, February 11). *The US Patriot Act and the privacy of Canadians*. Delivery text, Privacy and Security—Synergies in an e-Society Conference, Victoria, Canada.

Demchak, C.C. (1999). "New security" in Cyberspace: Emerging intersection between military and civilian contingencies. *Journal of Contingencies and Crisis Management,* *7*(4), 181-198.

Denning, D. (2003). Information technology and security. In M. Brown (Ed.), *Grave new world—Security challenges in the 21ˢᵗ century*. Washington, DC: Georgetown University Press.

De Rosa, M. (2003). Privacy in the Age of Terror. *The Washington Quarterly*, *26*(3), 27-41.

Desouza, K., & Vanapalli, G. (2005). Securing knowledge in organizations: Lessons from the defense and intelligence sectors. *International Journal of Information Management*, *25*(1), 85-98.

Dutta, A., & McCrohan, K. (2002). Management's role in information security in a cyber economy. *California Management Review, 45*(1), 67-87.

EGovernment Observatory. (2002). *Survey on e-government services to enterprises.* Brussels: European Commission Enterprise Directorate General.

Ferguson, Y.H., & Barry Jones, R.J. (Eds.). (2002). *Political space—Frontiers of change and governance in a globalizing world.* Albany: State University of New York Press.

Fitzgerald, A.M. (2004). *Addressing the security-development nexus: Implications for joined-up government.* Montreal, Canada: Institute for Research on Public Policy.

Fountain, J. E. (2001). *Building the virtual state: Information technology and institutional change.* Washington, DC: Brookings Institution Press.

Gerhart, B., & Torok-Apro, R. (2005). *The Canadian Passport System: Assessing the interface between technology, security and mobility.* Doctoral thesis, School of Public Administration, University of Victoria.

Giddens, A. (2002). Runaway *world—How globalization is reshaping our lives.* London: Profile Books.

Gill, P. (2004). Securing the globe: Intelligence and the post-9/11 shift from "Liddism" to "Drainism." *Intelligence and National Security. 19*(3), 467-489.

Grabbe, H. (2005). Conclusion: The politics of freedom, security and justice in the enlarging EU. In K. Henderson (Ed.), *The area of freedom, security and justice in the enlarged Europe.* New York: Palgrave Macmillan.

Hart-Teeter. (2003). *The new e-government equation: Ease, engagement, privacy and protection.* Washington, DC: Council for Excellence in Government.

Hart-Teeter. (2004). *From the home front to the front lines: America speaks out about Homeland Security.* Washington, DC: Council for Excellence in Government.

Hayden, P. (2005). *Cosmopolitan global politics.* Burlington, VT: Ashgate.

Henderson, K. (2005). *The area of freedom, security and justice in the enlarged Europe.* New York: Palgrave Macmillan.

Henrich, V. C., & Link, A.N. (2003). Deploying Homeland Security technology. *Journal of Technology Transfer, 28,* 363-368.

Heymann, P.B. (2001/02). Dealing with terrorism: An overview. *International Security, 26*(3), 24-38.

Holden, S. (2004). *Understanding electronic signatures: The keys to e-government.* Washington, DC: IBM Center for the Business of Government.

Jorgensen, K.E., & Rosamond, B. (2002). Europe: Regional laboratory for a global polity. In M. Ougaard & R. Higgott (Eds.), *Towards a global polity.* London: Routledge.

Joshi, J.B.D., Ghafoor, A., & Aref, W.G. (2002). Security and privacy challenges of a digital government. In W.J. McIver & A.K. Elmagarmid (Eds.), *Advances in digital government—Technology, human factors and policy*. Boston: Kluwer Academic.

Kernaghan, K., & Gunraj, J. (2004). Integrating information technology into public administration: Concepts and practical considerations. *Canadian Public Administration, 47*(4), 525-546.

Kruger, E., Mulder, M., & Korenic, B. (2004). Canada after 11 September: Measures and "preferred" immigrants. *Mediterranean Quarterly, Fall*, 72-87.

Loukidelis, D. (2004). *Identity, privacy, security—Can technology really reconcile them?* An address by B.C.'s Privacy Commissioner. Victoria: Office of the Privacy Commissioner, Retrieved from http://www.oipc.bc.ca

Marche, S., & McNiven, J.D. (2003). E-government and e-governance: The future isn't what it used to be. *Canadian Journal of Administrative Sciences, 20*(1), 74-86.

Marx, G.T. (2004). Some concepts that may be useful in understanding the myriad forms and contexts of surveillance. *Intelligence and National Security, 19*(2), 226-248.

McLuhan, M., & Firoe, Q. (1968). *War and peace in the global village*. New York: McGraw-Hill.

Meyers, D.W. (2003). Does "smarter" lead to safer? An assessment of the U.S. border accords with Mexico and Canada. *International Migration, 41*(1), 5-44.

Nugent, J.H., & Raisinghani, M.S. (2002). The information technology and telecommunications security imperative: Important issues and drivers. *Journal of Electronic Commerce Research, 3*(1), 1-14.

O'Connor, D. (2006). *Report of the events to Maher Arar: Analysis and recommendations*. Commission of Inquiry into the Actions of Canadian Officials in Relation to Maher Arar: Ottawa, Retrieved from www.ararcommission.ca

O'Harrow, R. (2004). *No place to hide*. New York: Free Press.

Ougaard, M., & Higgott, R. (Eds.). (2002). *Towards a global polity*. London: Routledge.

Paquet, G. (1997). States, communities and markets: The distributed governance scenario. In T.J. Courchene (Ed.), *The nation-state in a global information era: Policy challenges the Bell Canada Papers in economics and public policy* (pp. 25-46). Kingston: John Deutsch Institute for the Study of Economic Policy.

Pastor, R. (2001). *Toward A North American community*. Washington, DC: Institute for International Economics.

Pastor, R. (2004). North America's second decade. Foreign affairs. Council on Foreign Relations. Retrieved July 18, 2007, from *www.foreignaffairs.org*

Pavlichev, A., & Garson, G.D. (Eds.). (2004). *Digital government: Principles and best practises*. Hershey, PA: Idea Group.

Preyer, G., & Bos, M. (Eds.). (2002). *Borderlines in a globalized world*. Dordrecht, Holland: Kluwer Academic.

Reid, J. (2004). Holding governments accountable by strengthening access to information laws and information management practices. In L. Oliver & L. Sanders (Eds.), *E-government reconsidered: Renewal of governance for the knowledge age*. Regina, SK: Canadian Plains Research Center.

Ronchi, S. (2003). *The Internet and the customer-Supplier relationship*. Aldershot, UK: Ashgate.

Roy, J. (2005a). Services, security, transparency and trust: Government online or governance renewal in Canada? *International Journal of E-Government Research, 1*(1), 48-58.

Roy, J. (2005b). E-governance and international relations: A consideration of newly emerging capacities in a multi-level world. *Journal of Electronic Commerce, 6*(1), 44-55.

Salter, M. (2004). Passports, mobility and security: How smart can the border be? *International Studies Perspective, 5*, 71-91.

Scholl, H. (2005). Motives, strategic approach, objectives and focal points in e-government-induced change. *International Journal of E-Government Research, 1*(1), 59-78.

Sirmakessis, S. (2004). *Text mining and its applications*. Heidelberg: Springer.

Shearman, P., & Sussex, M. (2004). European *security after 9/11*. Aldershot, UK: Ashgate.

Smith, M. (2004). *Europe's foreign and security policy—The institutionalization of cooperation*. Cambridge, MA: Cambridge University Press.

Su, S. et al. (2005). Transnational information sharing, event notification, rule enforcement and process coordination. *Journal of E-Government Research, 1*(2), 1-26.

Waugh, W.L. (2003). Terrorism, Homeland Security and the National Emergency Management Framework. *Public Organization Review, 3*, 373-385.

Endnotes

[1]   This estimate was reported by "GlobalSecurity.org," an American observatory and research group devoted to security, defense, and intelligence matters.

[2]   Main findings of an August 2004 Report by the Office of the Inspector General (OIG-04-31).

3   In 1999, for example, 126,809,769 pages of government information were de-classified. By 2004, this number has dropped to 28,413,690. Source—Secrecy Report Card—An Update, April 2005, www.openthegovernment.org).

4   The United Kingdom has recently adopted a plan to introduce a new, mandatory identification card, along with biometrically-enabled passports. Indeed, pilots are already underway in Scotland, and over the next several years, the plan will be complemented by the creation of a National Identification Registry.

5   The International Civil Aviation Organization (www.icao.int) is the leading intergovernmental organization examining biometric standards for travel documentation.

6   In the hours following the terrorist attacks, the small town of Gander, New-foundland (with a population of roughly 11,000) welcomed some 6,000 unexpected travelers from diverted aircrafts—mostly Americans (2 years later, many American would return to participate in an organized gathering of goodwill to mark the occasion). One week later, nearly 100,000 Canadians gathered on Parliament Hill in Ottawa (along with the American Ambassador to Canada) to pay homage to the human loss of September 11.

7   Estimates peg bilateral commercial exchanges across the border in excess of $2 billion per day, with approximately 200 million border crossings each year.

8   From Gerhart and Torok-Apro (2005)—The Smart Border agreement gener-ally speaks to: the secure flow of people; the secure flow of goods; secure infrastructure; and coordination and information sharing in the pursuit of these objectives. The first action commits the two countries to: "jointly develop on an urgent basis common biometric identifiers in documentation such as perma-nent resident cards, NEXUS (a pilot initiative of prescreening frequent border crossers), and other travel documents to ensure greater security (Department of Foreign Affairs, Government of Canada). The second action item calls for the instillation of biometric security measures on Permanent Residency Cards.

9   Specifically, in the 2001 Federal Budget the government allocated $7.7 billion in new funds over 5 years on a range of initiatives and reforms centred on public security and safety and antiterrorism. Following the Auditor General's report, one public opinion poll conducted in April 2004 showed rising support among Canadians for higher spending on antiterrorism (55% of those surveyed) and military defence (54%) (Fife, 2004).

10   Bill C-36 adds a definition of "terrorist activity" to the criminal code. The defi-nition will cover an action that is, "taken or threatened for political, religious or ideological purposes and threatens the public or national security by killing, seriously harming or endangering a person, causing substantial property dam-age that is likely to seriously harm people, or in interfering with or disruption an essential service, facility or system." The new Bill gives police the power

to: detain a suspected terrorist for 72 hours without charge; compell Canadians to testify during an investigation; and intercept a wider range of private conversations for a longer period of time. The bill affects other legislation like the Income Tax Act. Organizations supporting terrorist groups which claim to be charities can now be stripped of their charitable status. The bill also allows the government to store the DNA of suspected terrorists, to compile lists of terrorists and their organizations, and to freeze and take away their assets (Source of this summary: http://www.cbc.ca/fifth/featurestories/protest/laws.html).

[11]   http://www.oag-bvg.gc.ca/domino/reports.nsf/html/20050201ce.html—The focus of this audit included five key areas: cooperation and information-sharing among lead organizations on IT security; development and implementation of IT security standards to support policy; effectiveness of the Government Security Policy and existing security measures; contingency planning; and risk management.

[12]   Indeed, the Senate Committee report went further in underscoring the absence of an intergovernmental architecture for cooperation and the resulting dearth of resources and capacities on the front line (i.e., local level governments and emergency service providers).

[13]   Information on the various players and initiatives is available at—www.safecanada.ca. Within the realm of cyber-security, one new initiative created in February 2005 is the Canadian Cyber-Incident Response Centre (http://www.ocipep.gc.ca/ccirc/index_e.asp).

[14]   The Minister is also responsible for a portfolio of six agencies: Canada Border Services Agency, Canada Firearms Centre, Canadian Security Intelligence Service, Correctional Service of Canada, National Parole Board and the Royal Canadian Mounted Policy.

[15]   http://www.cbsa-asfc.gc.ca/newsroom/factsheets/2004/0124passenger-e.html

[16]   The Privacy Commissioner of BC has voiced his concern against surveillance and data-mining efforts, underlining "function creep" as a serious threat (Loukidelis, 2004). He also underscores problems of secrecy and complexity that impede public accountability and the raise the prospect of unintended consequences.

[17]   In 2000, many Mexicans—led by President Fox, hailed the arrival of President Bush as a major turning point: the American President would break with the tradition of making Canada his first official foreign visit, opting for Mexico instead.

[18]   Canadian representative, John Manley, was formerly Deputy Prime Minister and Finance Minister and the person who negotiated the smart border accord

with then-U.S. Secretary Tom Ridge in the aftermath of 9/11. The trilateral commission made six key recommendations, covering new institutions, a unified border action plan, a common external tariff, an economic stimulus focus for Mexico, a continental energy and national resource strategy, and deepened educational ties.

[19]   This view was put forth by former Canadian Ambassador to the United States, Allan Gotleib, in his critique of the North American partnership (April 13, 2005, the Globe and Mail). He question's the new initiative's seriousness in light of numerous generalities and shortcomings, notably an absence of central authority in each country assigned with responsibility for moving forward and the refusal of the three leaders to regularize their annual meeting (as a basis for monitoring performance and updating actions).

[20]   In his first week as Canada's new Ambassador in Washington, Frank McKenna caused a political firestorm in Ottawa by stating that Canada was already apart of ballistic missile defence by virtue joint North American defence structures (a view categorically denied by the Government as during the same week Prime Minister Martin would announce Canada's decision to not partake in the system). Other examples reviewed early—notably the formation of joint border security units, also underscore this point.

[21]   Within Canada, the Auditor General brought to light this danger in her 2005 audit of national security, lamenting her lack of authority over information pertaining to new passenger screening systems installed in airports (the results of the testing of this new equipment were withheld under national security laws protecting such information as sensitive).

[22]   The mandate of the "National Security Committee of Parliamentarians" (as proposed in March 2005, subject to legislative adoption) would be to review the security and intelligence apparatus of departments and agencies engaged in security and intelligence activities to fulfill their responsibilities. The committee would submit reports to the Prime Minister who, in turn, would table them in Parliament (the prerogative to censor or modify these reports is unclear).

[23]   Along with the Parliamentary Committee are three existing review bodies: the Security Intelligence Review Committee (an independent body reporting to Parliament on the Canadian Security Intelligence Service); the Communications Security Establishment (CSE) Commissioner (reviewing the CSE); and the Commission for Public Complaints against the RCMP. The latter office in particular has been criticized for lacking authority, as it operates within the RCMP (much of the criticism has come from the Commissioner herself), and this position is subject to review by the Arar Commission.

[24]   Arar's deportation and torture in Syria are not disputed. However, the reasons for this deportation remain unclear due to national security laws limiting the

divulging of government documents in public. Arar's camp claims that the basis for his ordeal was groundless, perhaps involving misinformation gathered within public authorities in Canada and then shared with U.S. officials. The Canadian government appointed the Commission of Inquiry to independently examine the actions of Canadian officials and authorities.

[25] Specifically, by agreeing to the government's wishes, the government, in turn, withdrew its legal challenge from the Federal Court of Canada to keep the information in question secret (the information pertains to testimony of various government officials made in camera: the Commission maintained its view that the information should be released, and emphasized that it would seek public disclosure at a time and in a manner that would not interfere with the Inquiry proceedings. Details of the agreement, along with all proceedings of the Inquiry may be viewed at: www.ararcommission.ca).

[26] This comment was made by a former federal Cabinet Minister, Ron Atkey, acting as amicus curiae ("friend of the court") in the Inquiry process (reported in the Globe and Mail newspaper on May 3, 2005).

[27] The only security-related agency not under the purview of this Minister is the Communications Security Establishment (CSE), the national cryptologic agency (providing two key services: foreign signals intelligence in support of defence and foreign policy, and the protection of electronic information and communication. The Minister of National Defence is accountable to Cabinet and to Parliament for all of CSE's activities. The Minister also provides direction to CSE concerning the performance of its functions. The Minister of National Defence is supported by two Deputy Ministers. The National Security Advisor is accountable for CSE's policy and operations. The Deputy Minister of National Defence is accountable for administrative matters pertaining to CSE.

[28] Still, proponents of this direction, inspired by the work of Pastor (2003) and others, point to modest steps in recent times such as the trilateral vision endorsed by prominent representatives of Canada, the U.S., and Mexico and released by the Council of Foreign Relations (at a time chosen in part to coincide with the North American Leaders Summit in Waco, Texas, in March 2005). From this summit, North American leaders agreed to form the Security and Prosperity Partnership of North American (www.spp.gov).

An earlier version of this chapter appeared in Social Science Computer Review, 23(4), pp. 463-479, copyright 2005 by Sage Publications. Reprinted by permission of Sage Publications Inc.

Chapter VIII

Information Technology and Surveillance:
Implications for Public Administration in a New World Order

Akhlaque Haque, University of Alabama at Birmingham, USA

Abstract

The Patriot Act of 2001 has introduced significant legislative changes impacting how public managers collect, disseminate, and evaluate information for decision making. The chapter describes the theoretical underpinnings of information gathering and decision making and argues that more information gathering and subsequent use of sophisticated information gathering tools serves as an important myth promoting greater legitimacy and confidence in the government's ability to provide security to the citizens. The chapter suggests that the rational choice approach to security is limited in its ability to evaluate values that are embedded into the decision making processes. However, being cognizant of the nonrational rulings placed on technology-based policy initiatives, public managers can be guided toward "responsible values" to avoid the dark path of control, surveillance, and the loss of freedom.

Introduction

The Patriotic Act of 2001 has introduced significant legislative changes impacting the role of information technology (IT) in government. Although most changes have directly affected law enforcement agencies by giving them increased surveillance and investigative powers, more generally, the increased security environment has transformed ways in which public managers collect, disseminate, and evaluate information for decision making. What was initially spurred by the 9/11 terrorist attacks has now fundamentally changed how information technologies can be used in security and surveillance. Former HSD Secretary Tom Ridge termed the "War on Terrorism" as the "War of Information and Intelligence." Because of immediate threat and limited resources, government policy has been focused toward centralization of federal authority in security, robustness, and reliability of the information infrastructure. Such reforms are reflected in the establishment of individual executive entities such as the National Intelligence Authority (NIA) and the Department of Homeland Security (DHS).

The purpose of the chapter is two-fold: First, the chapter argues that more information gathering and subsequent use of greater IT provides an important myth giving greater legitimacy to and confidence in the government's ability to provide security to the citizens. Second, the increasing role of IT in security matters suggests that at the height of turbulence, the deterministic ruling of rational choice may become quite common. However, being cognizant of the implications of the values placed on technology-based policy initiatives, public managers can be guided toward "responsible values" to avoid the dark path of technology-driven "control, surveillance and the loss of freedom."

The chapter has been divided into three sections. The first section brings to light earlier literature on information management and technology in public organizations. It is argued that the value placed on information gathering starts as strategic or symbolic in nature, yet can become functional necessity for making decisions. The second section discusses the implications of the Patriot Act and the centralization policy bias of the U.S. federal government. The final section highlights the new challenges for public administration in the new world order.

Information Gathering:
A Strategic Choice for Organizations

Martha Feldman and James March in their seminal study "Information in Organizations as Signal Symbol" (1981) argued that the link between decisions and information is weak, and most organizations and individuals often collect more information than they use or can reasonably expect to use in making good decisions (p. 174). They cite three reasons why information gathering is of value to organizations and why a weak link between information and decision making will lead to information overflow. First, traditionally people who collect information in organizations are not the ones who generally use it. This apparent gap between information gathering and decision making in organizations provides positive incentives for gathering more information, underestimating the cost of information relative to the perceived benefit. Second, most information is gathered for surveillance or monitoring, not decision making. This is justified in terms of expected decisions which are beyond the control of the decision-maker. Third, due to the potential consequences of decisions, information is used by organization for *strategic misrepresentation* in persuading others to act—"Competition among contending liars turns persuasion into a contest in (mostly unreliable) information" (p. 177).

Increased information supports rational choice in decision-making, but what is more profound, according to Feldman and March, is having more information that carries social and individual significance. Organizations having greater information resources are a symbol of organizational legitimacy, and it creates confidence that the organization will make quality decisions. Decision-makers will view requesting information, gathering information, and citing information as indicative of sound decision-making in the organization. The symbolic role of information resources leads the organization to engage in "conspicuous overconsumption of information" (p. 182). This behavior is a "signal" but could also become a "functional necessity for making good decisions" (p. 180). This strategic behavior of organizations can create new realities and organizational processes and bias in favor of departments that are responsible for managing and processing information. More importantly, as Feldman and March noted "it is possible that norms that are changing will be simultaneously losing symbolic significance and gaining instrumental importance" (p. 184).

Based on imperfect information, organizations seek information that would improve the likelihood of desired consequences and which will enact future preferences. The desire to improve decisions is based on the strategic framework of information relevance as it relates to expected future outcomes and choices. We can expect that certain organizations will limit the boundaries of information collection based on their expected decisions. This "system of surveillance" is defended by organizations based on their expected decisions and anticipated environments (Feldman & March, 1981, p. 176). This can be further attributed to the ever-increasing sophistication of technologies demanded for the survival of the surveillance system. In other words, more sophisticated monitoring tools tend to become part of the strategic framework for better decisions.

The implication of Feldman and March's work in today's information age is quite striking. An organization's information gathering capability is directly reflected in its information technology sophistication: more sophisticated information technology leads to more information gathering, in turn leading to qualitatively better decisions. At the same time, recent years have shown that having separate information management units (e.g., e-government initiatives) or having a Chief Information Officer may serve as a symbolic alternative to more substantive action (Moon, 2002). Substantive government activity such as citizen participation in decision making, decreasing security threats, protecting client rights and privacy, and managing and controlling internal and external organization stake holders, may all take second place to the organization's promotion of symbolic alternatives. During times of crisis, however, organizations are often observed to overuse technology for results. As Brown and Brudney (2003) note, as decision uncertainty escalates and task routine diminishes, decision-makers gravitate toward richer information sources. Also, as uncertainty increases, so does the drive to use more sophisticated technology to solve the problem. Brown and Brudney conclude that the environmental context in which the organization resides may be more important for improving the quality of decision-making than is sophisticated information technology.

Information Management Post 9/11

The 9/11 terrorist attacks have been identified as the single most important incident of the century in terms of changing the "mood of the nation" and opening avenues for furthering new ways of information management and dissemination. The 9/11 tragedy raised significant concerns about the government's ability to make decisions based on collected information. Unlike past interest in citizen data for effective use of policy mandates, recent overhaul of the government's decision-making apparatus redefines the purpose of information gathering to emphasize better security and protecting the national interest. The USA PATRIOT Act of 2001 paved the way for the creation of the Department of Homeland Security (DHS), which has centralized 180,000 personnel from 22 different organizations throughout the federal government, making it the largest government reorganization since the beginning of the Cold War.

Sweeping changes in surveillance regulations, authorized under the Patriot Act, have given DHS unprecedented access to information through use of existing high-tech surveillance tools, and through tools yet to be developed. According to the strategic plan of the DHS, "data collection and analysis capabilities will be supported through investment in, and development of, leading-edge information analysis, data mining, data warehousing and threat/vulnerability mapping applications and tools, and recruiting, training and retaining human analysts" (DHS, 2004b, p. 10). The Department of Homeland Security is subdivided into five divisions, including the Information Analysis and Infrastructure Protection division, and Science and Technology division. In recent years, the federal government has allocated considerable resources to homeland security, the size which has been increasing at the rate of 40% a year.[1]

A significant portion of the USA PATRIOT Act requires investment in information technology and sophisticated monitoring devices. The act introduced sweeping changes to U.S. law and expanded the authority of the law enforcement officers, some of which have raised concerns about citizen's rights.[2] For example, the Electronic Communications Privacy Act (ECPA) authorizes government to access stored e-mail and other electronic communications. Within ECPA, the Pen Register statute supports real-time interception of "numbers dialed or otherwise transmitted on the telephone line to which such device is attached." Although the use of such devices requires a court order, it does not require probable cause. A government attorney need only certify to the court that the "information likely to be obtained by such installation and use is relevant to an ongoing criminal investigation" (*To deter and punish terrorist acts in the United States and around the world, to enhance law enforcement investigatory tools, and for other purposes*, Pub.L. 107-56, Page 115 STAT. 272, 2001). Section 217 of the act permits government interception of the "communications of a computer trespasser" if the owner or operator of a "protected computer" authorizes the interception. In this case, the "authorization" permits wiretapping of the intruder's communications without any judicial oversight.

A significant portion of recent sweeping changes has been subsumed by a new environment of surveillance. Nelson (2002) notes: "No longer is new technology necessarily viewed as a threat to individual privacy; rather, it is perceived as serving the common good and protecting freedom as reflected in legislative reactions such as the USA PATRIOT Act" (p. 69). Technology takes the role of panacea to the problem, making it appear "universal in its invasion and objective in its application" (p. 69). With technology of central facet of business and governmental operations, CIOs are increasingly taking leadership roles. With technical skills that are critical to agency functioning and which are now increasingly part of the policy-making core, a successful CIO may be expected to lead as a CEO in the coming years of the information age (Peterson, 2003).

State funding for police, fire, and emergency has dramatically increased. Since September 11, 2001, state-level police, fire, and emergency services received 13.1 billion dollars from the federal government—a 990% increase over the $1.2 billion spent by the federal government for similar programs in the preceding 3 years of terrorist threat (Ripley, 2004). Local governments increasingly find themselves spending more money on surveillance technology than on parks and streets (*Government Technology*, 2004, p. 20). The result in some cases have been overoptimistic use of technology, even giving GIS functionality and push-to-talk capable tools to "street crews sweeping the streets" (McKay, 2004, p. 22).

With promises of lucrative contracts for homeland defense, technology giants have rushed research and development efforts related to information technology and security. For example, Boeing created a new Homeland Security group in July 2002 as part of its $23 billion Integrated Defense Systems business. The new group is expected to install explosive-detection systems at 429 airports identified in the Transportation Security Administration's $500 million contract award to the Boeing-Siemens team. Raytheon, another defense contractor and technology investment giant, now focuses "on providing customers with technologies, solutions and services to protect airports, ports, airspace, computer networks and to assist first responders in crises and disaster" (Airport Review, 2002, p. 1).

Patriotic Information Systems and Implications for Public Administration

Today public administration is at odds with the post-9/11 surveillance society. As argued elsewhere, government efforts to get closer to the people means more confidence in government, leading to more stable communities (Haque, 2004; Putnam, 2000). Centralized information systems guarantee only more information, not an open and more secure society. More importantly, a narrow definition of the target population and types of information to be collected may designate a certain class of citizens identified as "high risk." The implications for public administration here are very far-reaching.

The essential thrust of the Patriot Act has been to use new regulations to control and monitor information flow and the use of high-tech surveillance technology to better understand and predict man-made catastrophes. The net effect of this transformation threatens to destabilize the status-quo, especially as it relates to diversity, by introducing control values. Indeed, following the rational path will necessary be at odds with calls for understanding and embracing diversity among us. Its repercussions in the adaptive process will raise fundamental issues of freedom and privacy in a democratic society.

This argument in no way supports the notion that the government should not react or should do nothing to counter terrorism. Rather, it is the approach and intensity of federal information strategy that constrains us to make drastic changes to the existing way of life. As Charles Lindblom (1959) reminded us, every decision-making process begins anew without regard to past experiences or reliance on past decisions or actions. While trying to *control* the apparent instability by surveillance methods, we could do more harm than good in the health of our democratic system.

Values can be understood in many ways, especially when such values are part of the information that is being gathered for decision making. The root word for values comes from Greek *axios,* meaning axis, direction or guidance. There are two types of values that are noteworthy here, values that are set for control (fixed) and values that are developmental (continuous) to bring new emerging values for different situations (Rokeach, 1973). In a democratic society, "values of the regime" are one of the desired characteristics of a public manager. Control-oriented values within regime values include discipline, efficiency, responsibility, punctuality, and so forth. Development-oriented values include constitutional principles, values of freedom, creativity, integrity, and trust. The weight of any of the two sets of values must be balanced, as it will fundamentally influence the emerging political culture.

If we decide to invest more in nurturing control-oriented values in order to foresee and control our destiny (a rational choice), we must forego some of our democratic rights that we cherish. Whether we overestimate the power of surveillance and control and the technological supremacy to fight terror, we will be undermining the role of democracy in the information age. The imbalance in values will ultimately shift our priorities, forcing us to move into territories where the emerging values are not compatible to democratic values.

Conclusion

Harry Hammitt (2000), describing the legislative foundation of information access policies in the U.S., argues that "the most important and far-reaching statute, and the foundation for the entire access policy, is a 1966 law—the Freedom of Information Act (FOIA) 5 U.S.C. 552" (p. 27). The 1950s journalists' movement for the *People's Right to Know* (Harold Cross, 1953) came to fruition when President Lyndon Johnson signed FOIA into Law in July 4, 1966. The Patriot Act of 2001 opens another chapter to the information access literature—the "Government's Right to Know." The creation of the Department of Homeland Security adds a new layer of bureaucracy posing challenges for diversity within governments and citizens. As Alvin Toffler (1984) would suggest, diversity is essentially desirable, as it can ensure a secure and stable civilization. Centralization of a part of government's decision-making apparatus through DHS threatens to overshadow the traditional importance of diversity and creativity within public administration.

References

Airport Review, (2002). "Homeland security promises lucrative contracts, Sep. 10, 2002, p. 1". Retrieved March, 2004, from http://www.janes.com/aerospace/civil/news/jar/jar020910_1_n.shtml

Brown, M.M., & Brudney, J. (2003). Learning organizations in the public sector? A study of police agencies employing information and technology to advance knowledge. *Public Administration Review, 63*(1), 30-43.

Cross, H. (1953). *The people's right to know: Legal access to public records and proceedings.* NY: Columbia University Press.

Department of Homeland Security, DHS. (2004a). *DHS budget in brief - Fiscal year 2005.* Retrieved July 18, 2007, from http://www.dhs.gov/dhspublic/display?theme=12&content=3131

Department of Homeland Security, DHS. (2004b). *Securing our homeland. U. S. Department of Homeland Security strategic plan 2004.* Retrieved July 18, 2007, from http://www.dhs.gov/interweb/assetlibrary/DHS_StratPlan_FINAL_spread.pdf

Feldman, M.S., & March, J.G. (1981). Information in organizations as signal and symbol. *Administrative Science Quarterly, 26*(2), 171-186.

Peterson, S. (2003). Rising to the top: CIOs might be well suited to lead more than just technology agencies.*Government Technology , 16*(16), 14-19.

McKay, J. (2004). Balancing act. *Government Technology, 17*(2), 19-22.

Hammitt, H. (2000). The legislative foundation of information policy: Balancing access against privacy and confidentiality. In D. Garson (Ed.), Handbookof public information systems (pp. 27-39).NewYork: Marcel Dekker.

Haque, A. (2004). Ethics and administrative discretion in a unified administration: A Burkean perspective. *Administration Society, 35*, 701-716.

Lindblom, C.E. (1959). The science of muddling through. *Public Administration Review, 19*, 79-88.

Moon, M.J. (2002). The evolution of e-government municipalities: Rhetoric or reality? *Public Administration Review, 62*(4), 424-33.

Nelson, L. (2002). Protecting the common good: Technology, objectivity, and privacy. *Public Administration Review, 62*(Special Issue), 69-73.

Putnam, R. (2000). *Bowling alone: The collapse and revival of American community.* New York: Simon & Schuster.

Ripley, A. (2004). How we got homeland security wrong. *Time Magazine OnlineEdition.* Retrieved July 18, 2007, from http://www.time.com/time/covers/1101040329/nhomeland.html#

Rokeach, M. (1973). *The nature of human values.* New York: MacMillan.

Toffler, A. (1984). *The third wave.* New York: Bantam House.

Endnotes

[1] Including supplemental funding, the federal government allotted $17 billion to homeland security in 2001. This amount since then has increased to $29 billion, $38 billion, and $46 billion in 2002, 2003, and 2004, respectively (Average increase $7.25 billion/year) (DHS, 2004a).

[2] The Electronic Privacy Information Center (EPIC USA) has some extensive analysis on the surveillance powers of this legislation (See http://www.epic. org/privacy/terrorism/usapatriot).

This chapter was previously published in Social Science Computer Review, 23(4), pp. 480-485, copyright 2005 by Sage Publications. Reprinted by permission of Sage Publications Inc.

Chapter IX

The Little Chip
That Could:
The Public Sector and RFID

David C. Wyld, Southeastern Louisiana University, USA

Abstract

This chapter provides an overview of RFID (radio frequency identification) and the emerging use of the technology in the governmental sector. It examines the fundamental aspects of what RFID technology is, why there is a need for it, and how it is advantageous vs. present bar code technology. The chapter provides a look at how RFID is being used today, both at the federal and state/local levels of government. It looks at the major RFID initiatives being undertaken in the military and the governmental supply chain, as well as creative uses of the technology for improving public administration. The purposes of the chapter were to raise governmental executives and academicians' understanding and awareness of RFID technology and to spotlight the technological, business, and privacy considerations that will be raised over the next decade with the advent of what has been described as nothing less than a "weird new media revolution."

Introduction

What if…:

- A worker at a distribution center could instantly identify each and every one of the items contained in every box on a pallet on the tongs of the forklift she is driving?
- A librarian could locate a book that had been hopelessly misshelved?
- A worker at a livestock processing facility could instantly access the identity and history of a cow?
- A hospital could locate critical medical devices instantly, wherever they are located throughout the facility?
- A pharmacist could tell that two bottles in his supply of a high in demand, highly addictive prescription drug are counterfeit?
- A military contractor in Baghdad could instantly locate the necessary spare to repair a Blackhawk helicopter for an imminent mission?
- A golfer could instantly locate his errant shot and retrieve the ball from the thicket where it landed?

These scenarios are not science fiction. In fact, all are fast becoming possible today through the advent of RFID (radio frequency identification) technology.

What is RFID? Surveys have consistently shown a lack of RFID awareness and an overall lack of understanding about the actual capabilities—and limitations—of automatic identification technologies. Less than half of the general public (41%) have an awareness of RFID technology (Collins, 2005). Likewise, board-level executives were roughly equally divided between those who were up to speed on RFID technology (45%) and those who had no idea what it was (43%) (Best, 2004). There is also an "RFID gender gap," as men are more than twice as likely as women to be aware of RFID and significantly more likely than women to perceive the whole concept of using RFID to track products as being a "good idea." Thus, as has been the case with other radical technologies (cell phones, the Internet, high-definition television), men tend to be in the lead in terms of their overall knowledge of and interest in the technology (Wyld, 2004a).

This chapter is aimed at informing public sector executives and policymakers about this important technology. We will overview what RFID is, how it came to be, how it works, and what you need to know about the technology that will likely becoming a driving force in the economy of the 21ˢᵗ century. We will examine some of the emerging uses of RFID in the public sector, as well as some of the privacy concerns that accompany the technology. Finally, we will look at the proper role for government with what is emerging a new media technology.

RFID 101: The Basics of Technology

The Roots of RFID

Throughout history, there has been a need to identify "things." By identifying things, we can sort, classify, request, ship, account for, look for, and so forth, specific objects. We can do so for our personal use, for business purposes, and even for governmental functions.

As a society, we have come to expect that certain "things" would be—must be—uniquely identified. For instance, each and every automobile has a VIN—a vehicle identification number. Built on a coded system of letters and digits, the VIN conveys information on the specific vehicle in question. As such, it enables the vehicle to be traded, to be owned, to be maintained, and to be insured. Today, with a VIN, one can quickly pull up the complete history of a vehicle on the Internet. Without the power of the VIN to uniquely identify every automobile ever produced, much of the automotive industry and how we think about cars and car ownership would be far different (i.e., "That's really *my* Hummer!").

As with cars, people must be uniquely identified. This need for unique identification of people has existed throughout history. For instance, in the Middle Kingdom of Ancient Egypt, the Pharaoh Khasekem faced great difficulty in effectively distributing rations among the approximately 100,000 men "on duty" for constructing a pyramid project. Paralleling today's headlines, fraud was a common concern in this food distribution program. As such, Khasekem faced great accounting and inventory management difficulties, in that some workers would attempt to receive a daily food allowance several times. To combat this problem, Khasekem's administrators developed a system for identifying each of the workers (Ezzamel, 2004).

Our individual names may not be unique, and any James Johnson, Michael Smith, Miguel Torres, Emily Washington, or Youssef Islam (Cat Stevens) can relate stories—some humorous and some far more serious—where they have been mistakenly identified by their name. Today, we are uniquely identified by a variety of entities, including:

- By the government, through our Social Security numbers,
- By our employers, through our employee ID numbers,

- By universities, through our student ID numbers, and
- By insurers, banks, credit card companies and other financial institutions, through our account numbers.

While we have seen it historically necessary to uniquely identify such highly important assets as ourselves and our vehicles, the vast majority of "things" have remained identified by their class, category, or type. Until 3 decades ago, the human eye served as the primary mechanism for discriminating between objects of different types, whether they be different species of trees, different brands of ketchup, or different forms of munitions. However, with the advent of new technology in the 1970s, for the first time, machines—in addition to people—could identify things.

Automatic Identification, or *Auto-ID*, represents a broad category of technologies that are used to help machines identify objects, humans, or animals. As such, it is often referred to as automatic data capture, as Auto-ID is a means of identifying items and gathering data on them without human intervention or data entry. As can be seen in Figure 1, the omnipresent bar code is itself a form of Auto-ID technology.

RFID is thus fundamentally another form of Auto-ID technology. Sometimes referred to as dedicated short range communication (DSRC), RFID is "a wireless link to identify people or objects" (d'Hont, 2003, p. 1). RFID is, in reality, a subset of the larger radio frequency (RF) market, with the wider market encompassing an array of RF technologies, including: cellular phones, digital radio, the Global Positioning System (GPS), High-Definition Television (HDTV), and wireless networks (Malone, 2004a).

RFID is a technology that already surrounds us. First off, if you have an automobile that was manufactured after 1994, the car uses RFID to verify that it is your key in the ignition. Otherwise, the car won't start. If you have an Exxon/Mobil SpeedPass™ in your pocket, you're using RFID. If you have a toll tag on your car, you're using RFID. If you have checked out a library book, you've likely encountered RFID. If you've been shopping in a department store or an electronics retailer, you've most certainly encountered RFID in the form of an EAS (Electronic Article Surveillance) tag.

RFID is by no means a "new" technology. It is fundamentally based on the study of electromagnetic waves and radio, which was rooted in the 19th Century work of pioneers such as Michael Faraday, James Clerk Maxwell, and Guglielmo Marconi. The idea of using radio frequencies to reflect waves from objects dates back as far as 1886 to experiments conducted by Frederick Hertz. Radar as we know it was invented in 1922, and its practical applications date back to World War II, when the British used the IFF (Identify Friend or Foe) system to identify enemy aircraft on its coasts (Landt, 2001).

Figure 1. The family of automatic identification technologies

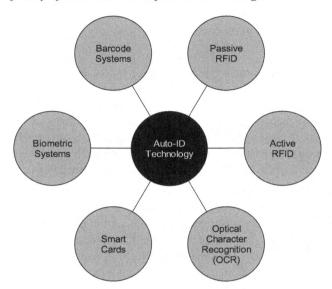

There is even a school of though that attributes the first use of RFID to spy work done in the Former Soviet Union by an imprisoned American musical inventor, Léon Theremin (Glinsky, 2000).

Many, however, point to a seminal academic paper as having laid the foundation for RFID. In 1948, Harry Stockman published "Communication by Means of Reflected Power," in which he laid-out the basic concepts for radio frequency identification. However, Stockman (1948) predicted that "considerable research and development work has to be done before the remaining basic problems in reflected-power communication are solved, and before the field of useful applications is explored" (p. 1202). In fact, it would take decades of development in a variety of different fields—computers, radar and radio technology, supply chain management, transportation, quality management, and engineering—before RFID technology became a reality, seeing limited use in asset management, livestock tracking, transportation, and even payments.

RFID vs. Bar Code Technology

Conceptually, bar codes, and RFID are indeed quite similar, as both auto-ID technologies which are intended to provide rapid and reliable item identification and tracking capabilities. The primary difference between the two technologies is the way in which they "read" objects. With bar coding, the reading device scans a printed label with optical laser or imaging technology. However, with RFID, the reading device scans, or interrogates, a tag using radio frequency signals. Thus, referring to RFID as "radio bar codes"—as many do—is a disservice to the technology, confusing the basics of the technology.

The specific differences between bar code technology and RFID are summarized in Table 1. In summary however, there are five primary advantages that RFID has over bar codes. These are:

1. Each RFID tag can have a unique code that ultimately allows every tagged item to be individually accounted for,

2. RFID allows for information to be read by radio waves from a tag, without requiring line of sight scanning or human intervention,

3. RFID allows for virtually simultaneous and instantaneous reading of multiple tags,

4. RFID tags can hold far greater amounts of information, which can be updated,

5. RFID tags are far more durable (Wyld, 2005a).

Table 1. RFID and bar codes compared

Bar Code Technology	RFID Technology
• Bar Codes require line of sight to be read	• RFID tags can be read or updated without line of sight
• Bar Codes can only be read individually	• Multiple RFID tags can be read simultaneously
• Bar Codes cannot be read if they become dirty or damaged	• RFID tags are able to cope with harsh and dirty environments
• Bar Codes must be visible to be logged	• RFID tags are ultra thin and can be printed on a label, and they can be read even when concealed within an item
• Bar Codes can only identify the type of item	• RFID tags can identify a specific item
• Bar Code information cannot be updated	• Electronic information can be over-written repeatedly on RFID tags
• Bar Codes must be manually tracked for item identification, making human error an issue	• RFID tags can be automatically tracked, eliminating human error

Figure 2. Anatomy of a bar code

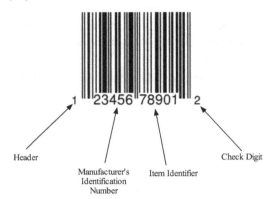

Header

Manufacturer's
Identification
Number

Item Identifier

Check Digit

The principal difference lies in the potential of RFID to provide *unique identifiers* for objects. While the bar code and the UPC (Universal Product Code) have become all-pervading and enabled a host of applications and efficiencies (Brown, 1997), they only identify a "thing" as belonging to a particular class, category, or type. Due to its structure (as shown in Figure 2), a bar code cannot uniquely identify the specific object before you. For instance, while the bar code on a box of cereal can tell you the type, size, and producer of that box of corn flakes, it cannot tell you:

• Where the cereal was boxed?
• When the cereal was produced?
• The lot or production run during which the cereal was made?
• Where the cereal box had traveled in its journey to the shelf?

In sum, a bar code on an item can identify *only* the product and its manufacturer. Thus, a bar code on any one package of sliced meat in a grocery store is the same as on any other of a particular type/size from a particular firm. Likewise, the bar code on a case or pallet of military supplies cannot tell one shipment from another. As such, it is impossible to tell from the bar code such important questions as:

• Where was that particular item manufactured?
• In which lot/shift was the item manufactured?
• When was the product manufactured?
• When will the product expire?

How Does RFID Work?

There are three necessary elements for an RFID system to work. These are tags, readers, and the software necessary to link the RFID components to a larger information processing system. In a nutshell, the technology works like this: the tag is the unique identifier for the item it is attached to. The reader sends out a radio signal, and the tag responds with it to identify itself. The reader then converts the radio waves returned from the tag into data that can be passed on to an information processing system to filter, categorize, analyze, and enable action, based on the identifying information. Kenneth Porad, who is in charge of Boeing's RFID program, explained the technology working "like shining a flashlight at a mirror and reflecting the light back" (quoted in Sternstein, 2005a, n.p.). While this analogy is an easy way to explain the technology to a lay audience, an engineer might readily object, as it is not *technically* correct. This is because with RFID, the communication occurs through the transference of data not through audio or light, but over electromagnetic waves in radio frequency communication.

What's in a Tag?

There are three essential components that combine to form an RFID tag:

• Chip

• Antenna

• Packaging

An RFID tag has at its heart an integrated circuit (IC), which contains the unique identifying data about the object to which it is attached. One of the identifiers—but not the only one—that can be used to identify the item uniquely with an RFID tag is the Electronic Product Code, or EPC, which will be discussed later. The IC is attached to a small antenna, which most commonly is a small coil of wires. The third element is the packaging of the tag that contains and protects the IC and the antenna. This packaging can come in a variety of sizes and forms, geared to meet the requirements of the specific application. In fact, RFID tags can take a variety of forms, including:

• Smart labels

• Keys or key fobs

• Watches

- Smart cards
- Disks and coins, which can be attached to an item with a fastening screw
- Mount-on-metal, with special construction that creates a buffer between the tag and the item to reduce interference and heighten readability
- Glass transponders, which can be implanted under the skin of a human or animal

Hitachi has even developed the mu-chip, a very tiny (.4 millimeter square) RFID tag that is the size of a grain of rice (Anonymous, 2004a).

RFID tags and labels can work effectively, even in harsh environments with excessive dirt, dust, or moisture, and in temperature extremes. They can function in both extreme heat and cold, with a functional temperature range between -25° Celsius and 70° Celsius. Some tags specifically designed for industrial applications can function well beyond the boiling point—up to 250° Celsius. Most tags can withstand the high-power pasteurization process and X-rays. The only caveat to the latter would be that most silicon-based electronic circuits are erased by the gamma radiation commonly used for sterilization (Zebra Technologies, 2004).

There are two basic categories of tags, passive and active. A summary of the differences between the two general categories is presented in Table 2. *Passive tags* are already very familiar to us, as we see simple examples of such in the form of the EAS tags used throughout the retail industry. With a passive tag, the tag basically has no power source, and as such, it is only "on" and able to transmit information when it is within range of an RFID reader. Passive tags function through a process known as "energy harvesting," wherein energy from the reader is gathered by the tag, stored momentarily, and then transmitted back to the reader at a different frequency.

In brief, the science of a passive RFID system works like this. The reader sends out electromagnetic waves, and a magnetic field is formed when the signal from the reader "couples" with the tag's antenna. The passive RFID tag draws its power from this magnetic field, and it is this power that enables the tag to send back an identifying response to the query of the RFID reader. When the power to the silicon chip on the tag meets the minimum voltage threshold required to "turn it on," the tag then can respond to the reader through the same radio frequency (RF) wave. The reader then converts the tag's response into digital data, which the reader then sends on to the information processing system to be used in management applications. Writing in *Wired*, Singel (2004, n.p.) likened passive RFID to a "high-tech version of the children's game 'Marco Polo.'" In a passive RFID system, the reader sends out a signal on a designated frequency, querying if any tags are present in its read filed (the equivalent of yelling out "Marco" in a swimming pool). If a chip is present, the tag takes the radio energy sent-out by the reader to power-it-up and respond with the electronic equivalent of kids yelling "Polo" when they are found.

Table 2. Differentiating passive and active RFID tags

Passive Tags	Active Tags
• Operate without a battery	• Powered by an internal battery
• Less expensive	• More expensive
• Unlimited life (because of no battery)	• Finite lifetime (because of battery)
• Less weight (because of no battery)	• Greater weight (because of battery)
• Lesser range (up to 3-5 meters, usually less)	• Greater range (up to 100 meters)
• Subject to noise	• Better noise immunity
• Derive power from the electromagnetic field generated by the reader	• Internal power to transmit signal to the reader
• Require more powerful readers	• Can be effective with less powerful readers
• Lower data transmission rates	• Higher data transmission rates
• Less tags can be read simultaneously	• More tags can be read simultaneously
• Greater orientation sensitivity	• Less orientation sensitivity

All of this happens almost instantaneously. In fact, today's RFID readers are capable of reading tags at a rate of up to 1,000 tags per second. Through a process known as "simultaneous identification," most RFID systems can capture data from many tags within range of the reader's antenna almost simultaneously. In reality however, the tags are responding individually—within milliseconds of one another—in a manner to prevent tag and reader collision in their signals through response protocols.

"Smart labels" are a particularly important form of passive RFID tag. A smart label is an adhesive label that is human and, quite often, also machine readable through the inclusion of a bar code. However, the label is also embedded with an ultra-thin RFID tag "inlay" (the IC and a printed antenna). Smart labels combine the functionality of passive RFID tags with the convenience and flexibility of that they can be either be preprinted and precoded for use or printed "on-demand." Looking ahead, analysts have predicted that the vast majority of all RFID tags will come in the form of smart labels. In fact, it has been estimated that smart labels will constitute 99.5% of the trillion tags forecast to be in use a decade from now (Anonymous, 2005).

An *active tag* functions in the same manner as its passive counterpart, but it contains a fourth element—an internal battery that continuously powers the tag. As such, the tag is always "on" and transmitting the information contained on its silicon chip. The active tag is only readable, however, when it is in the reading field of an RFID reader. However, the battery significantly boosts the effective operating range of the tag. Thus, while a passive tag can only be read at a range of a few yards, active tags can be read at a distance of 10-30 yards, or more. However, while the useful life of an active tag is limited by the life of he on-board battery (typically 5 years at present), a passive tag has an unlimited life span. Due to the need for a battery, active tags will always cost more and weigh more than a passive tag.

There is a third tag category. With *semi-passive tags*, the RFID tag is combined with sensor, enabling the semi-passive tag to sense the environment. This sensing capacity can be for environmental monitoring. Like an active tag, this category of tag has a battery, which both powers the sensing capability and extends the readability range of the tag. Semi-passive tags have found uses where it is critical to monitor both the location and condition of an item. As tag prices fall, it is very likely that there will be more and unique uses for such tags. A decade from now, the very nature of RFID will likely change, as the technology evolves to what has been labeled "Super RFID," integrating today's microchip technology with sensors that can alert systems for condition changes critical to that item (Best, 2005). Sensors could be geared to a wide variety of conditions, including:

- altitude
- chemical and electrical properties
- flow
- imaging
- level
- motion
- positioning
- pressure
- proximity
- shock and vibration
- speed
- temperature (Malone, 2004b)

Ricadela (2005) predicts that the market for such "multisensor fusion" will be strong, considering that high value products and hazardous materials are especially suited for such sophisticated types of monitoring.

RFID tags can also be classified by their memory capabilities, which can come in three forms:

- **Read-only tags:** Store data that cannot be changed.

- **Read/write tags:** Store data that can be altered or even rewritten over the original data.

- **Combination tags:** Have some data that is permanently stored on the tag, along with additional memory capacity that is available for updates or sensing data.

As such, the tags are intentionally designed not to be the repository of this unique item information. Rather, through a coding system known as the Electronic Product Code (EPC), the tag serves as an electronic "license plate" for each tagged item, directing the user via the Internet to the specific database where complete descriptive information about the item is housed (Aitoro, 2005). While most tags function in this "license plate" mode, with limited memory capacity (generally 96 or 128 bits at present), far more sophisticated tags are available to meet the needs of specific applications.

What is the Electronic Product Code?

The Electronic Product Code is designed to be the unique, item-level identifier for the item to which it is attached. As described earlier, the EPC information on the RFID tag is the pointer to where the complete information on the item is stored. As can be seen in Figure 3, there are 4 elements that comprise the 96-bit capacity Electronic Product Code. These are:

Figure 3. The electronic product code (EPC)

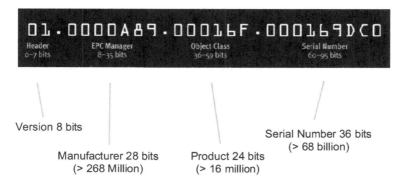

Table 3. EPC tag classes

EPC Tag Class	Tag Class Capabilities
Class 0	EPC number is factory programmed onto the tag and is read-only
Class 1	Read/write-once tags are manufactured without the EPC number (user programmable)
Class 2	Class 1, plus larger memory, encryption, and read/write capabilities
Class 3	Class 2 capabilities, plus a power source to provide increased range or advanced functionality (such as sensing capability)
Class 4	Class 3 capabilities, plus an active transmitter and sensing
Class 5	Class 4 capabilities, plus the ability to communicate with passive tags (essentially a reader)

1.   **The Header (or Version):** This section identifies the length of the EPC number including the code type and version in use (up to 8 bits).

2.   **The EPC Manager (or Manufacturer):** This section identifies the company or entity responsible for managing the next two EPC elements (up to 28 bits).

3.   **The Object Class (or Product:** This section identifies the class of item (e.g., the Stock Keeping Unit {SKU} or consumer unit) (up to 24 bits).

4.   **The Serial Number:** This section identifies a unique serial number for all items in a given object class (up to 36 bits).

There are literally hundreds of trillions of unique identifications possible in the 96-bit EPC structure, and thus, manufacturers should not have to worry about running out of EPC numbers for unique identifiers for each of their product types for many decades or more. The EPC data structure can generate approximately 33 *trillion* different unique combinations, which according to Helen Duce of Cambridge University, would be enough to label all of the atoms in the universe (cited in Anonymous, 2003, p. 39). In fact, according to projections from the National Research Council's Committee on Radio

Frequency Identification Technologies (2004), this will allow for each of the billions of people on earth to have billions of tags each. This can be contrasted with the 12-bit structure of the current UPC data structure. As can be seen referring back to Figure 2, there is a "memory" limitation on bar codes, as with their coding structure, they can identify "only" 100,000 products for each of 100,000 manufacturers. As Parkinson (2003) points out, this may simply not be enough for companies operating in the global, modern economy.

The EPC framework outlines six classes of tags, with an ascending range of capabilities. These are outlined in Table 3.

The EPC has advanced to a second generation of RFID technology, dubbed "Gen2." The Gen2 standard allows for greater interoperability of RFID tags and readers, less collision with wireless devices, increased read rates and enhanced security protocols (Borck, 2006).

What is an RFID Reader?

RFID tags are read by a device known as an RFID reader. These readers have three essential components. These are the:

- Antenna
- Transceiver
- Decoder

RFID readers, which are also referred to as interrogators, can differ quite considerably in their complexity, form, and price, depending upon the type of tags being supported and the functions to be fulfilled. Readers can be large and fixed or small, hand-held devices. However, the read range for a portable reader will be less than the range that can be achieved using a fixed reader, as the effective read range is determined by the size of the antenna, the efficiency of that antenna, and the power of the transmitter. Readers can have a single antenna, but multiple antennas allow for: greater operating range, greater volume/area coverage, and random tag orientation. The reader, either continuously (in the case of a fixed-position reader) or on demand (as with a hand-held reader), sends out an electromagnetic wave to inquire if there are any RFID tags present in its active read field. When the reader receives any signal from a tag, it passes that information on to the decoding software and processes it for forwarding to the information system it is a part of. Recently, it has been forecast that very soon, RFID readers will not be just distinct, dedicated devices. Rather, RFID reading capabilities will soon be capable of being integrated into cell phones, PDAs (personal digital assistants), and other electronic devices, technology that is being tested even today (Thomas, 2005).

"What's the Frequency, Kenneth?"

Frequency designates the intensity of the radio waves used to transmit information. Frequency is of primary importance when determining data transfer rates (bandwidth), in that the higher the frequency, the higher the data transfer rate. In principle, any RF system works much akin to your car radio (assuming you don't have satellite radio!). For instance, all FM radio stations in the United States must operate between 88 and 108 MHz. Thus, if you are currently tuned to 97.1 FM, it means that your radio is tuned at the moment to receive waves repeating 97.1 million times per second.

There are four common frequencies used in RFID systems. Each of the four frequencies has its own properties, and there are a variety of reasons why each is used in specific applications. An overview of the characteristics of each frequency range is provided in Table 4. While work is progressing to harmonizing world standards in each of the four frequency ranges, frequency restrictions imposed by governments around the world have been a significant obstacle facing RFID development (Moore, 2003). For instance, while Europe uses 868 MHz for UHF systems, and the U.S. uses 915 MHz. Japan and China currently do not allow any use of the UHF spectrum for RFID. National governments also regulate the power of the readers to limit interference with other devices (Fox & Rychak, 2004).

The radio frequencies involved in RFID are all in the safe range. 13.56 MHz is between the AM and FM frequencies that have been used for years in commercial radio transmissions, without any known problems. The maximum power level in the United States and most countries is limited to 4 watts. 915 MHz is around the analog cell phone spectrum and has not been found to cause any health concerns at levels below one watt. 2.45 GHz is around the frequency of the newer digital cell phones. At 1 watt or less, there have been no proven health concerns (Wyld, 2005a).

The *read range* refers to the working distance between a tag and a reader. The range that can be achieved in an RFID system is determined by five variables. These are:

1.   The frequency being used.
2.   The power available at the reader.
3.   The power available within the tag.
4.   The size of the reader and tag antennas.
5.   Environmental conditions and structures.

As seen in Table 5, higher frequencies tags have far greater read ranges than tags operating at lower frequencies. This is because all things being equal, power is the key element in this process. In the previously described energy harvesting technique that is employed to power passive tags, it is important to note that the process only returns the signal with a fourth of the power transmitted to power it up. Thus, with the relative—and unavoidable—inefficiency of the process, in order to double the

Table 4. Characteristics and applications of RFID frequency ranges

Frequency Band	Read Range/Speed	Example Applications
Low (LF) 100-500 kHz (Typically 125 to 134 KHz worldwide)	• Short read range (to 18 inches) • Low reading speed	• Access control • Animal identification • Beer keg tracking • Inventory control • Automobile key/ antitheft systems
High (HF) (Typically 13.56MHz)	• Short to medium read range (3 – 10 feet) • Medium reading speed	• Access control • Smart cards • Electronic article surveillance • Library book tracking • Pallet/container tracking • Airline baggage tracking • Apparel/laundry item tracking
Ultra High (UHF) 400-1000 MHz (Typically 850-950 MHz)	• Long read range (10-30 feet) • High reading speed	• Item management • Supply chain management
Microwave 2.4-6.0 GHz (Typically 2.45 or 5.8 GHz)	• Medium read range (10+ feet) • Similar characteristics to UHF tags, but with faster read rates	• Railroad car monitoring • Toll collection systems

read range, the power used must be increased 16 times (Committee on Radio Frequency Identification Technologies, National Research Council, 2004).

Finally, as is the case with so many technologies, while the physics are relatively simple, the devil is in the details to get readers and tags to properly communicate. While the goal for the technology to be "automatic" and hands-off necessitates 100% read rates, such has not always been the case in pilots and early implementations (Sliwa, 2005). There are several variables that can dramatically affect read rates in practice. These include: tag selection and placement, antenna selection and placement, and reader (interrogator) settings (Sirico, 2005). According to Clarke (2005), it must be remembered that experiments and pilots of tags and readers in controlled circumstances "represent the best possible scenarios for readability" and, as the shift is made to an actual warehouse conditions and higher quantities/higher speeds, readability can be significantly challenged" (n.p.).

There are many seemingly extraneous factors which can complicate the reading process. Firstly, when metal or water is present, either in the item itself or in the reading field, this can cause significant declines in read rates. This is because liquids absorb radio waves and metal reflects them. Much has been written about the technical problems of dealing with both problems. For instance, when dealing with the tagging of aircraft parts (Wyld, 2004b) and even luggage tracking (Wyld, 2005b), the metals present in the aircraft must be taken into consideration. Likewise, there are problems in dealing not just with the presence of water and humidity in the environment, but high water content in the packaging and in the items being tagged, labeled. These include, but by no means are limited to:

- fruits (Maenza, 2005)
- vegetables (Downey, 2006)
- beer (Roberti, 2005)
- wine (Wyld, 2005c)

In any setting in which RFID is used, there is the potential for radio signal interference to occur. When this happens, the read rates—and therefore the functionality of the system—can be hampered on anything from a minor to catastrophic level. For instance, Douglas Martin, an Executive Consultant with IBM Global Services, observed that in IBM's work with Wal-Mart on a pilot project involving the backrooms of seven stores' grocery operations, IBM consultants experienced interference from a number of sources. These included: walkie-talkies, forklifts, cell phone towers, and bug zappers (Sullivan, 2004a). Likewise, Hewlett-Packard has reported that in some cases, when HP's forklift drivers would use their cell phones, this would cause misreads of RFID tags (Albright, 2005a). Finally, there is the simple matter that sometimes, the people element comes into play, as workers need to be informed that it is important that they drive the forklift at a certain speed past a certain point or apply a smart label at a precise location on a carton, in order for the RFID tags to be read properly.

In the end, making RFID systems work in practice—meaning produce 100% read accuracy—is thus a complex matter. In fact, L. Allen Bennett, the President and CEO of System Concepts, an RFID integrator providing services to the Social Security Administration and other organizations, provided an apt analogy when he stated, "It's a little like Chinese cooking," in that all the ingredients have to be prepared "right" and be combined in the proper manner (quoted in Olsen, 2005, n.p.). Every location where RFID is to be used and every item to be read by RFID thus presents its own unique set of circumstances. Thus, at present, there is no "one best way" to accomplish RFID, whether your setting is a distribution center, an airport, a hospital, a parking lot, or a retail location. Carey Hidaka, an RFID specialist at IBM Global Services, observed that "in many ways, these (RFID) deployments are more art than science, although the science is very important." Hidaka stressed that when working with RFID, it is vital to remember that "these are not plug-and-play systems" (quoted in Albright, 2005b, n.p.).

The Move to RFID in the Public Sector

The push for RFID has been propelled by the mandates that have been issued for the use of the technology in the supply chain. Various retailers, both in the U.S. and abroad, have issued RFID mandates, including:

- Wal-Mart
- Target
- Best Buy
- Albertson's
- Metro (Germany)
- Tesco (United Kingdom)

The early results found by Wal-Mart have shown marked improvements in supply chain management and item availability (Wyld, 2006a, 2006b). In contrast to the American approach that has leading organizations mandating the use of RFID in their supply chains, the European marketplace has indeed seen a more collaborative approach being taken between large retailers and their major suppliers in the case of Metro and Tesco (Goodman, 2005).

However, it is the U.S. Department of Defense (DoD) that has issued the largest and most sweeping RFID mandate. While the RFID mandates from Wal-Mart, Target, Albertson's, and other retailers will be important, the Defense Department's RFID mandate is far more reaching than that of any retailer, due to the sheer size and scope of the military supply chain. The U.S. military's supply chain is a worldwide operation, which moves almost $29 billion worth of items worldwide each year. The military supply chain is not just bullets, bombs, and uniforms, as it involves a wide panoply of goods, the majority of which are consumer goods as well. The DoD's directive will ultimately affect approximately 60,000 suppliers, the vast majority of which are not the Lockheed's and Boeing's of the world, but small businesses, many of which employ only a few people (Wyld, 2005d). As such, the DoD's RFID mandate has been rightly categorized as the likely "tipping point" for widespread use of RFID in supply chains (Roberti, 2003). As of the end of 2006, the DoD will have all 19 of its centralized distribution depots in the U.S. mainland RFID-enabled (O'Connor, 2006a).

An RFID Agenda for Government

At this early stage in the widespread use of RFID technology, there are far more questions than answers, far more pilots than implementations, and far more interested observers than users of RFID. Indeed, we are early on in the lifespan of RFID technology. In fact, many leading industry experts expect full-fledged implementation of RFID to take 10-15 years, or more (Emigh, 2004). According to Amar Singh, Vice President of SAP's Global RFID Initiative, observed that at present, no one knows the what the true and lasting impact of RFID on the overall business of companies yet simply because "no one has done it yet" (cited in *RFID News & Solutions*, 2004, p. R8). However, as Alan Estevez, the Assistant Deputy Under Secretary for Supply Chain Integration for the Department of Defense bluntly put it: *"Here's the real lesson learned: the technology works"* (quoted in Albright, 2005a, n.p.).

However, there are several areas where government can aid in the progress of the RFID revolution. These are in the areas of:

• Best Practices
• Standards
• Research
• Education
• Privacy

In many instances, these efforts should be, by design, joint undertakings by the public and private sectors, due to the fact that it may be hard to separate the visible hand of government from the invisible hand of the economy in regard to many aspects and applications of this technology. National and even provincial/state governments are taking an even more direct role in the promotion of RFID technology, including:

• China (O'Connor, 2006b)
• United Kingdom (AIM Global, 2003)
• Singapore (Shameen, 2004)
• South Korea (Ilett, 2005)
• Scotland (O'Connor, 2005a)
• Victoria (Australia) (Anonymous, 2005a)

Best Practices

If we look at what is necessary for RFID to be tried, tested, and evaluated in the public sector, the primary need is for executive leadership. Champions must emerge at all levels of government who are willing to set a path toward RFID. Perhaps the greatest function that the public sector can serve is that of a testing ground for RFID technologies, and champions need to emerge who are willing to evaluate if the technology can improve their operations.

In May 2005, the Government Accountability Office (GAO) (2005) issued a comprehensive survey of RFID interest and use across the federal sector, looking for planned and pilot uses beyond the Department of Defense. The GAO found that there were 28 planned or active RFID projects across 15 cabinet-level agencies. The GAO's findings are summarized in Table 5.

One example of a successful RFID program beyond the Department of Defense in the federal government is that of the Social Security Administration (SSA). The Social Security Administration has been a progressive federal agency in the use of RFID. The SSA piloted RFID in 2003 in its internal office supply store, individually tagging items and issuing RFID-enabled shopping cards to allow for automatic reconciliation of "shopping" activity. In the store operations, tagged items could be scanned at checkout, and the system provided greater inventory accuracy and enabled automatic reordering (Albright, 2004b). The SSA has now also implemented RFID in its warehouse management (for forms, flyers, supplies, etc.). In the SSA's warehouse operations:

- 98% of the orders are now processed within eight hours.
- Order processing time has been reduced from 45 days to 3.
- Order backlogs have been eliminated.
- Picking has increased from 500 lines per day to 1,500.
- Fill rates of 94% on normal orders and 98% on emergency orders have been accomplished, both with minimal safety stock.
- The agency has been able to reduce its warehouse space by 60,000 square feet through inventory optimization (Anonymous, 2005c; Olsen, 2005).

From the perspective of SSA Project Manager Gary Orem, the agency has been able to dramatically improve the accuracy of its inventory data, while providing labor savings on the order of 70%. According to Orem, "Initially, the SSA warehouse and supply chain operations were done manually and very labor intensive, which resulted in system inaccuracies and delays in getting product to our customers. The agency reaped significant benefits—including more production with less staff ...(and) an annual savings of $1 million" (quoted in Anonymous, 2007, n.p.).

Table 5. Federal agencies reported or planned use of RFID technology

Agency	Application
Department of Agriculture	• Animal identification program
Department of Defense	• Logistics support • Tracking shipments
Department of Energy	• Detection of prohibited articles • Tracking the movement of materials
Department of Health and Human Services	• Physical access control
Department of Homeland Security	• Border control • Immigration and customs • Location systems • Tracking and identification of baggage on flights
Department of Labor	• Tracking and locating case files
Department of State	• Electronic passports
Department of Transportation	• Electronic screening
Department of the Treasury	• Physical and logical access control • Records management (tracking documents)
Department of Veterans Affairs	• Audible prescription reading • Tracking and routing carriers along conveyor lines
Environmental Protection Agency	• Tracking radioactive materials
Food and Drug Administration	• Tracking pharmaceutical drugs for product integrity/anticounterfeiting
General Services Administration	• Distribution and asset management • Identification of contents of shipments • Tracking of evidence and artifacts
National Aeronautics and Space Administration	• Hazardous material management
Social Security Administration	• Warehouse management

Apart from its warehouse operations, the SSA has employed RFID for fleet management of an 86-vehicle pool, which receives over a thousand use requests monthly. The system employed RFID for key-management systems, and it provided greater availability of pool vehicles, while making for cost-operational efficiencies (Burnell, 2004).

RFID has been demonstrated by public sector users to be able to improve the tracking of both critical things and even critical people. In the former category, there are several exemplary public sector examples of RFID pilots and implementations that have already taken place. These include:

- Library materials
- Court documents and evidence
- Hazardous waste

Libraries have been at the vanguard of implementing RFID-based tracking, inventory, and check-out systems. For instance, in Virginia Beach, Virginia, the public library system in investing $1.5 million in an RFID-based inventory system and placing tags (at a cost of 50 cents each) in each of approximately 800,000 items at nine library locations (Sternstein, 2005b). Likewise, in suburban Frisco, Texas, the library system is outfitting its libraries with a similar RFID-based tracking system (Anonymous, 2005d).

The interest in RFID systems for libraries is high. This is because in library operations, RFID can:

- Enable self-checkout.
- Reduce the time librarians spend handling materials (by as much as 75% in Frisco, TX).
- Enable library staff to more easily locate lost/misplaced items;
- Reduce repetitive stress injuries.
- Empower librarians to engage in more "value-add" services with library patrons (research assistance, storytelling, etc.) (Wyld, 2005a).

Dr. Ron Heezen, Director of the Frisco Public Library, commented that: "We wanted to redesign our library for the next generation, as it became very clear to me that all public libraries will have to make do with fewer employees and tighter budgets in the future" (quoted in Anonymous, 2005d, n.p.).

Yet, there is a civil liberties aspect to implementing the technology in public libraries. In fact, privacy concerns led the San Francisco Board of Supervisors to deny funding in July 2005 for an RFID system that would have replaced bar code based tracking at 12 of the 28 branches of the San Francisco Public Library. Similar concerns were also brought to the fore across the bay when the Berkeley Public Library actually installed an RFID pilot system in 2004 (O'Connor, 2005b).

One of the most promising applications of RFID technology is in the area of file tracking. While many government agencies are attempting to move to a paperless environment, the fact remains that for most, the ubiquitous manila folder is at the heart of their operations. However, building upon systems designed for law firms to better organize and track their files by employing RFID tagging, legal agencies are taking the lead in the public sector to better manage their paper files.

The DeKalb County, Georgia Juvenile Court works with more than 9,000 children in their system annually. To do so, the court system faces the task of tracking over 12,000 manila file folders. DeKalb County estimates that on average, clerks spend about 10 hours each week simply searching for lost files. According to Juvenile Court Judge Robin Nash: "We have about 2,200 cases of neglect investigated every year, and between 1,100 and 1,200 kids in foster care at any given time. My assistant spends about two hours daily trying to track down files on the three floors of the courthouse, and we believe the RFID system will become a huge labor savings" (cited in Sullivan, 2005a). Thus, DeKalb County is spending $50,000 to tag file folders with RFID-labels and equip clerks with desk-mounted and handheld readers. DeKalb County is projecting that the payback on this system will come within 2 years, as it estimates that the reduction in lost files will save the Juvenile Court approximately $30,000 each year. When a new, far larger courthouse opens later in 2007, DeKalb County plans to outfit the building with an RFID file-tracking system throughout the facility (Sullivan, 2005a).

Across the country, similar results have been achieved in two reported installations of RFID-based file tracking systems in both Marin County, California, and Maricopa County (Phoenix), Arizona. Using 13.56 Mhz tags embedded in file labels, the tracking capabilities enable employees to track files. The main benefit of the file tracking system, in the view of Marin County District Attorney Ed Berberian Jr., is that it dramatically cuts down on the wasted time in locating misplaced and lost files, a cost his office estimates to be approximately 2,500 man hours per year. If an employee should not be able to locate a file in their office, the 3M system allows employees to use handheld devices to track the wayward file down. Likewise, in Marin County, staff members routinely screen each of the forty attorneys' offices several times a week to catalog the files in their possession. The systems employed in both jurisdictions enable employees to be alerted if a file is physically misfiled or placed out of order in a storage drawer or file cabinet. They also use reading pads that can successfully scan a stack of files a foot high (Swedberg, 2005)!

With a high critical value, RFID has proven to have significant potential in improving the handling of the most critical things, like hazardous waste. For example, the Department of Energy is currently overseeing the clean-up of the Hanford Nuclear Site, the former plutonium production facility in Washington State. With its private contractor, Bechtel Hanford, the DOE is transporting 4,000 tons of radioactive waste daily from around the 586-square-mile, 200-mile-long Columbia River Corridor area to a central landfill facility. Prior to the May 2005 introduction of the RFID-based system, as the trucks bearing the hazardous waste were weighed prior to entering the landfill, operators had to manually key in the identity codes for both the truck and each of the up to ten steel cans bearing tons of waste for over 200 truckloads daily. The system utilizes active tags operating at 315Mhz, with a range of 100 feet. Steve Teller, who directed the RFID deployment for Bechtel Automation Technology, reports that the system is presently achieving a 98% read rate, in spite of the challenge of dealing with the metal cans. Teller stated that: "We use cans with four different designs. If you look at them, you wouldn't think the designs are very different, but those little differences become big differences when you're using RFID, because the radio waves are bouncing off everything" (OConnor, 2005c, n.p.).

At the Dryden Flight Research Center at Edwards Air Force Base in California, a team of NASA innovators has shown how RFID can be combined with sensor technology to enhance the safety of handling hazardous materials. Ralph Anton, NASA Dryden's Chemical Program Manager, commented that: "When we heard about RFID, we saw its potential. But instead of just producing a PowerPoint slide show of what RFID could enable, we went ahead and developed a working solution to prove it" (quoted in Collins, 2004, n.p.). Their pilot in late 2004 demonstrated how RFID tags, augmented by temperature sensors, could be used to monitor the proper storage of hazardous chemicals in one of Dryden's five storage facilities. The system developed by the NASA engineers tied-in to the existing hazardous materials management system, enabling alerts to be triggered if a tagged chemical bladder, container, or cardboard box holding a chemical was moved, stored incorrectly, or reached a threatening temperature. The Dryden test showed that safety could be enhanced while producing labor savings in the physical monitoring of the hazardous chemicals. Perhaps even more importantly, the pilot demonstrated that RFID-labeling could enable emergency responders could more quickly access information on the chemicals they were dealing with, should an incident occur off-site (Collins, 2004). The initial NASA test further demonstrated the value proposition for RFID in the handling of even nonhazardous chemicals, and the agency is planning to extend it to cover all chemical storage at the Dryden facility. According to NASA's Anton: "Storing at the correct temperature can extend the useful life of chemicals. Given that for every $1 spent buying a chemical it costs about $10 to dispose of it, monitoring the temperature can save the government money in future" (cited in Collins, 2004, n.p.).

RFID can be also be used to track the most critical possible thing, namely people. In Mexico, Attorney General Rafael Macedo de la Concha made headlines last year when it was announced that he and 160 federal prosecutors and drug investigators were implanted with subcutaneous RFID chips to provide the most secure access possible to Mexico's new federal anticrime information center. The number of chipped officials in Mexico reportedly grew to include key members of the Mexican military, the federal police, and even staffers in the office of Mexico's then President, Vicente Fox (Anonymous, 2004b).

While nothing like this would be a widespread practice for government in this country, due to the obvious civil liberty concerns, there are several exemplary public sector examples of the use of external RFID tags for what might be categorized as "critical people." First, borrowing from the same RFID concepts that have been successfully used at theme parks (Dignan, 2004) and sports venues (Wyld, 2006c) with RFID-enabled smart bands, patients can be tracked using RFID-equipped smart brands or bracelets. For instance, the U.S. Navy used smart bands to identify the wounded aboard hospital ships in the Iraq War in 2003, replacing the "Civil War technology" of tracking patients through the use of paper-based charts (Ewalt, 2003). The Los Angeles County Sheriff's Department has earmarked $1.5 million dollars to a program to monitor inmates, using active RFID bracelets. The sheriff's office feels that the technology is a good investment, due to the fact that it will aid in enhancing security and in decreasing violent incidents (Sullivan, 2005b). Finally, after pilot testing an RFID-enabled access card program at the Marshall Space Flight Center in Alabama, National Aeronautics and Space Administration (NASA) plans to implement a system to deploy 100,000 "smart cards." With RFID-enabled access cards, NASA hopes to achieve improved security and access control (Bacheldor, 2004).

In sum, the government—at all levels—should be a test-bed for RFID technologies. Much of the message today is that it is important to begin to experiment with, to pilot, and to plan for implementation of RFID, even if the business case for doing so can be categorized as being "fuzzy." In the view of the President of EPCglobalUS, Mike Meranda: "You learn by doing, even though the technology is not perfect" (quoted in Albright, 2005a, n.p.). Speaking in April 2005, Former U.S. Department of Homeland Security Secretary Tom Ridge commented that: "The return on investment most businesses want is a little bit different than the return on investment you might find in the public sector....This (RFID) will improve efficiency. This will improve accountability. This will improve the bottom line. And, oh, by the way, as a direct consequence, this will also enhance security" (quoted in Wasserman, 2005a, n.p.). Thus, government can and should undertake RFID projects that may produce ROI over a longer period than could be done by their private sector counterparts, and work to "push the envelope" and expand the knowledgebase on RFID technology in the process. We have also seen the federal government become an active partner in industry-wide initiatives to make use of RFID to improve supply chain security, including animal identification (Wyld, 2006d) and pharmaceuticals (Wyld & Jones, 2007).

RFID should be viewed as part of a larger wave of wireless technologies that are fast-becoming a significant part of the governmental IT market. Writing in *Washington Technology*, Welsh (2005) observed that "RFID is quickly moving from being viewed as a standalone technology to one that can be blended with complementary technologies into more robust solutions" (n.p.). However, he also cautioned that it will be difficult for governments to pursue these solutions when they are struggling with their own budgets. Thus, it is very likely that there will be a role for the federal government to play in encouraging governmental applications of RFID technology at the state and local level. This could be done through grant programs and demonstration projects from various agencies. However, as we have seen the potential for government to aid in programs that foster both technological and economic growth (such as President Bush's hydrogen car initiative), the stage would seem to be set for a wider RFID initiative at the federal level. Such a Presidential initiative would certainly place RFID on the national agenda, and spotlight its potential to find new ways to do things in better ways, and create companies, jobs, and technological progress in the process.

Privacy is a huge issue as RFID moves forward. As Paul O'Shea (2003) reminds us, RFID is a technological tool, and "as with all technology, it can be used to manipulate our world or be abused for unwarranted control" (n.p.). The fears of a "Big Brother" use of the technology are widespread. It is only inflamed by references to the Biblical "Mark of the Beast" (Jones, 2005, April 3) and to Orwellian popular culture examples, such as in the movies *A Beautiful Mind* and *Minority Report*. From a procedural perspective, privacy must be a consideration in *all* federal RFID initiatives. The E-Government Act of 2002 requires that each agency must undertake a privacy impact assessment (PIA) when they decide to employ undertake an information technology project or redesign a business process to incorporate new technologies. These PIAs must be published and made available to the public. Thus, in the view of Kenneth Mortensen, an attorney with the U.S. Department of Homeland Security's (DHS) Privacy Office who spoke on the subject at a privacy forum in July 2005, "We have privacy baked in" on any federal RFID project. He cited as an example the DHS US-VISIT (United States Visitor and Immigrant Status Indicator Technology) program, which will incorporate RFID and biometric technology at border crossings with Canada and Mexico. His office filed the PIA for the project in January 2004 and continues to work with project managers and technologists, asking questions like: "'What is the purpose?'...and 'Why am I using or collecting or storing this information?" to help project teams incorporate privacy considerations into their proposed designs and solutions (quoted in Wasserman, 2005b, n.p.).

Certainly, privacy will continue to be a huge issue in the development of RFID, especially as the technology begins to migrate to the consumer level. We have seen this again and again, from when the first shoppers began encountering RFID tags at Wal-Mart's Sam's Wholesale Clubs in Texas (Sullivan, 2004b) to the recent controversy over the U.S. State Department's attempts to place RFID chips in U.S. passports (Zappone, 2006; Wyld, 2005e). It will behoove both those in the public and private sector to maintain a "finger on the pulse" of the public and workers to gauge their understanding of and misapprehensions about the capabilities of RFID technology. However, there is a significant risk to have policy go beyond protecting individual rights and hamper the full use and deployment of the technology, which could perhaps delay or make impossible breakthroughs that could aid the public in retail, health care and many other arenas of their lives. Further, with significant concern over identity theft and other forms of hacking, as cases of such are reported with RFID (Hesseldahl, 2004), calls for encryption and other forms of protection for RFID tags may be furthered.

Conclusion: "Uncle Sam's Guiding Hand"

For at least a decade to come, we are likely to see the U.S. government's investment in automatic identification technologies and its formal and informal mandates create profound changes in the way *all of us* conduct business and even live our lives. If so, it would be history repeating itself. When we look at federal programs, the direct ROI for the spending is often miniscule when compared to the spin-off effects of the technological developments. This has occurred several times over the past few decades, including:

- The 1960s and 1970s with NASA and the space program;
- The 1980s and 1990s with the Defense Department and ARPANET, which laid the foundations for the Internet; and
- The present, post-September 11th environment, where the push for greater homeland security is leading to large investments in wireless technologies, scanning, imaging, and data mining, which is already producing technology transfer to private enterprise and public benefit.

A couple of years ago, noted futurist Paul Saffo (2002), the Director of the Institute for the Future, characterized RFID as being this decade's entry into the pantheon on the new technologies that have come along to reshape the information technology landscape.

As Dan Mullen, President of AIM Global, put it: "The government was a huge driver in the development of the bar code market, and there is an incredible amount of parallel in how the RFID market is developing." As such, the government "can serve as a model for others who want to explore new opportunities to improve" (quoted in Burnell, 2004, p. 16). Likewise, the Department of Defense's commitment to be an early adopter of RFID technologies throughout its complex, worldwide, multilayered supply chain is likely to advance not just the pace of automatic identification technology development, but the scope, standardization and utility of RFID technologies in general. In the end, we may well judge that the U.S. government's push for RFID technology—through both the military's mandate and the host of other mandates and initiatives across federal agencies—will perhaps be *the* key driver to make automatic identification a reality throughout consumer-facing industries in the very near future.

Writing on the subject of "Uncle Sam's Guiding Hand," Greenemeier (2004) argues that the government's role in technology adoption can be a complex one, which both fosters and retards innovation. He shows that throughout history, government—by issuing mandates, by acting as a major purchaser, and by helping to set standards—can be a positive force in advancing technology. However, if regulations and mandates are too constrictive, government can stifle innovation and actually slow the progress and acceptance of the technology. Dave Wennergren, The Navy's Chief Information Officer, remarked that the proper role of government when technology is new and in flux is a leadership position, helping "to help make some order out of chaos." Wennergren points out that "in a networked world, government can use its size in a united way" to advance the technology and set standards (opinion cited in Hasson, 2004, n.p.).

In the end, the current push for RFID may be a small part of a larger mosaic. Indeed, Paul Saffo foresees that much of the focus on RFID today is on doing old things in new ways, but the truly exciting proposition is the new ideas and new ways of doing things that will come from RFID. RFID makes possible "an Internet of things" (Schoenberger, 2002) or a "wireless Internet of artifacts" (Gadh, 2004), Saffo sees RFID as making possible what he terms "the sensor revolution." This is based on viewing RFID as a *media technology*, making it possible for what he categorizes as "'smartifacts' or intelligent artifacts, that are observing the world on our behalf and increasingly manipulating it on our behalf." Saffo thus stresses the importance of thinking outside the box on RFID and looking beyond today's problems to find "unexpected applications," which is where "the greatest potential for RFID lies" (quoted in O'Connor, 2005d, n.p.). Indeed, Saffo urges people to take a 20-year perspective on RFID, believing that we are in the early stages of "a weird new kind of media revolution," in that "RFID will make possible new companies that do things we don't even dream about" (quoted in Van, 2005, B1).

If we indeed take the long-view of history, we can see that some of today's biggest industries, most pedestrian technologies, and most indispensable parts of our lives come from sparks of imagination on how to use a technology in unimagined ways. Indeed, we have seen bar coding itself used in applications far beyond the supply chain functions it was created for (Brown, 1997). Who would have dreamed that GPS systems would today be routinely used by business executives, lost in their rental cars in big cities, and by fisherman and hunters on the bayou? Who would have dreamed that people around the globe, from Moscow, Russia to Moscow, Idaho and every place in between, would have their own cell phone? In the 1950s, when people gathered around a lumbersome black and white television to watch "I Love Lucy," who could have dreamed of a 500-channel universe? Could anyone at DARPA have envisioned the multitude of opportunities for companies such as eBay, Amazon, and Google that would be spawned by the Internet? As with the RFID-enabled golf balls discussed earlier in this chapter, we are today seeing the first fruits of this "weird" new media revolution that RFID is sparking.

There will undoubtedly be an "RFID Revolution." How far and how fast it will move, and at what cost (both in dollars and privacy) and benefit (to the contactless of our commerce to our own health) remain to be seen. The trajectory and the timeline for this revolution may be uncertain, and the ultimate scale of RFID's impact on business, society, and indeed our everyday lives spans a very wide margin of error (from minor conveniences to total transformation).

Yet, we can benefit today from being cognizant of the long view of history, knowing how the government has played a role in advancing other communications media. Thus, the public sector should have a different ROI equation on its RFID investments than any private sector entity can—and perhaps even should—have at present. While companies such as Wal-Mart can look at their internal investments in RFID and hope that others in its supply chain will follow, they must ultimately make their decisions on RFID on what is going-on within their own four walls. Yet, we ultimately do not—and really cannot—live in a "slap and ship" world. In supply chains, the move has been toward greater integration and cooperation. Likewise, the power of the network has been shown over and over again, with the Internet, the Web, mobile telephones, electronic media, and so forth. As shown in Figure 4, the larger the net cast by RFID becomes (linking organizations internally and their external supply chain partners, both upstream and downstream), the higher the overall value proposition becomes.

RFID thus presents a classic "chicken and egg" problem, in that wider RFID adoption will likely lower the costs associated with RFID and markedly increase the beneficial aspects. The author of a recent book on RFID, Steven Shepard (2005) categorized the current supply chain as operating under what he aptly described as "The Kevin Costner Effect." Adapting the famous line from the movie *Field of Dreams*, he described the layers of players in the supply chain as operating under the philosophy that, "If you build it, they will come" (p. 7).

In the long-view then, it is likely that an "RFID multiplier" will emerge, whereby one lead entity's RFID spending will cause ripple effects in the form of RFID investments by others in its supply chain, and then on to a next-level of derivative supply chain partners down-line. Yet, while this concept applies to government RFID investments as well, RFID ROI in the public sector will come not only from the RFID multiplier in the supply chain, but from a larger spark in those new ideas and new companies that will pursue them in the marketplace. This will lay the ground for job and wealth creation, and make government investments in what Saffo termed a "weird new kind of media revolution" an enticing economic development tool. The public sector's efforts to pilot and implement RFID today and over the next decade will help to advance the RFID knowledge base, establish best practices, overcome some of RFID's technological quirks and physics problems, and set the standards to provide the common set of tracks for the RFID industry.

Thus, federal, state and local officials must rightly examine each prospective use of RFID, from the battlefield to the warehouse to the library to the hospital for the implementation and ongoing costs vs. the tangible service gains and cost savings that can be achieved to determine the short-term ROI of their project. Yet, they should also know that by making the decision to implement ROI in their venue for their purposes and for the benefit of their stakeholders, they are helping to advance the technology and ultimately, they will help to not only give the technology the lift needed to fly over the long-term. Thus, they will help lay the foundation not only for

Figure 4. The increasing value of automatic identification interconnectivity

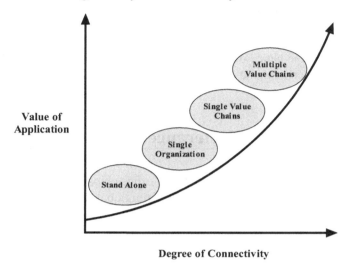

future RFID uses in their own organization and aid the development of the people and companies that will prosper in the midst of this RFID revolution.

Will RFID be "the next big thing?" At this point in the technology's life cycle, it is too early for anyone to tell, but the stars certainly seem to be in alignment for the next decade to be a tremendously exciting one. As Under Secretary Alan Estevez (2005) recently wrote: "The real value of RFID lies not in what it can do today but in what it will do in the future" (n.p.). As Albright (2005b) so aptly characterized the RFID challenge, "We're in the very early stages of a marathon" (n.p.). Many share the sentiment of Kuchinskas (2005) that: "RFID will change business and society as much as cell phones and the Internet have. While the technology will transform business processes, it also will ease some of life's daily annoyances" (n.p.). One blogger captured the latter sentiment regarding RFID exquisitely when he wrote: "I'm serious. I don't really care much for Wal-Mart's inventory problems. RFID could solve *my* inventory problems" (emphasis in the original, n.p.). He desired a smart home that could help one locate "unhappy objects," such as a forgotten coffee cup or the TV remote, made intelligent with RFID. For instance, if he couldn't find his bag for a trip, he'd like to have the smart home system prompt him with: "Dude. You left the suitcase in the bathroom, under the sink again" (Grosso, 2004, n.p.). If we reach that point, RFID will have arrived.

RFID may prove to be one of the true technological transformations of our time. As the successor to bar code technology to identify "things," each and every day, new applications are being developed for the technology, both in the supply chain and beyond. Just as it has with the space program, the Global Positioning System, the Internet, and indeed, with the use of bar codes, the federal government is playing a significant role in the advancement of RFID technology and in the development of best practices and models that can be used both in the public and private sectors. Thus, the "visible hand" of government is once again an important factor in technological advancement and commercialization.

References

AIM Global. (2003, October). The U.K. home office chips in. *RFID Connections*. Retrieved July 19, 2007, from http://www.aimglobal.org/technologies/rfid/resources/articles/oct03/homeoffice.htm

Aitoro, J. (2005, February 25). The government and RFID: What you need to know. *VARBusiness*. Retrieved July 19, 2007, from http://www.varbusiness.com/sections/governmentvar/govt.jhtml?articleId=60403591

Albright, B. (2004, March 1). Social Security Administration gives RFID a try. *Frontline Solutions*. Retrieved July 19, 2007, from http://www.frontlinetoday.com/frontline/article/articleDetail.jsp?id=88916

Albright, B. (2005a, April 12). RFID worth the risk: The technology is providing real solutions today, even if the business case isn't yet clear for everybody. *Frontline Solutions*. Retrieved July 19, 2007, from http://www.frontlinetoday.com/frontline/article/articleDetail.jsp?id=156139

Albright, B. (2005b, March 23). Business intelligence vendors sitting out RFID rush. *Frontline Solutions*. Retrieved July 19, 2007, from http://www.frontlinetoday.com/frontline/article/articleDetail.jsp?id=152787

Anonymous. (2003, May). Pushing the envelope. *Management Today*. Retrieved August 30, 2004, from http://www.managementtoday.co.uk/search/article/412314/techknow-people- products-shaping-future-pushing-the-envelope-smart-labels/.

Anonymous. (2004a). Micro tracker. *Technology Review, 107*(3), 18.

Anonymous. (2004b, July 14). Mexico tagging federal crime fighters with RFID chips. *SiliconValley.com*. Retrieved July 19, 2007, from http://www.siliconvalley.com/mld/siliconvalley/living/9154114.htm

Anonymous. (2005a, July 13). Victoria eager to become RFID hotspot. *Image and Data Manager Online*. Retrieved July 19, 2007, from http://www.idm.net.au/story.asp?id=6520

Anonymous. (2005b, March 23). RFID unites the supply chain. *Business Process Management Today*. Retrieved July 19, 2007, from http://bpm-today.newsfactor.

com/scm/story.xhtml?story_title=RFID-Unites-the-Supply-Chain&story_id=
31672&category=scm#story-start

Anonymous. (2005c, February 1). Social Security RFID. *SecureIDNews*. Retrieved July 19, 2007, from http://www.secureidnews.com/library/2005/02/01/social-security-rfid/.

Anonymous. (2005d, June 16). Frisco Public Library deploys RFID technology to help manage books. *Government Technology*. Retrieved July 19, 2007, from http://www.govtech.net/news/news.php?id=94309

Anonymous. (2007, January 18). Social Security Administration uses Intermec RFID technology to improve data collection accuracy, reduce labor costs. *MSN/Money*. Retrieved July 19, 2007, from http://news.moneycentral.msn.com/provider/providerarticle.aspx?Feed=BW&Date=20070118&ID=6354695

Bacheldor, B. (2004, July 19). NASA to test RFID-enabled access cards: The access cards will be used to regulate entry at the space agency's Marshall Space Flight Center in Alabama. *InformationWeek*. Retrieved July 19, 2007, from http://www.informationweek.com/showArticle.jhtml?articleID=26100614

Best, J. (2004, October 8). Senior management "clueless" about RFID. *Silicon.com*. Retrieved July 19, 2007, from http://news.zdnet.co.uk/business/management/0,39020654,39169620,00.htm

Best, J. (2005, January 25). 2015: RFID is all over—Make way for super RFID. *Silicon.com*. Retrieved July 19, 2007, from http://networks.silicon.com/lans/print.htm?TYPE=story&AT=39127336-39024663t-40000017c

Borck, J.R. (2006, April 13). The long road to RFID interoperability: The Gen2 standard means vendors and customers finally have a common platform. *InfoWorld*. Retrieved July 19, 2007, from http://www.infoworld.com/article/06/04/13/77022_16FErfidsoftgen2_1.html?DATA+MINING

Brown, S. (1997). *Revolution at the checkout counter: The explosion of the bar code*. Cambridge, MA: Harvard University Press.

Burnell, J. (2004, January). Of the people, by the people, for the people—with help from technology. *Realtime*. Retrieved July 19, 2007, from http://epsfiles.intermec.com/eps_files/eps_realtime/jan_04/jan_04_trends.pdf

Clarke, R. (2005, January-February). Assessing readability problems with RFID systems: Frequency, distances and angles, type of tag, location and orientation, influences of moisture and metals, and pallet patterns all play a part in readability. *RFID Product News*. Retrieved July 19, 2007, from http://www.rfidproductnews.com/issues/2005.01/feature/readability.php

Collins, J. (2004, December 14). NASA tries RFID for HAZMAT: At Dryden Flight Research Center, NASA is exploring ways to reduce costs and risk by using RFID to automatically identify and track hazardous materials. *RFID*

Journal. Retrieved July 19, 2007, from http://rfidjournal.com/article/articleview/1288/1/1/

Collins, J. (2005, April 8). Consumers more RFID-aware, still wary: A recent survey finds that more U.S. consumers have heard about RFID, but worries about privacy remain. *RFID Journal*. Retrieved July 19, 2007, from http://www.rfidjournal.com/article/articleview/1491/1/1/

Committee on Radio Frequency Identification Technologies, National Research Council (2004). Radio frequency identification technologies: A workshop summary. Washington, D.C.: National Academy of Sciences, National Academies Press. Retrieved July 19, 2007, from http://www.nap.edu/catalog/11189.html

Dignan, L. (2004, May). Riding radio waves: Are radio frequency identification tags good just for cutting costs in the supply chain? Not hardly. Theme park operators think they can boost sales. *Baseline, 1*(30), 22-24.

d'Hont, S. (2003). The cutting edge of RFID technology and applications for manufacturing and distribution: A white paper from Texas Instruments. Retrieved July 19, 2007, from http://www.ti.com/tiris/docs/manuals/whtPapers/manuf_dist.pdf

Downey, L. (2006, November 13). Can RFID Save the Day for Spinach? *RFID Journal*, Retrieved December 6, 2006, from http://www.rfidjournal.com/article/articleview/2802/1/82/.

Emigh, J. (2004, December 1). Full-scale RFID could take a decade. *eWEEK*. Retrieved July 19, 2007, from http://www.extremetech.com/print_article2/0,2533,a=140277,00.asp

Estevez, A.F. (2005, May-June). RFID vision in the DOD supply chain. *Army Logistician*. Retrieved July 19, 2007, from http://www.almc.army.mil/alog/rfid.html

Ewalt, D. (2003, June 9). Navy puts RFID into service: Doctors and nurses at Iraq military hospital use the technology to track and treat patients. *InformationWeek*. Retrieved July 19, 2007, from http://www.ti.com/tiris/docs/news/in_the_news/2003/6-9-03.shtml

Ezzamel, M. (2004). Work organization in the Middle Kingdom, Ancient Egypt. *Organization, 11*(4), 497-537.

Fox, R., & Rychak, L. (2004, May). The potential and challenges of RFID technology. *Advisory*. Retrieved July 19, 2007, from http://www.mintz.com/publications/detail/264/Communications_Advisory_The_Potential_and_Challenges_of_RFID_Technology/

Gadh, R. (2004, August 11). The state of RFID: Heading toward a wireless Internet of artifacts. *Computerworld*. Retrieved July 19, 2007, from http://www.computerworld.com/mobiletopics/mobile/story/0,10801,95179,00.html

Glinsky, A. (2000). *Theremin—Ether music and espionage*. Champaign, IL: University of Illinois Press.

Goodman, B. (2005, March 17). Is RFID taking off, or just taking its time? *Integrating the Enterprise*. Retrieved July 19, 2007, from http://www.itbusinessedge.com/content/3Q/3qpub2-20050317.aspx

Government Accountability Office (GAO). (2005, May). Report to Congressional requesters—INFORMATON SECURITY: Radio frequency identification technology in the federal government. Retrieved July 19, 2007, from http://www.gao.gov/new.items/d05551.pdf

Greenemeier, L. (2004, December 13). Uncle Sam's guiding hand: Government mandates increasingly translate directly into IT initiatives, setting the top priorities at many companies. *InformationWeek*. Retrieved July 19, 2007, from http://www.informationweek.com/story/showArticle.jhtml?articleID=55301001

Grosso, B. (2004, November 15). Intelligent objects versus unhappy objects. *RFID Buzz*. Retrieved July 19, 2007, from http://www.rfidbuzz.com/news/2004/intelligent_objects_versus_unhappy_objects.html

Hasson, J. (2004, September 27). The next big thing for government. *Federal Computer Week*. Retrieved July 19, 2007, from http://www.fcw.com/fcw/articles/2004/0927/news-next-thing-09-27-04.asp

Hesseldahl, A. (2004, July 29). A hacker's guide to RFID. *Forbes*. Retrieved July 19, 2007, from http://www.forbes.com/2004/07/29/cx_ah_0729rfid_print.html

Ilett, D. (2005, June 24). Korea dishes out $800m on RFID. *Silicon.com*. Retrieved July 19, 2007, from http://networks.silicon.com/mobile/0,39024665,39131408,00.htm

Jones, J. (2005, April 3). Is the "RFID" chip the mark of the beast? *Political Gateway*. Retrieved July 19, 2007, from http://www.politicalgateway.com/main/columns/read.html?col=323

Kuchinskas, S. (2005, January 12). RFID tags a booming biz. *Internetnews.com*. Retrieved July 19, 2007, from http://www.internetnews.com/wireless/article.php/3458331

Landt, J. (2001). Shrouds of time: The history of RFID. Retrieved July 19, 2007, from http://www.aimglobal.org/technologies/rfid/resources/shrouds_of_time.pdf

Maenza, T. (2005, June). Supply chain visibility exposes weak links, hidden costs. *Insights*. Retrieved July 19, 2007, from http://www.unisys.com/commercial/insights/insights__compendium/supply__chain__visibility__exposes__weak__links__hidden__costs.htm

Malone, R. (2004a, August). Reconsidering the role of RFID. *Inbound Logistics*. Retrieved July 19, 2007, from http://www.inboundlogistics.com/articles/supplychain/sct0804.shtml

Malone, R. (2004b, December). Sensing the future. *Inbound Logistics, 24*(12), 18-19.

Moore, B. (2003, February). RFID: Not a perfect world. *Material Handling Management, 58*(2), 50.

O'Connor, M.C. (2005a, January 26). Scotland provides RFID support: The government-supported Wireless Innovation Demo Lab at Scotland's Hillington Park Innovation Centre fosters RFID applications. *RFID Journal.* Retrieved July 19, 2007, from http://www.rfidjournal.com/article/articleview/1358/1/1/

O'Connor, M.C. (2005b, July 11). SF Library denied funds for RFID: The San Francisco Board of Supervisors' Budget Committee rejected a request by the city's library system to reserve funds for an RFID project in the coming fiscal year. *RFID Journal.* Retrieved July 19, 2007, from http://www.rfidjournal.com/article/articleview/1708/1/1/

O'Connor, M.C. (2005c, May 13). RFID helps Hanford manage waste: Bechtel Hanford has deployed an active-tag RFID system to identify a fleet of trucks and containers transporting 4,000 tons of radioactive waste daily. *RFID Journal.* Retrieved July 19, 2007, from http://www.rfidjournal.com/article/articleview/1592/1/1/

O'Connor, M.C. (2005d, April 13). RFID and the media revolution: Renowned futurist Paul Saffo predicts that RFID's biggest impact will come from surprising applications. *RFID Journal.* Retrieved July 19, 2007, from http://www.rfidjournal.com/article/articleview/1508/1/1/

O'Connor, M.C. (2006a, July 28). DOD getting Gen 2-ready: The Department of Defense is expanding its RFID requirements and infrastructure while it takes steps toward transitioning its requirements to support the EPC UHF Gen 2 standard. *RFID Journal.* Retrieved July 19, 2007, from http://www.rfidjournal.com/article/articleview/2530/1/1/

O'Connor, M.C. (2006b, August 16). Will China's RFID standards support EPC protocols, systems?: China has yet to release its much-anticipated RFID standards; some observers say it has produced too little, too late. *RFID Journal.* Retrieved July 19, 2007, from http://www.rfidjournal.com/article/articleview/2593/

Olsen, F. (2005, January 5). Social Security Administration utilizes RFID. *USA Today.* Retrieved July 19, 2007, from http://www.usatoday.com/tech/news/techpolicy/2005-01-05-rfid-to-track-ssa_x.htm

O'Shea, P. (2003, June). RFID comes of age for tracking everything from pallets to people. *ChipCenter.* Retrieved July 19, 2007, from http://www.chipcenter.com/analog/ed008.htm

Parkinson, J. (2003, September). Tag! You're it! The value of RFID goes way beyond the supply chain. Imagine knowing exactly how old that carton of milk really is. Or how safe your tires really are. *CIO Insight, 1*(30), 37.

RFID News & Solutions. (2004, August). RFID—Powering the supply chain: Questions every user needs to answer before implementing RFID. *Reed Business Information, 5*(8), R1-R16.

Ricadela, A. (2005, January 24). Sensors everywhere: A "bucket brigade" of tiny, wirelessly networked sensors someday may be able to track anything, anytime, anywhere. *InformationWeek.* Retrieved July 19, 2007, from http://www.informationweek.com/story/showArticle.jhtml?articleID=57702816

Roberti, M. (2003, October 6). The tipping point: The U.S. Military's decision to require suppliers to use RFID tags will have an even bigger impact than Wal-Mart's RFID mandate. *RFID Journal.* Retrieved July 19, 2007, from http://www.rfidjournal.com/article/articleprint/607/-1/2/

Roberti, M. (2005, February 8). The puzzle of putting RFID tags on beer. *RFID Journal.* Retrieved July 19, 2007, from http://www.rfidjournal.com/article/articleview/1393/1/1/

Saffo, P. (2002, April 15). Smart sensors focus on the future. *CIO Insight.* Retrieved July 19, 2007, from http://www.cioinsight.com/print_article/0,3668,a=25588,00.asp

Schoenberger, C.R. (2002, March 18). RFID: The Internet of things. *Forbes.* Retrieved July 19, 2007, from http://www.mindfully.org/Technology/RFID-Things-Forbes18mar02.htm

Shameen, A. (2004, July 12). Singapore seeks leading RFID role: With the goal of becoming Asia's foremost center for RFID technology, the island-republic will invest millions on research and training. *RFID Journal.* Retrieved July 19, 2007, from http://www.rfidjournal.com/article/articleview/1024/1/1/

Shepard, S. (2005). *RFID: Radio frequency identification.* New York: McGraw-Hill.

Singel, R. (2004, October 21). American passports to get chipped. *Wired.* Retrieved July 19, 2007, from http://www.wired.com/news/privacy/0,1848,65412,00.html

Sirico, L. (2005, February 3). Numbers that please the palate. *RFID Operations.* Retrieved July 19, 2007, from http://www.rfidoperations.com/newsandviews/20050203.html

Sliwa, C. (2005, January 24). Retailers drag feet on RFID initiatives. *Computerworld.* Retrieved July 19, 2007, from http://www.computerworld.com/printthis/2005/0,4814,99170,00.html

Sternstein, A. (2005a, June 20). FAA gives go-ahead to RFID. *Federal Computer Week.* Retrieved July 19, 2007, from http://www.fcw.com/article89316-06-20-05-Print

Sternstein, A. (2005b, March 4). Virginia Beach sees RFID payoff. *Federal Computer Week*. Retrieved July 19, 2007, from http://www.fcw.com/article88216-03-03-05-Web

Stockman, H. (1948, October). Communication by means of reflected power. In *Proceedings of the IRE (Institute of Radio Engineers)* (pp. 1196-1204).

Sullivan, L. (2004a, October 25). IBM shares RFID lessons: Disruption to radio signals comes from surprising sources as IBM Global Services rolls out the technology in Wal-Mart tests. *InformationWeek*. Retrieved July 19, 2007, from http://www.informationweek.com/shared/printableArticle.jhtml?articleID=51000091

Sullivan, L. (2004b, October 28). Wal-Mart takes RFID to Sam's Club: The retailer will soon begin putting RFID-tagged cases and pallets in its chain of club outlets. *InformationWeek*. Retrieved July 19, 2007, from http://informationweek.com/story/showArticle.jhtml?articleID=51201255

Sullivan, L. (2005a, January 24). Georgia court system hopes to trial RFID: The DeKalb County Juvenile Court wants to use RFID to track thousands of file folders on more than 9,000 children processed through the system each year. *InformationWeek*. Retrieved July 19, 2007, from http://www.informationweek.com/story/showArticle.jhtml?articleID=57703442

Sullivan, L. (2005b, June 20). Where's RFID going next?: Supply-chain projects spurred development. Now chips are turning up in ever-more-innovative uses. *InformationWeek*. Retrieved July 19, 2007, from http://www.informationweek.com/story/showArticle.jhtml?articleID=164900910&tid=5978

Swedberg, C. (2005, April 5). Marin County DA saves with RFID: The District Attorney for Marin County, California says his Department Will Trim 2,500 Man-hours a Year Thanks to a 3M RFID System That Lets It Locate Legal Files." *RFID Journal*. Retrieved July 19, 2007, from http://www.rfidjournal.com/article/articleview/1486/1/1/

Thomas, L. (2005, January 26). RFID cell phones? Maybe in 2007. *Mobile Magazine*. Retrieved July 19, 2007, from http://www.mobilemag.com/content/100/102/C3673/

Van, J. (2005, April 16). RFID spells media revolution, futurist says. *Chicago Tribune*, B1.

Wasserman, E. (2005a, April 11). Ridge says RFID can protect the U.S.: At RFID Journal's Conference in Chicago, the Former Secretary of Homeland Security says that through innovation, RFID can strengthen both the nation's security and its economy. *RFID Journal*. Retrieved July 19, 2007, from http://www.rfidjournal.com/article/articleview/1499/1/1/

Wasserman, E. (2005b, July 18). Agencies affirm privacy policies for RFID: A panel of government officials explained how agencies are trying to build privacy safeguards into potential U.S.-issued RFID-enabled IDs. *RFID Journal*.

Retrieved July 19, 2007, from http://www.rfidjournal.com/article/articleview/1747/1/1/

Welsh, W. (2005, March 21). Growin' on empty: RFID's many uses outpace available funds. *Washington Technology*. Retrieved July 19, 2007, from http://www.washingtontechnology.com/news/20_6/statelocal/25834-1.html

Wyld, D.C. (2004a, December). What's the buzz on RFID?: New research reveals Americans' knowledge, attitudes and concerns about the growth of automatic identification technology. *Global Identification*, (18), 14-19.

Wyld, D. (2004b). Soaring benefits from RFID. *Global ID Magazine*, (18), 46-52.

Wyld, D.C. (2005a, October). *RFID:* The right frequency for government. The IBM Center for the Business of Government. Retrieved July 19, 2007, from *http://www.businessofgovernment.org/main/publications/grant_reports/details/index.asp?gid=232*

Wyld, D.C. (2005b). Delta Airlines tags baggage with RFID. *Re:ID Magazine*, *1*(1), 63-64.

Wyld, D.C. (2005c, March). Beyond the bar code: How the use of RFID (radio frequency identification) will give wine marketers unprecedented visibility at each step in the supply chain. *Wine Business Monthly*. Retrieved July 19, 2007, from http://winebusiness.com/html/MonthlyPrinterFriendly.cfm?issue id=98479&aid=98728

Wyld, D.C. (2005d, February 24). Supporting the "Warfighter." *RFIDNews*. Retrieved July 19, 2007, from http://www.rfidnews.org/library/2005/02/24/supporting-the-warfighter/

Wyld, D.C. (2005e, June). A smarter way to travel or a "bulls-eye" on the backs of Americans abroad?: The U.S. Government moves on RFID-enabled passports. While the technology is ready, privacy activists and business groups are balking at the prospect of "contactless" travel. *IDPeople*, (3), 22-24.

Wyld, D.C. (2006a, November). Better than advertised: The early results from Wal-Mart's RFID efforts are in, and the technology may be outperforming even some of the most optimistic forecasts for improving retail…And the best is yet to come. *Global Identification*, (30), 10-13.

Wyld, D.C. (2006b, September). Delivering at the "moment of truth" in retail: How RFID can reduce out-of-stocks and improve supply chain performance to store shelves, benefiting both retailers and product manufacturers. *Global Identification*, (28), 50-53.

Wyld, D.C. (2006c, October). Sports 2.0: A look at the future of sports in the context of RFID's weird new media revolution. *The Sport Journal*. Retrieved July 19, 2007, from http://www.thesportjournal.org/2006Journal/Vol9-No4/Wyld.asp

Wyld, D.C. (2006d, October). The National Animal Identification System: Ensuring the competitiveness of the American agriculture industry in the face of mounting animal disease threats. *Competition Forum, 4*(1), 110-115.

Wyld, D.C., & Jones, M.A. (2007). RFID is no fake: The adoption of radio frequency identification technology in the pharmaceutical supply chain. *International Journal of Integrated Supply Management*, (in press).

Zappone, C. (2006, July 13). E-passports: Ready or not here they come—The State Department expresses confidence in "e-passports' while technologists fret about their security risks. *CNN/Money*. Retrieved July 19, 2007, from http://money.cnn.com/2006/07/13/pf/rfid_passports/

Zebra Technolgies. (2004). RFID tag characteristics. Retrieved July 19, 2007, from *http://www.rfid.zebra.com/faq_RFID_tag_characteristics.htm*

Section IV

Conclusion

Chapter X

Out of Control?
The Real ID Act of 2005

Todd Loendorf, North Carolina State University, USA

Abstract

The tragic events of September 11, 2001, created an environment that was conducive to the expansion of surveillance operations. Furthermore, the Bush Administration's belief that the power of the presidency allows for any action, in the name of national security, led to the gathering of information about both terrorists and ordinary citizens. The Real ID Act of 2005 is a piece of legislation that requires, among other things, that state licensing agencies verify, collect, store, and share an increased amount of personal information. Opponents of this legislation are concerned about the financial, technological, privacy, and security implications of a law that was enacted with little to no due diligence. Currently, the requirements of the Real ID Act have been forced into an immigration bill in the Senate. Fortunately for those opposed to the Real ID Act, the Democratic majority currently in Congress appear to be more concerned with protecting the freedoms and liberties of American citizens than the Republican majority was when they originally passed the Real ID Act legislation in 2005. Ultimately, this chapter seeks to provide the reader with a thorough discussion into the many concerns associated with the Real ID Act.

Introduction

Daniel Webster once said "that good intentions will always be pleaded for every assumption of authority. It is hardly too strong to say that the Constitution was made to guard the people against the dangers of good intentions." In a day and age when a majority of Americans seem willing to trade personal liberties for the prospect of security, it is important to remember the words of Webster. Certainly, the terrible events of 9/11 contributed to the willingness of a nation to turn a deaf ear to Webster and other protectors of personal liberty. This is a logical reaction to a very tragic sequence of events as we all tend to become more conservative and seek safety when we are threatened (Maslow, 1943). Unfortunately, a major problem in America today is that some would have us believe that our personal safety is at risk around every corner and in every facet of our daily life. In fact, security concerns fuel a multibillion dollar industry for everything from car alarms to home protection systems to Internet virus protection. Some might say that, as a society, we are more scared and less free than our rhetoric might suggest.

This growing culture of fear has provided ample opportunity for those determined to engineer safety through increased control. Examples of new age controls for safety are everywhere. Red light cameras, parking lot cameras, employee badges and background checks, antivirus software, and biometric scanners are a few of the ways we have created to protect our safety. To be clear, these measures are not the problem. In fact, they can do a lot of good. The problem lies in the way in which the information collected by these devices is so easily mismanaged.

In February 2007, 1,400 members of the California National Guard found this out the hard way. A computer hard drive containing Social Security numbers, home addresses, birth dates, and other identifying information of these troops deployed to the U.S.-Mexico border was stolen on February 23, 2007. Considering the sensitive nature of the work performed by these troops, a breach in the safety of their personal information is unacceptable. Furthermore, it casts a very dark cloud over any attempts to collect and store personal information. This is especially true considering this breach came on the heels of another security infraction in the military community in California. In January 2006, a report containing the names and Social Security numbers of more than 1,000 high-ranking California National Guard officers was in a briefcase stolen from a car in Sacramento. Unfortunately, the issues surrounding mismanaged data and the security of personal information are not contained to the military community in California. In fact, the issues are propagating throughout our society at an alarming rate despite the increasing awareness about the importance of information security. For this reason, we must heed the sage advice given to us by Webster over 200 years ago and carefully consider the impacts associated with any attempt to collect and store personal information in the name of security.

One such effort, intended to engineer safety from threat of terrorism, is the Real ID Act of 2005. The Real ID Act began as H.R. 418. One of the key objectives of H.R. 418 was to create a National ID Card by establishing and implementing regulations for state driver's license and identification cards that would, in theory, prevent terrorists and illegal immigrants from entering the United States. This piece of legislation, written by policy entrepreneur James Sensenbrenner (WI-R), received solid support in the republican controlled House and was passed by a margin of 261-161 with 11 representatives choosing to not vote. The bill then moved to the Senate, where it stalled in the Judiciary Committee. Approximately 1 month later, Sensenbrenner pressed forward and attached his pet solution to another piece of legislation, H.R. 1268.

The primary purposes of H.R. 1268 were to make emergency supplemental appropriations for the war in Iraq and for the devastating Tsunami in the Indian Ocean. Knowing that it was highly unlikely that anyone would vote against making more money available for these causes, the sponsors found a way to ensure that this legislation became law. By using this opportunity to stuff an increasingly unpopular plan into an appropriations bill, the process to pass an unfunded mandate down to the states started with little or no understanding about the impacts on states and citizens. The reality here is that financial considerations are but one of the issues that should have been evaluated in regard to this piece of legislation. In fact, the collision of privacy, security, and technology concerns that is manifested in the Real ID Act has sparked an ongoing debate on a wide range of controversial topics and set into motion a coalition of powerful forces opposed to this legislation. This chapter will proceed by identifying the national security concerns that serve as the basis for this legislation before moving on to an analysis of the financial impacts, technology and privacy concerns, security issues, and other implementation obstacles. Finally, the current state of activity around the Real ID Act is provided with a look toward the future.

A Matter of National Security?

Another protector of personal liberty, Thomas Jefferson, once said "it behooves every man who values liberty of conscience for himself, to resist invasions of it in the case of others: or their case may, by change of circumstances, become his own." In the 21st century, national security issues have dominated the political landscape at an alarming rate. In fact, national security issues have permeated every facet of American life. One example familiar to many can be found in the airline industry.

The process of arriving at the airport and boarding your plane has degenerated from a fairly simple activity to an exercise in patience and obedience. By now, most people are well aware of the increased scrutiny placed upon travelers as they pass through airport security check points. Thanks, in part, to the failed attempt of the infamous shoe bomber, Richard Reid, airport security now requires all travelers to take off their shoes and have them scanned. Richard Reid was found trying to detonate explosive material hidden in his shoes while traveling on a commercial flight from Paris to Miami on December 22, 2001. Of course, this failed attempt came very close on the heels of the tragic events of September 11, 2001, and thus, the policy requiring that all passengers have their shoes scanned is an understandable reaction.

Unfortunately, shoes are not the only items receiving increased attention at security check points. Laptops must be taken out of computer bags, and the list of allowable carry-on items has gone through many iterations. Currently, some of the items that travelers are not allowed to carry-on flights include mace key chains, lighters, knives, corkscrews, nail files, nail cutters, scissors, razors, and wrapped packages. Initially, gels, liquids, and aerosols were also banned as carry-on items. Fortunately for many road warriors, these items are now allowed, but there are some key restrictions. All liquids, gels and aerosols must be in three-ounce or smaller containers and must be placed in a single, quart-size, zip-top, clear plastic bag. Larger bags or ones that do not zip are not allowed. Additionally, each traveler can use only one approved bag and it must be removed from carry-on luggage and placed in a bin or on the conveyor belt for X-ray screening. In response to the long lines created by these security measures, airlines now recommend that travelers arrive at the airport at least two hours before domestic flights and three hours before international flights. This represents a major increase in time and a major inconvenience for many Americans.

Still, when it comes to national security, many Americans are willing to put up with being inconvenienced. Presently, two of the main areas of concern, in regard to national security, are the war on terror and illegal immigration. The Hobbesian strategy of the current administration can be summed up in the words of Louis Freeh, former Director of the Federal Bureau of Investigations. Freeh said that "the American people must be willing to give up a degree of personal privacy in exchange for safety and security." Thomas Hobbes was a seventeenth century philosopher who believed that a social contract exists between citizens and the government such that citizens must willingly relinquish some personal rights in order for the government to ensure peace and a common defense.

An ABC News/Washington Post poll in January 2006 revealed that this sentiment is reflected in the opinions of the American public. In this poll of 1,001 American adults, 63% said that the government was either not intruding on privacy rights or that they were justified in any intrusions. Additionally, 65% said it was more important for the government to investigate terrorism than to protect personal privacy. Even though this percentage is down from a similar poll in 2002 that showed 79% willing to trade privacy for the ability to investigate terrorism, it still represents a sobering view of public perception of the privacy vs. security debate. With public opinion on their side, those determined to fight terrorism and illegal immigration via increased controls and decreased personal privacy are trying to make hay while the sun shines.

The war on terrorism has been going on for ages; however, the "War on Terror" policy of the Bush administration has thrust these issues into the limelight. The primary focus of this policy has been on groups such as al-Qaeda; however, the policy is much broader and wide-reaching in nature. In fact, the Bush administration was able to use the threat of potential terrorist activities from Iraq as a means to convince the American public and the Congress to invade Iraq and remove Saddam Hussein from power. The objectives of this policy can be characterized as a multiprong attack on terrorism. Everything from attacking terrorists and terrorist organizations to attempting to control organizations and nations that sponsor terrorism are part of the Bush administration "War on Terror" policy.

The creation of the United States Department of Homeland Security (DHS) was a momentous step for the Bush administration "War on Terror." DHS is also a crucial component in the debate over the Real ID Act because the agency is responsible for determining the standards that must be adhered to by the states. The two primary sets of DHS standards, in regard to driver's licenses and identification cards, are document standards and issuance standards. Basically, document standards are the items that must be contained on the ID card and issuance standards are the items that must be verified and collected when the ID is issued to a citizen. The standards listed below are subject to change as debate over the potential implementation of the Real ID Act progresses; however, at present time, the minimum document standards for driver's licenses and identification cards are:

- Person's full legal name
- Person's date of birth
- Person's gender
- DL/ID number
- Digital photograph
- Person's address of legal residence
- Person's signature
- Physical security features designed to prevent tampering, counterfeiting, or duplication for fraudulent purposes
- A common machine-readable technology with defined data elements

The minimum issuance standards are:

- A photo identity document (except that a nonphoto identity document is acceptable if it includes both the person's full legal name and date of birth).
- Documentation showing the person's date of birth.
- Proof of the person's social security account number (SSN) or verification that the person is not eligible for an SSN.
- Documentation showing the person's name and address of principal residence.
- A state shall not accept any foreign document other than an official passport.
- A state shall subject each DL/ID applicant to mandatory facial image capture.
- A state shall refuse to issue a DL/ID to a person holding a DL/ID from another state without confirmation that the person is terminating the other state's DL/ID.
- A state shall limit the period of validity of all DL/IDs that are not temporarily issued to a period that does not exceed eight (8) years.

The conventional wisdom is that the collection of an increased amount of personal information coupled with an increased focus on verification will prove to be a winning combination in the "War on Terror" and the problem of illegal immigration.

In fact, an additional set of standards has been crafted to help address the problem of illegal immigration. These require that the state verify that the person:

- Is a U.S. citizen
- Is an alien lawfully admitted for permanent or temporary residence
- Has a conditional permanent resident status
- Is a refugee or has been granted asylum
- Has a valid, unexpired nonimmigrant visa or nonimmigrant visa status
- Has a pending application for asylum
- Has a pending or approved application for temporary protected status
- Has approved deferred status
- Has a pending application for adjustment of status to that of an alien lawfully admitted for permanent residence or conditional permanent resident status

Instead of clarifying the situation, these standards have had the opposite effect on those responsible for implementing the Real ID Act. Additionally, they have given rise to a powerful movement opposed to this legislation and have created more questions than answers. Questions centered on financial, technological, privacy, and security concerns. Questions that should have been more carefully considered by the Congress, but were pushed aside in favor of hasty appropriations for military funding. After all, this is a matter of national security.

Impacts and Obstacles

Financial Concerns

Initially, the proponents of the Real ID Act projected that the cost would be approximately $100 million. For this reason, little to no Federal money was set aside for the implementation. States quickly responded by performing their own financial analysis with varying results. Pennsylvania and Washington both found that they would spend roughly $100 million each, while Virginia projected their cost to be closer to $230 million. Even the National Conference on State Legislators (NCSL) got into the estimation game. They found that the initial cost of implementing these new standards would be between $500 and $700 million dollars over the first 5 years. With all of the variance associated with the estimates, state officials began to reject the idea setting up new standards for driver's licenses.

Later, in September 2006, the NCSL teamed up with the American Association of Motor Vehicle Administrators (AAMVA) and the National Governors Association (NGA) to perform a thorough study of the issue. The resulting report, entitled "The Real ID Act: National Impact Analysis," was 60 pages of bulletin board material for the opponents of the legislation.

To ensure Congress and the federal government understand the fiscal and operational impact of altering these complex and vital state systems, the American Association of Motor Vehicle Administrators (AAMVA) in conjunction with the National Governors Association (NGA) and the National Conference of State Legislatures (NCSL) conducted a nationwide survey of state motor vehicle agencies (DMVs). Based on the results of that survey, NGA, NCSL and AAMVA conclude that Real ID will cost more than $11 billion over five years, have a major impact on services to the public and impose unrealistic burdens on states to comply with the act by the May 2008 deadline. (NCSL, 2006)

To be clear, these figures are also most likely underestimated because the standards that the states would have to implement have not been fully defined by DHS. Specifically, states were left to make their best guesses as to the:

- Facility security requirements
- Development of federal verification systems and transaction costs
- Expansion of the AAMVA net system
- Law enforcement training and technology deployment
- Expanded public education/data privacy protection
- Increased customer demand/care/advocacy

Furthermore, the legislation will affect everyone, not just terrorists and illegal immigrants. All drivers will be required to verify their documents in person at a motor vehicle office. This process, called re-enrollment, would create a nightmare for motor vehicles offices and citizens and cost over $8 billion.

States based their analysis on the assumption that to implement Real ID, all 245 million U.S. DL/ID holders must be re-credentialed within five years of the May 2008 compliance deadline. This standard will require an in-person visit by every current DL/ID holder as well as new applicants to review and verify all required identification documents and re-document information for the new license including place of principal residence, new photographs and new signatures.

Efficiencies from alternative renewal processes such as Internet and mail will be lost during the re-enrollment period, and states will face increased costs from the need to hire more employees and expand business hours to meet the five year re-enrollment deadline. (NCSL, 2006)

DHS now concedes that the initial estimate of $100 million is way off and that the cost will most likely be closer to that presented in the National Impact Analysis mentioned above. DHS has said that they may make grants to a state to assist the state in conforming to the minimum federal standards; however, this should provide little comfort to citizens who will end up bearing the lion's share of the costs associated with this legislation if it is ultimately implemented. In fact, it is very likely that the cost of a driver's license or identification card would rise to over $100 per card.

While the debates rage on over what the final cost of this legislation will be and exactly who will have to shoulder the financial burden, the only thing that is certain is that there will be disagreement. Assuming, for arguments sake, that legislative and financial hurdles can be cleared through some incredible cooperation and compromise between the federal government and the states, there are still incredible challenges presented by the issues swirling around the convergence of technology, privacy, and security.

Technology Concerns

Before beginning this section, it should be made clear that this is not an antitechnology chapter. The world would not be nearly as fun without technological advancement. This is especially true in situations where the technology is being created for willing recipients. Unfortunately, that is not the case here. The responses to the AAMVA National Impact Analysis surveys sent out to state agencies indicated an overwhelming concern for financial and technological issues. In other words, the states do not want to be forced to deal with the headaches associated with technology implementation. Clearly, the proponents of the Real ID Act did not include the end users or key stakeholders in the planning process. In committing this cardinal sin in regard to strategic planning and project management (Markus, 1983; Tait & Vessey, 1988), a huge tactical mistake occurred and the support for Real ID continued its downward spiral. One is left to wonder exactly how the proponents saw this all playing out with little to no support at the state agency level.

Basically, the states were concerned that the new standards would surpass their current abilities, thus forcing new technology into organizations along with the cost, time delays, issues, need for training, and possible failures that are so often a part of any new technology implementation. Simply put, technological implementations, of any sort, always look easier on the surface than they are in reality and are often destined for failure (Lundquist, 2005). This is a time tested axiom and can be seen again and again in both the public and private sector. The real question is:

Will we ever use our "lessons learned"?

The potential for technological problems can be lumped into two distinct buckets. First, there are the cards and their required readers. Then, there are the databases and data mining tools needed to store and analyze the mountain of data that would be generated by this legislation.

Cards and Readers

A recent and very relevant example of issues with identification documents occurred in an RFID pilot project performed by DHS. In 2005, the agency began testing

RFID-enabled I-94 forms in its United States Visitor and Immigrant Status Indicator Technology (US-VISIT) program to track the entry and exit of visitors (*for a thorough discussion into RFID technology please refer to the chapter by David Wyld in this text*). Fortunately, for those concerned about privacy issues, the project failed miserably. This is a key reason why this technology did not become the standard for the proposed driver licenses and identification cards in Real ID implementations. In the words of DHS Secretary Michael Chertoff, "yes, we're abandoning it. That's not going to be a solution"(Chertoff, 2007).

In the pilot project, RFID-enabled forms were used to store personal information. This information was then linked to databases containing additional information on foreign visitors. The core issue with the project is the lack of security associated with RFID technology. Ultimately, any unauthorized person could easily access personal information contained on the RFID-enabled form.

According to a recent report from the Electronic Privacy Information Center (EPIC), the failure with the US-VISIT pilot is just the tip of the iceberg in regard to technological issues.

Homeland Security's failure with the US-VISIT pilot test is just one of several instances where the agency has stumbled with identification systems. The Transportation Security Administration said recently that Secure Flight, a federal passenger screening program, would be delayed until 2010, at least five years behind schedule. Secure Flight was suspended a year ago after two government reports detailed security and privacy problems. One report found 144 security vulnerabilities. About $140 million has been spent on the program, and the TSA is seeking another $80 million for proposed changes. Homeland Security also has problems with its bloated watch lists. More than 30,000 people who are not terrorists have asked the Transportation Security Administration to remove their names from the lists since September 11, 2001. In January, the head of TSA said that the watch lists were being reviewed, and he expected to cut in half the watch lists (estimated to contain about 325,000 names). (EPIC, 2007)

Another program that has recently come under increased scrutiny because of technological deficiencies is the Transportation Workers Identification Credential (TWIC) program. This program relies on smart cards and their companion readers. Smart card technology has been gaining in popularity because of their ability to store a large amount of information on a small chip that is integrated into the card. Getting past the potential privacy issues for the moment, this program faces two other major technological issues.

Two problems are paramount. First, there are worries that TWIC smart cards, which use a personal identification number and must be inserted into a reader, won't work properly in the harsh, salty air of marine environments. DHS officials, in response, withdrew the card readers from the initial TWIC deployment. They now are working with industry and port authority officials to develop standards for contactless TWIC readers to avoid the problems of corrosion from salt air and water.

Second, serious concerns are surfacing about the 1 percent system error rate inherent in FIPS 201. That figure reflects a 1 in 100 false acceptance rate, and 1 in 100 false rejection rate. Those rates are published in the National Institute of Standards and Technology's Special Publication 800-76, incorporated in the FIPS 201 standard.

NIST established those error rates in its test of the FIPS 201 requirement for interoperability among cards produced by different vendors. To meet that requirement, NIST tested fingerprint minutiae templates, which are digitized versions of fingerprints showing features such as ridges and whorls.

Based on the published error rates, for every 100 people presenting the TWIC card to enter a facility, the system is nearly certain to make at least one false reading. At a busy port welcoming 300 trucks an hour, that would be at least three false reads per hour. (Lipowicz, 2006)

On their own, technological issues related to cards and readers create a major barrier for the implementation of the Real ID Act. That being said, they pale in comparison to the issues created by requirements for databases and data mining.

Databases and Data Mining

The current DHS standards specify requirements in two key areas. The first is data retention and storage. At a minimum, DHS is mandating that states maintain a state motor vehicle database that contains:

- All data fields printed on DL/IDs issued by the state
- Motor vehicle drivers' histories, including motor vehicle violations, suspensions, and points on license

The second major requirement in this area is the linking of databases within and across states. Specifically, states must provide electronic access to all other states in regard to information contained in the motor vehicle database of licensing state. Together, these technology requirements have coupled with concerns about personal privacy and the security of personal information to cast a dark cloud over the implementation process.

You do not have to search very hard to find examples of privacy and security infractions in relation to databases. Over the past 5 years, Web sites have been completely devoted to tracking the expanding list of breaches. Credit card, banking, and consumer marketing companies are frequent targets for hackers attempting to gain unauthorized access to personal information. The list of breached companies grows on a daily basis.

Recently, TJX Companies Incorporated, a major retailer, acknowledged that at least 45.7 million credit and debit cards were stolen over an 18-month period by hackers who managed to penetrate its network. The cost to TJX for this infraction is currently over $25 million and rising. TJX is not alone as their plight only adds to the growing list of private organizations, such as ChoicePoint, Visa, Pfizer, and many others, who have had their systems breached by hackers. Increasingly, however, government organizations are the targets.

In May 2007, a database containing private police information was stolen in Houston, Texas:

The handiwork of a few Houston burglars left 229,000 Texas law enforcement officers at risk for identity theft, reports WFAA, a Dallas-based ABC television affiliate. The robbers not only got their hands on officers' names and Social Security numbers, but their addresses and telephone numbers, too. A police detective interviewed by WFAA calls the slip-up "really disturbing."

Burglars scored the sensitive data during a breaking-and-entering spree that targeted 23 separate buildings in one section of Houston. While there is no indication that they specifically sought the officers' information, it's little consolation for those who could potentially be affected by resulting identity-related fraud. (Stoler, 2007)

In May 2006, an employee of the State Department opened a malicious e-mail that contained an attachment that installed a Trojan Horse. "I believe the infiltration by foreign nationals of federal government networks is one of the most critical issues confronting our nation," Rep. James Langevin, D–RI, said at a hearing of the House Subcommittee on Emerging Threats, Cybersecurity, Science and Technology. "Over time, the theft of critical information from government servers could cost the United States our advantage over our adversaries."

Of course, the unauthorized access of personal information is but one of the problems associated with databases and data mining. There is the additional problem of authorized individuals using incorrect information to make very poor decisions that directly impact innocent citizens.

About 6:30 a.m., June 18, 2004, federal agents at the port of Miami boarded the Fascination, a cruise ship returning from Cozumel, Mexico, awakened Hope Clarke in her cabin, handcuffed and shackled her, kept her in detention for nine hours before turning her over to U.S. marshals who brought her before a federal magistrate.. Clarke's "terroristic" offense? She had been cited by the National Park Service more than a year earlier for not putting away hot chocolate and marshmallows while staying at Yellowstone National Park—the park has rules that are designed to reduce interaction between humans and wildlife.

Clarke had paid the $50 fine the same day, but one of the federal databases still had an outstanding warrant on her. It was that warrant that led federal law enforcement to arrest her. Before Magistrate John O'Sullivan, Assistant U.S. Attorney Peter Outerbridge admitted there may have been some "discrepancies," but still asked that the defendant be returned to a federal court in Wyoming to clear her record. O'Sullivan, who secured a copy of Clarke's citation which indicated the fine had been paid, just as Clarke had stated, refused to accede to the government's request and then apologized to Clarke. (Brasch, 2005)

Unfortunately, issues similar to those mentioned above continue to plague efforts in the field of database and data mining technology. These types of infractions will continue to provide ample ammunition for those charged with protecting personal liberty. It is unfortunate and potentially very harmful when an unauthorized person gains access to personal information. It is equally problematic when authorized individuals have access to incorrect information. One final scenario that needs to be considered is the access to personal information by those in government that claim to have the authority but who are, in reality, standing on very shaky ground. It is undeniably tragic and most likely unconstitutional when those elected to defend our freedom turn out to be the biggest thieves.

Privacy Concerns

Not since the dismantling of the Total Information Awareness (TIA) project has there been a movement with privacy implications as severe as in the Real ID Act. TIA was first concocted by in 2002 by the Defense Advanced Research Projects

Agency (DARPA), the research and development agency of the United States Department of Defense. The primary goal of TIA was to strengthen the U.S. counterintelligence capability via increased data collection, storage, and analysis. This massive surveillance system was halted by Congress in 2003. The ACLU stated that TIA "may be the closest thing to a true 'Big Brother' program that has ever been seriously contemplated in the United States." Even though privacy concerns over the program eventually shut TIA down, one of the more disturbing findings in this research is the continued willingness of governmental agencies to violate the privacy of American citizens:

Millions of JetBlue passenger records were used in a military effort whose methods closely resemble those employed in the notorious Terrorism Information Awareness überdatabase program, the Army confirmed Monday.

Last week, defense contractor Torch Concepts came under heavy scrutiny after Wired News revealed that the company had crunched fliers' private data without their knowledge.

On Monday, Army spokesman Maj. Gary Tallman said the information was used by Torch Concepts to test a prototype of a data-mining system designed to screen out terrorists who might want to infiltrate or attack Army bases worldwide. (Shachtman & Singel, 2003)

An investigation by Nuala O'Connor chief privacy officer of the Department of Homeland Security concluded:

TSA employees involved acted without appropriate regard for individual privacy interests or the Spirit of the Privacy Act of 1974. In doing so, it appears that their actions were outside normal processes to facilitate a data transfer, with the primary purpose of the transfer being other than transportation security. Such sharing exceeds the principle of the Privacy Act which limits data collection by an agency to such information as is necessary for a federal agency to carry out its own mission. While these actions may have been well intentioned and without malice, the employees arguably misused the oversight capacity of the TSA to encourage this data sharing.

More recently, parents in Earlville, Illinois, have taken up the fight for privacy in demanding that the local school system gain parental approval before gathering biometric information about students:

Shepherded by State Rep. Bob Pritchard (R–Sycamore) and passed to State Senator Kimberly Lightford (D–Chicago), the Senate unanimously agreed with the House Tuesday that parents must consent before schools take student biometric info, such as finger or iris scans.

First brought to the attention of Rep. Pritchard by parents in the Earlville area schools, district children refusing finger scans were denied hot school lunches. As a child would approach the lunch checkout, the child would place his or her finger to be scanned electronically. The cost of the child's lunch would automatically be deducted from his lunch account.

Parents complaining their children's biometric information was obtained without parents' prior knowledge were brushed off and scoffed by school officials (Illinois Review, 2007).

All of this secrecy and deception in regard to personal information adds credence to those who claim that we are increasingly living in a "Surveillance State" and conger up images of Orwell's *1984*:

There was, of course, no way of knowing whether you were being watched at any given moment. ... You had to live—did live, from habit that became instinct—in the assumption that every sound you made was overheard, and except in darkness, every movement scrutinized. (George Orwell, 1984)

In many cities in America, one can be easily reminded of this fact by noticing the presence of stop-light cameras. Although stop-light cameras are not very invasive and do present a great opportunity in regard to freeing up police human resources for use in more important areas, one important question remains. Will the information being collected on these devices be used for more than catching citizens as they "run a red light"? Can we trust government when it tells us that they will not be used for surveillance? One thing is certain, the longer these devices are pointed at citizens the more likely that citizen expectation of privacy and freedom will erode.

One of the more recent and highly publicized assaults on personal privacy by the Bush Administration involved warrantless wiretaps of American citizens. This troubling story begins and ends with the administration's firm belief that they have the Executive Privilege to perform any action they deem is in the best interest of national security. This troubling posture by the Executive Branch has consistently moved it toward an expansion of power. Another recent example that is closely related to the warrantless wiretapping scandal is the expanded use of National Security Letters (NSL).

NSL's have been a tool used by our government for many years to gather information in support of terrorism and espionage investigations. One of the more controversial aspects of NSL's has been that they contain a gag order that prevents the recipient of the letter from disclosing that the letter was ever issued. Imagine that you are a librarian and you receive one of these letters requesting information about a patron. Not only must you comply with the request, but you cannot divulge the request for information to anyone. This, of course, was intended to mask the activities of the investigating agency. Another issue many have with these letters is that they do not require prior judicial approval or even probable cause. Additionally, the Patriot Act includes a provision that made these letters much more powerful than was originally intended. After the Patriot Act, NSL's could be used to gather data about all citizens and visitors to the U. S. even if they are not suspected in any criminal investigation.

This fact is troubling considering the findings of a recent internal FBI audit. The FBI found that it violated the law more than 1,000 times while collecting data about domestic phone calls, e-mails, and financial transactions in recent years. This finding is even worse than a report previously produced by the Justice Department, one that ignited criticism aimed at both the department and the Attorney General, Alberto Gonzales:

Alberto Gonzales is challenged on his testimony about FISA, in which he sharply contradicts Deputy Attorney General James Comey. His response is predictable: Gonzales is sticking with the sworn account he furnished earlier, which is to say, he's sticking with his lies. Gonzales's conduct wonderfully sums up the Bush Administration's attitude towards the national surveillance state it has crafted: don't worry about the fact that it's illegal. When your own lawyers tell you it's illegal, fire them. When newspapers expose the illegality, you commence surveillance of the reporters in question, engage in thuggish harassment, and threaten to prosecute the newspapers—using the heavy hand of the state to coerce their silence. And when you're caught in lies under oath to Congress by the testimony of government officials who serve alongside of you, and have foolish qualms about lying under oath to Congress—you persist in your lies and denigrate your former colleagues for their disloyalty. (Horton, 2007)

As a side note to the Alberto Gonzales story, in 2007 he was called to testify for his role in another agency scandal. One that involved the firing of Federal Judges who did not share the goals of the Bush Administration. At present time, the Congress is calling for his resignation and the possibility of impeachment proceedings exists. Despite all of the criticism, President Bush is standing by his man, in true cowboy fashion.

Ultimately, the unfettered attack on personal liberty by the Bush Administration and other governmental agencies provides one of the more compelling arguments against the implementation of the Real ID Act. It is simply another attempt by overzealous, power hungry bureaucrats who believe that gathering, storing, and analyzing information about citizens is the path to security. The reality is that these deceptive efforts chip away at our trust in government and makes us feel less secure.

Security Concerns

Security is another important part of this debate for both advocates and critics of the Real ID Act. In the information age, the exact definition of security has been blurred as both information security and physical security must be considered. For the Real ID Act, the discussion of security in this chapter will focus in on information security, as it pertains to the protection of personal data, and physical security, as it pertains to theft and forgery of identification cards. Security, then, will be viewed as a tool to help protect our personal information from being viewed by those who are not properly authorized to view the information.

Information security is the nexus between privacy and technology. Without information security, the technology that advances the lives and livelihood of millions of people can, in one fail swoop, destroy or at least severely inconvenience the lives and livelihood of millions of people. So, why the contradiction? How can technology be so good and so bad in the same breath? The answer is surprisingly simple and it goes back to something we all learned as children. No matter how smart or determined you are there is always someone smarter or more determined.

Many of the principles that govern information security are built on economics and game theory. Game theory, simply put, is an analysis tool used to evaluate deci-

Figure 1. Information security defense curves

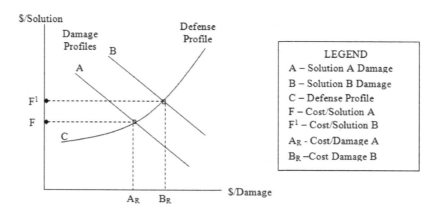

sions to be made during a conflict or competitive situation. Game theory can help analyze the (Grant, 2005):

- Identity of the players (adversaries)
- Specification of each player's options
- Specification of the payoffs from every combination of options

All of this information then contributes to building attack trees and simulations that are used to inform security experts about potential risks (Schneier, 1999). They are also used to help build complex intrusion detection systems. The economic principles that underlie these models are fairly straightforward.

After the formulas of game theory have been tabulated and run several times, using different scenarios, the end result is an equilibrium point. The movement of player A and player B, in reaching this equilibrium point, is analogous to the movements of leader and follower in economic modeling. Eventually, their playing options narrow into the Nash equilibrium. At this point, the same supply and demand curve that has been reviewed and studied for years can be used, as a defense and attack curve, to illustrate responses to information security incidents (Figure 1).

The object for the attacker is to move away from the equilibrium point (F, A_R) along the defense profile curve (C) to a point that makes it more difficult for the defender (B_R). This should force those being attacked into the role of follower and increase the cost of prevention (F^1). The game between attacker, or more appropriately "hacker," and potential victim then becomes one of cost. How much is the potential victim willing to spend to make the efforts of the hacker to cost prohibitive? Conversely, how much is the attacker willing to lose in order to achieve their goals? This question exposes one of the major shortcomings of game theory in regard to information security. Namely, that it assumes that the players will always attempt to maximize their position.

The proceeding discussion on the economics of information security is not intended to be exhaustive. Instead, it is simply provided to help illustrate the following point. Those who believe that they can completely engineer a way to keep criminals out of our country, or out of our private lives, are living in a dreamland. In fact, in the words of security expert Bruce Schneier, "they are living with a false sense of security."

Criminals hell-bent on causing problems and willing to sacrifice themselves, in other words, to act irrationally, will always be able to find a way around, over, or through a set of rules. Likewise, there is always someone out there willing to do something they know they should not do in order to advance themselves or their families. Some might argue that this is actually rational, not irrational, behavior. Although that might be true on some level, it would present an impossible scenario to model and make it very difficult, if not impossible, to detect and handle.

Unfortunately, for proponents of information security, there is another issue that is even more problematic than the game with potential attackers. Human involvement, at any level, will always expose a system to failure. There is just no way around it. We are, after all, imperfect beings.

Organizations are doing little to address the most serious threat to their information security and technology infrastructure, according to new research released today by the Computing Technology Industry Association (CompTIA).

Human error was responsible for nearly 60 percent of information security breaches experienced by organizations over the last year, according to the fourth annual CompTIA study on information security and the workforce. That figure is significantly higher than one year ago, when 47 percent of security breaches were blamed on human error alone.

Yet despite the prominent role that human behavior plays in information security breaches, just 29 percent of the 574 organizations that participated in the survey said that security training is a requirement at their company. Only 36 percent of organizations offer end-user security awareness training.

Virus and worm attacks were the most commonly mentioned security problem, as they have been through all four years of the CompTIA study on information security. A lack of user awareness, browser-based attacks and remote access were the next most frequently mentioned security problem areas. (Technology News Daily, 2006)

Even if every computing device known to man was made secure from human error, the physical security of identification cards would continue to be an issue. No matter how tamper-proof, someone will create counterfeit cards that will eventually surface and make it into the hands of those not authorized to have the "real ID." Recently, an employee of the Indiana Bureau of Motor Vehicles was charged with selling fraudulent state identification cards to illegal immigrants at the local motor vehicle branch in South Bend:

Julian Marie Sanchez, 28, of South Bend, told police she was known in the local Hispanic community as someone who could provide Indiana photo ID cards to people who came into the Indiana Bureau of Motor Vehicles branch at 4646 Western Ave. with bogus Social Security numbers, according to court documents.

About a dozen supporters attended her initial court hearing Monday.

"I did it for my people," Sanchez told supporters afterward on the courthouse steps. "I know what I did was wrong." (Parrott, 2007)

As the heat continues to rise with respect to illegal immigration, the problem of fake identification cards is not likely to go away. In December 2006, Ohio conducted the largest bust of fake identification cards in the state's history:

Authorities said an illegal immigrant went into the Butler County Sheriff's Department looking to get a background check.

The staff at the sheriff's office noticed something about the ID that set off a red flag, and helped authorities bust the largest fake I-D case in the state of Ohio.

Sheriff Richard Jones said investigators they found the business and 4,000 blank ID cards just feet away from the Butler County Jail.

The cards were going for $100 to $200 a piece.

The sheriff said the blank cards were being turned into Ohio driver's licenses, Mexican driver's licenses, and green cards.

Authorities said they arrested three people who face 18 charges in connection with allegedly making the fake ID's. (WHIOTV, 2006)

Finally, despite all of the concerns put forth against the Real ID Act, the direction put forth by the proponents of the legislation lives on today in the most recent Senate bill on immigration. With some luck, this will be the Real ID's last stand.

Current State

At the time of writing this chapter, The U.S. Senate is preparing to consider immigration bill (S. 1348), also known as the Secure Borders, Economic Opportunity and Immigration Reform Act of 2007. Among other things, this bill contains a section (Title III) entitled Worksite Enforcement that will require all Americans to present a Real ID card before they can get a job.

Workplace Enforcement Tools: As required through all the provisions of Title III of this Act, the Department of Homeland Security has established and is using secure and effective identification tools to prevent unauthorized workers from obtaining jobs in the United States. These tools shall include, but not be limited to, establishing:

(i) strict standards for identification documents that must be presented in the hiring process, including the use of secure documentation that contains a photograph, biometrics, and/or complies with the requirements for such documentation under the REAL ID Act; and

(ii) an electronic employment eligibility verification system that queries federal and state databases to restrict fraud, identity theft, and use of false social security numbers in the hiring process by electronically providing a digitized version of the photograph on the employee's original federal or state issued document or documents for verification of the employee's identity and work eligibility.

The pressure to implement a Real ID system continues on despite major opposition from the states. This opposition springs from the abundance of concerns outlined in this chapter. Currently, 16 states have passed legislation that opposes the Real ID Act (Tennessee, South Carolina, Nebraska, New Hampshire, Illinois, Missouri, Nevada, Colorado, Georgia, Hawaii, North Dakota, Washington, Montana, Arkansas, Idaho, and Maine). These states, along with more than 60 other organizations, have spoken out against this legislation and form a powerful coalition, a coalition that is strong enough to finally extinguish the Real ID Act.

To that end, the Baucus-Tester Amendment to the Secure Borders, Economic Opportunity and Immigration Reform Act of 2007 is one of several amendments that would eliminate the Real ID language from the bill. In supporting this amendment, Senator Patrick Leahy (D–VT) gave the following speech on June 7, 2007, on the Senate floor:

Mr. President, I rise today in support of the Baucus-Tester-Sununu-Leahy-Akaka-Collins amendment to strip the references to the problematic REAL ID program from the underlying immigration bill.

We may agree or disagree about the merits of the actual REAL ID program, but as hearings in the Judiciary Committee and the Homeland Security and Government Affairs Committee have shown, REAL ID is far from being ready for primetime. In fact, the Department of Homeland Security has not even released final regulations directing the States on REAL ID implementation. With 260 million drivers in this country, I do not see how we could have the massive national databases required by REAL ID and this immigration bill up and running by the 2013 deadline set in this bill.

In addition to numerous privacy and civil liberties concerns, REAL ID is an unfunded mandate that could cost the States in excess of $23 billion. Opposition spans the political spectrum, from the right to the left. A large number of States have expressed concerns with the mandates of the REAL ID Act by enacting bills and resolutions in opposition. Georgia, Washington, Oklahoma, and Montana have gone so far as to indicate that they intend to refuse compliance with it. The National Conference of State Legislatures and the National Governors Association have expressed concerns about the costs imposed on the States. The reaction to the unfunded mandates of the REAL ID Act is a good example of what happens when the Federal government imposes itself rather than working to create cooperation and partnership.

On top of that, even though they are not even in production yet, REAL ID cards are rapidly becoming a de facto national ID card—since they will be needed to enter courthouses, airports, federal buildings, and now workplaces all across the country. In my opinion, REAL ID raises multiple constitutional issues whose legal challenges could delay final implementation for years.

For any new immigration measures to be effective, they must be well designed. Forcing employers, employees, and the States to use this troublesome national ID card will slow down the hiring process, stifle commerce, and not serve as an effective strategy. As a result, we should not jeopardize the future success of the immigration reforms sought in this legislation by tying REAL ID too closely to it. I do not see how it is possible for all of the States to have their new license programs up and running by the 2013 deadline called for in this bill. Thus, I think that instead of mandating REAL ID in this bill, we should support the Baucus-Tester amendment to strip REAL ID from this bill and put together a workable employment verification system that does not needlessly burden every legal job seeker in this country with the onerous and problematic requirements of REAL ID.

A close reading of this speech reveals many of the concerns already outlined in this chapter. Clearly, the forces opposed to the Real ID Act are prepared for a fight. For this reason, it is highly unlikely that the current immigration bill will make it out of the Senate.

The Beauty of Democracy

On September 11, 2001, Osama Bin Laden executed a calculated attack on America. For a terrorist, the core reason for committing such atrocious acts is to instill fear into the victim and slowly take away their freedom. Sadly, Osama Bin Laden was very successful in his mission. Consider all that has changed in America since the attacks.

We are at war in Iraq. Not with Iraq, but with terrorists inside of Iraq. Our position as respected world leader is in question because of our unilateral policies. The price of gas is over $3.00 per gallon. The Department of Homeland Security was created to keep us secure. We have to take off our shoes before boarding an airplane and have many restrictions on what we can carry onto the plane. Red-light cameras watch city streets. The President has the power to wiretap anyone if he feels it is a matter of national security.

In this concluding chapter for *Patriotic Information Systems: Access, Privacy, and Security Issues of Bush Information Policy*, many of the concerns surrounding the Real ID Act have been presented in order to provide the reader with a thorough discussion into the history and progression of this legislation. This summary is intended to compliment the other authors who, throughout this book, have presented original research and summaries on a variety of topics. These topics provide the reader with a very dark and disturbing look into the out of control information policies of the Bush Administration. The insight that can be gained is quite clear. The Bush Administration has, and will most likely always, do what they want with little respect for the opinions of others.

Recently, the midterm elections of 2006 sent a very strong message that the country was ready for a change. To be clear, the war in Iraq was the major factor in the election; however, the growing dislike for the Bush Administration was evident. Additionally, in a poll conducted by the Pew Research Center between the dates of May 30—June 3, 2007, the approval rating for President Bush was reported as 29% with 10% unsure. This mirrors a poll conducted a week later by NBC/Wall Street Journal that also reported a 29% approval rating with only 5% unsure. These ratings are among the lowest recorded for a president since the resignation of Richard Nixon. Perhaps Abraham Lincoln put it best when he said that "you may fool all the people some of the time, you can even fool some of the people all of the time, but you cannot fool all of the people all the time." This is the enduring beauty of democracy. Eventually, the majority will rule. In this case, the opponents of the Real ID Act represent the majority and are lined up to protect the freedoms that many of us take for granted. After raging against the dying of the light for far too long, the Real ID Act, along with the Bush Administration, will both go gently into that good night.

References

Brasch, W.M. (2005). Fool's gold in the nation's data-mining programs. *Social Science Computer Review, 23*(4), 401-428.

Chertoff, M. (2007, February 9). Testimony at a hearing on the fiscal year 2008 Dep't of Homeland Security budget before the H. Comm. on Homeland Security, 110th Congress. Retrieved July 18, 2007, from http://www.epic.org/privacy/us-visit/chertoff_020907.pdf

Electronic Privacy Information Center. (2007). United States Visitor and Immigrant Status Indicator Technology (US-VISIT). *EPIC.* Retrieved July 18, 2007, from http://www.epic.org/privacy/us-visit/

Grant, R.M. (2005). *Contemporary strategy analysis* (5th ed.). Malden, MA: Blackwell.

Horton, S. (2007, May 17). Defending the national surveillance state: Torture, lies and secrecy. *Harpers Magazine.* Retrieved on July 18, 2007, from http://www.harpers.org/archive/2007/05/hbc-90000090

Illinois Review. (2007, May 1). General assembly agrees: Protect kids' biometric info. *Illinois Review.* Retrieved July 18, 2007, from http://illinoisreview.typepad.com/illinoisreview/2007/05/general_assembl.html

Lipowicz, A. (2006). More woes for TWIC: Error rates could stall rollout of transportation ID program. *Washington Technology, 21*(23). Retrieved July 18, 2007, from http://www.washingtontechnology.com/print/21_23/29754-1.html

Lundquist, E. (2005). Why projects fail. *eWeek, 22*(5), 24.

Lynne, M.M. (1983). Power politics and MIS implementation. *Communications of the ACM, 26*(6), 430-444.

Maslow, A.H. (1943). A theory of human motivation. *Psychological Review, 50,* 370-396.

NCSL. (2006). The real ID act: National Impact Analysis. Retrieved July 18, 2007, Retrieved from http://www.ncsl.org/print/statefed/Real_ID_Impact_Report_FINAL_Sept19.pdf

Parrott, J. (2006, November 14). BMV worker charged with taking bribes. *Tribune.* Retrieved July 18, 2007, from http://www.alipac.us/modules.php?name=News&file=article&sid=1695

Schneier, B. (1999). Attack trees. *Dr. Dobb's Journal, 24*(12), 21.

Shachtman, N., & Singel, R. (2003, September 23). Army admits using JetBlue data. *Wired News.* Retrieved July 18, 2007, from http://www.wired.com/politics/security/news/2003/09/60540

Stoler, S. (2007, May 19). Robbery puts police at risk from ID theft. *WFAA News*. Retrieved June 20, 2007, from http://www.wfaa.com/sharedcontent/dws/wfaa/latestnews/stories/wfaa070518_lj_stoler.81ee4b9a.html

Tait, P., & Vessey, I. (1988). The effect of user involvement on system success: A contingency approach. *MIS Quarterly, 12*(1), 91-108.

Technology News Daily. (2006, April 18). Information security breaches, human error. *Technology News Daily*. Retrieved July 18, 2007, from http://www.technologynewsdaily.com/node/2489

WHIOTV. (2006, December 8). Deputies bust fake ID manufacturing ring. Retrieved July 18, 2007, from http://www.whiotv.com/news/10498958/detail.html

About the Contributors

Todd Loendorf is a PhD student in the School of Public and International Affairs at North Carolina State University. He holds an MBA (information security) from James Madison University, and a BA in political science from the University of North Carolina at Greensboro. His primary research interests are at the intersection of technology, security, and democracy and in the development and use of spatial techniques in social science research.

G. David Garson is a full professor of public administration at North Carolina State University, where he teaches courses on American government, research methodology, computer applications, and geographic information systems. In 1995, he was recipient of the Donald Campbell Award from the Policy Studies Organization, American Political Science Association, for outstanding contributions to policy research methodology, and in 1997 of the Aaron Wildavsky Book Award from the same organization. He is author of *Guide to Writing Quantitative Papers, Theses, and Dissertations* (Dekker, 2001), editor of *Social Dimensions of Information Technology* (2000), *Information Technology and Computer Applications in Public Administration: Issues and Trends* (1999), and *Handbook of Public Information Systems* (1999), and is author of *Neural Network Analysis for Social Scientists* (1998) and *Computer Technology and Social Issues* (1995), and is author, co-author, editor, or co-editor of 17 other books, and author or co-author of more than 50 articles. For the last 20 years, he has also served as editor of the *Social Science Computer Review* and is on the editorial board of four additional journals.

* * *

Charles N. Davis worked for nearly 10 years as a journalist after his graduation from North Georgia College in 1986, working for newspapers, magazines, and a news service in Georgia, Florida, and Ireland. As a national correspondent for Lafferty Publications, a Dublin-based news wire service for financial publications, Davis reported on banking, e-commerce, and regulatory issues for 7 years before leaving full-time journalism in 1993 to complete a master's degree from the University of Georgia's Henry W. Grady School of Journalism and Mass Communication, and to earn a doctorate in mass communication from the University of Florida in 1995. As a member of the Missouri School of Journalism faculty since 1999, he has continued to write for business and legal publications while conducting scholarly research on access to governmental information and new media law, including jurisdictional issues, intellectual property, and online libel. His first edited book, *Access Denied: Freedom of Information in the Information Age*, was published in 2001 by Iowa State University Press. Davis has earned a Sunshine Award from the Society of Professional Journalists for his work in furthering freedom of information, and the University of Missouri Provost's Award for Outstanding Junior Faculty Teaching. In March 2003, he was inducted into the University of Missouri – Columbia chapter of the Golden Key International Honor Society.

Leigh Estabrook directs the Library Research Center at the University of Illinois at Urbana-Champaign. Her primary teaching is the core course, Libraries, Information and Society. Among her recent research projects are a series of studies of the impact of the USA Patriot Act on libraries, and a study of the book as a gold standard for promotion and tenure in the humanistic disciplines. She is the recipient of the 2003 Association for Library and Information Science Award for professional contributions to library and information science education, and the 2002 Beta Phi Mu Award from the American Library Association and Beta Phi Mu for distinguished service to education for librarianship. Her full vita may be found at https://netfiles.uiuc.edu/leighe/www/vita.html.

Abby A. Goodrum is the Velma Rogers Graham research chair in news media and technology and has a full-time faculty position in the School of Journalism in association with the Edward S. Rogers Sr. Graduate School for Advanced Communications. The Velma Rogers Graham Chair is funded by a $2,000,000 endowment established by Ted and Loretta Rogers for the purpose of conducting research that addresses the relationship of various aspects of emerging communications and information technology to news gathering and the practice of journalism. Dr. Goodrum went to Ryerson from Syracuse University, where she has been a professor in the School of Information Studies, as well as a research scientist at the Information Institute of Syracuse and research associate for the Convergence Center for Communication and Media Studies. While on leave in 2004/05, she was a visiting research professor at the Canadian Centre of Arts and Technology, University of Waterloo. Prior to her academic career, she worked for the Cable News Network (CNN), where she provided research for news and feature production staff at 8 domestic and 16 international bureaus. She holds a BS and MSLIS from the University of Texas, and a PhD from the Interdisciplinary Information Science Program, University of North Texas. Dr. Goodrum has authored or coauthored a book and more than 35 book chapters, journal articles, and refereed conference papers. She sits on the editorial boards of the *Journal of the American Society for Information Science & Technology* and the *Annual Review of Information Science & Technology*. Since 2000, she has acquired nearly $500,000 in research funding, and is currently the principal investigator for a $200,000 project that is examining the effect of the Patriot Act on privacy in U.S. libraries.

Harry Hammitt is editor and publisher of *Access Reports*, a biweekly newsletter on the Freedom of Information Act, open government laws and policies, and informational privacy issues. He has written and edited the newsletter since 1985. Hammitt has also written extensively on all aspects of the case law, legislation, and administrative practice. Besides *Access Reports*, he has written a monthly newsletter on access and privacy for Canada, and has served as the primary editor of *Litigation Under the Federal Open Government Laws*, a practice guide created for nongovernment users of FOIA and other federal access laws. In addition, Hammitt has lectured extensively on access and privacy issues in the United States and Canada. He has served as president and as a board member of the American Society of Access Professionals, a Washington-based professional organization.

Akhlaque Haque is an associate professor of government and director of graduate studies in public administration at the University of Alabama at Birmingham (UAB). He is also a senior research fellow with UAB Center for Urban Affairs. Born in Dhaka, Bangladesh, Dr. Haque received Bachelor of Social Science in Economics (Honors) from the University of Dhaka and MA (Economics) and PhD (Urban and Public Affairs) from Cleveland State University. His research interests are in the areas of administrative theory and behavior, electronic government and geographic information systems, public health, and the urban population. He is published widely in peer reviewed publications, some of which appear in the *Public Administration Review*, *Administration and Society*, *Public Administration Quarterly*, *International Journal of Public Administration*, *Journal of Ethics and Technology*, *Journal of Rural Health*, *Public Health Registry*, *Journal of Urban Technology*, *Annals of Epidemiology*, *Journal of Management History*, and *Public Personnel Management*. He is currently serving on the editorial board of *Public Administration Review*. He is serving a 3-year term in the National Council on Peer Review and Accreditation (COPRA) that reviews and determines accreditation for MPA Programs under the National School of Public Affairs and Administration (NASPAA). He is serving a 2-year elected term in the Pi Alpha Alpha National Council. Professor Haque has taught graduate courses in public administration theory and behavior, e-government, geographic information systems, public sector information technology, economic development, and policy analysis, public budgeting, research methods, and public economics. He is the recipient of several federal grants, including a grant from the U.S. Housing and Urban Development (1998-2002) and the Center for Disease Control (1998). He is currently working on an edited book on electronic government and civic engagement. Dr. Haque also holds two other appointments with School of Public Health and School of Social and Behavioral Science at UAB. He is married and has two children.

Brian S. Krueger (bkrueger@uri.edu) is an associate professor of political science at the University of Rhode Island. His research interests include conventional and unconventional political participation, political mobilization, and the impact of new technologies on politics and society.

Megan Mustafoff is the project coordinator in the Library Research Center, with expertise in data analysis and analytic methods. She holds the MS from the University of Illinois in community health. She also has survey design and implementation experience due to her consultant work for the University of Illinois.

Jeffrey Roy (jroy44@gmail.com) (PhD, Carleton; MBA, Ottawa; BA, Waterloo) is associate professor in the School of Public Administration at Dalhousie University in Halifax, Nova Scotia, Canada. He specializes in models of democratic and multistakeholder governance and electronic government reforms. Prior to joining Dalhousie, Professor Roy was associate professor at the University of Ottawa's School of Management. In 2004-2005, Professor Roy was a visiting faculty member of the School of Public Administration at the University of Victoria. He served as managing director of the Centre on Governance at the University of Ottawa in 2001-2002. He is also a member of the Organization for Economic Cooperation and Development's E-Government Network, associate editor of the *International Journal of E-Government Research*; a featured columnist in *CIO Government Review*, a Canadian publication devoted to the nexus between technology and government (www.itworldcanada.com); and author of a new 2006 book, *E-government in Canada: Transformation for the Digital Age* (University of Ottawa Press).

Lauren Teffeau, the Library Research Center project coordinator, has a M.A from the University of Georgia in mass communications. With experience in social scientific research methods, including surveys, focus groups, and content analysis, she has also served as a corporate communications consultant and has a background in publishing.

David C. Wyld currently serves as an associate professor of management at Southeastern Louisiana University in Hammond, Louisiana, where he teaches courses in business strategy and methods for dealing with contemporary workplace issues. He earned his doctorate in management from the University of Memphis in 1993. David has written over 60 journal articles on a wide variety of subjects dealing with contemporary management issues. These have appeared in many leading business, health care, and education journals, including: *Journal of Business Research*, *Journal of Business Ethics*, *Business and Public Affairs*, *American Business Review*, *Journal of Contemporary Business Issues*, *Marketing Intelligence & Planning*, *Journal of Services Marketing*, *The Entrepreneurial Executive*, *International Journal of Management*, *Management Research News*, *Futures Research Quarterly*, *International Journal of Value Based Management*, *Managerial Law*, *Labor Law Journal*, *Public Personnel Management*, *Hospital & Health Services Administration*, *The Health Care Supervisor*, and *The Cornell Hotel and Restaurant Administration Quarterly*. He has also presented over 80 papers at professional conferences, garnering four best paper awards for these efforts. In the area of grant writing, Dr. Wyld has served as principal investigator on two grants, securing over a quarter of a million dollars in funding to upgrade both the classroom presentation technology and computer labs of the College of Business at Southeastern Louisiana University. In recognition of these accomplishments, Dr. Wyld was awarded the campus-wide President's Award for Excellence in Research in 1998 at Southeastern Louisiana University. In addition to his traditional teaching duties and research efforts, Dr. Wyld has served as a consultant to major corporations on a myriad of topics. He has participated extensively in delivering college classes to nontraditional students in divergent settings, teaching in Executive MBA programs, and working with emerging online universities. David, along with his wife, Karla, and two young sons, Spencer (5) and Carson (1), live in Ponchatoula, Louisiana. He also is an avid runner, and has run three marathons to date.

Index